A Handbook of African Affairs

A Handbook of African Affairs

EDITED BY HELEN KITCHEN
Editor of *Africa Report*

Published for The African-American Institute

BY

FREDERICK A. PRAEGER, *Publisher*

New York

A Handbook of African Affairs is the first of a series of reference publications on contemporary Africa to be sponsored by The African-American Institute.

WALDEMAR A. NIELSEN
President
THE AFRICAN-AMERICAN INSTITUTE

BOOKS THAT MATTER
Published in the United States of America in 1964
by Frederick A. Praeger, Inc., Publisher
111 Fourth Ave., New York 3, N.Y.

Foreword

All of the materials in this book appeared originally in the monthly *Africa Report,* the most widely read magazine on African affairs published in the United States. Since its inception in 1956, *Africa Report* has been a project of The African-American Institute, the leading private agency in the United States concerned with African educational and cultural development. The magazine, available by subscription only, is published as a public service. The articles reprinted in this volume are without exception independently selected and edited by the editor; thus they do not necessarily represent the views of The African-American Institute on contemporary Africa.

Africa Report seeks to report, synthesize, and interpret political events and trends on the African continent for a readership that was originally largely American but now extends to five continents. Its articles are not usually concerned with African-American relations as such, except in those instances when American policy directly influences or seems likely to influence internal developments in any given African country. The resident magazine staff of nine persons is multiracial and multinational. Editorial offices are at 1346 Connecticut Avenue, Washington, D.C.

Approximately half of the sketches in Part One of this volume were written by the editor. The others were developed by the editor from longer articles previously published in *Africa Report* and/or from working papers contributed especially for this project by William Berry, David Burns, A. A. Castagno, Ann Dalsimer, Victor Du Bois, Stewart Edwards, Harvey Glickman, Manfred Halpern, Okon Idem, Raymond K. Kent, Victor T. LeVine, John Marcum, René Pelissier, Carl Rosberg, Jr., Clyde Sanger, Stuart Schaar, John Seiler, Samuel W. Speck, Jr., Georgiana Stevens, C. Thomas Thorne, Jr., J. H. A. Watson, Sally Willcox, M. Crawford Young, and I. William Zartman. In addition, my warmest thanks are extended to the many other scholars, journalists, and officials—in Africa and in Europe, in American universities, in U.S. Government agencies, and in African and European embassies in Washington—who gave so generously of their time to answer our queries and to comment on drafts-in-preparation.

The material on African armies in Part Two was compiled for *Africa Report* by George Weeks, African specialist in the Washington bureau of United Press International. Mr. Weeks collected and cross-checked data from a wide variety of sources. Among the most important were publications of the governments concerned and international agencies; interviews with several hundred African and non-African officials and students of politico-military affairs; reports compiled by African and European bureaus of United Press International; limited firsthand observations in Africa; and the research and newspaper files of the *Africa Report* library. William Gutteridge's *Armed Forces in New States* (Oxford University Press); Vernon McKay's *Africa in World Politics* (Harper & Row); *The Role of the Military in Underdeveloped Countries,* a RAND Corporation study published by Princeton University Press; *Europe Outremer,* No. 385 (Paris); and *Jane's Fighting Ships* were of special value in developing historical context for the current materials. We are indebted to the invaluable London weekly *West Africa* for the discussion of the French military role in Africa.

Part Three includes a collection of materials on the antecedents, documents, and accomplishments of the founding conference of the Organization of African Unity, held at Addis Ababa in May, 1963. Where appropriate, sources are cited.

Lewis Nkosi, whose articles on literary trends in South Africa and English-speaking West Africa open Part Four, was formerly on the staffs of *Drum* and the Johannesburg *Golden City Post.* He left South Africa in 1961 for a year's study at Harvard on a Nieman Fellowship, and is now living and writing in London. Paulin Joachim ("French-Speaking Africa"), a Dahomean, is editor of the Dakar monthly *Bingo,* the largest-circulation periodical published in French-speaking Africa. Jeanne Contini ("The Somalis: A Nation of Poets in Search of an Alphabet") lives in the Somali capital of Mogadiscio.

Finally, this book owes more than can be expressed here to my colleagues on the staff of *Africa Report*—especially Assistant Editors Gayle Quisenberry Sharabi and Glenford Mitchell, Research Assistant Okon Idem, Librarian Margaret O'Neill, and my secretary Reather Kelly. I am grateful for their loyalty, enthusiasm, and spirit of camaraderie; the refreshing lack of ethnocentrism in their approach to life and the task of understanding and reporting contemporary Africa; the healthy skepticism that presses them on to ever more diligent pursuit of the elusive "facts" of a continent still unformed; and the many man-hours each devoted to collecting, sifting, and cross-checking the materials included here through several stages of production.

HELEN KITCHEN

Contents

Contents

CHARTS

MAPS

(Following page 311)

A Handbook of African Affairs

Introduction

Throughout this book, the reader will repeatedly encounter the phrase "as of 1963" or "as of early 1964." This qualification is a conscious reminder on the part of the editor that there are few absolute truths in Africa of the 1960's. A few days before the final manuscript was completed, the section on Zanzibar—which, in the original draft stated prophetically that "political prediction is particularly risky here"—had to be revised to take account of a revolution whose ultimate character cannot even yet be conclusively evaluated. At this writing, Ghana and Tanganyika are in the midst of crises that could result in fundamental changes of political courses before this volume is published. Anyone who purports to produce a "concise handbook of African affairs" in this decade must somehow accommodate himself to the fact that the race with the clock will be a hopeless one.

In shaping the content of this book, therefore, I have given special attention to pressures for change and to delineating those political and social groups now marking time impatiently on the outskirts of power. At the same time, I have sought to deal equally honestly with economic realities, and the extent to which the range of political choice often remains circumscribed by continuing financial dependence on the former colonial power. In the sections on South Africa and the territories still under colonial rule, this book implicitly assumes that the *status quo* will not be maintained indefinitely, but is primarily concerned with characterizing and appraising the protagonists.

Within the limited space available for treatment of each country, an attempt has been made to supply precise, up-to-date, comparative data on political parties, governments, elections, and significant constitutional developments. On the other hand, a broad-stroke brush has been used to put political events and forces in a perspective that will be meaningful to the reader only newly arrived in African affairs, and, hopefully, may even offer new in-

3

sights to readers overly enmeshed in the day-to-day intricacies of a particular segment of this vast and varied continent.

While there is much uncertainty about the decade ahead in Africa, certain trends are evident. The first is that the more conservative African governments will continue to shift their domestic policies (but not necessarily their foreign policies) leftward in the hope of containing rising pressures for a more egalitarian, more "African" society. Authoritarian leaders and one-party states will remain dominant, but events of 1963 and early 1964 suggest that authoritarians who lose contact with the broadening base of the nationalist movement from which they sprang may find their days of power numbered, whatever the constitutional barriers to governmental change. The *évolués* who carried the African revolution through its first stage (i.e., independence) are already, as the London *Times* noted in a June, 1962, editorial, beginning to "look like a fading generation." It is no longer a decisive political advantage in Africa to be at ease in a European drawing room; those leaders who would survive or rise to power in the "second revolution" (i.e., Africanization) now in progress must, above all, be unapologetically at home in their own environment. In some of the more radical states, on the other hand, leaders whose Africanness has been demonstrated beyond doubt have been able to moderate their doctrinaire anti-colonialist policies of the late 1950's, particularly in the area of economic cooperation. The recent events in Zanzibar on the east coast, Guinea's experience on the west coast, and the Congo story in the center are helping to awaken the truly nonaligned of the African governing elites to a more sophisticated appreciation of the techniques and objectives of Communism in relation to developing countries.

Perhaps the safest prediction of all is that increasingly urgent attention will be given to the strengthening and political indoctrination of security forces. In the first glow of independence, most African leaders rejected the idea of a strong army as an unnecessary luxury in a continent where all resources ought logically to be thrown into the battle against ignorance, disease, and poverty. In any case, armies were associated in the African mind with the enforcement of colonial rule and the Cold War, and thus were to be relegated to a minor place in the new political society. Ghana's

Kwame Nkrumah was principal spokesman for the view that national armies were only a temporary phenomenon and that the real answer to Africa's political and security problems lay in pan-African arrangements. Most of France's former colonies gratefully accepted an offer from Paris of low-keyed protection in the form of military technical assistance and defense agreements. The exceptions to this general disinterest in military establishments were the Arab countries, where armies have been accepted as a crucial political force for many centuries; Ethiopia (and, more recently, the Somali Republic), where an external threat was believed to exist; and the white-governed bastions of the southern part of the continent.

By late 1962, however, armies had begun to take on a new political significance in tropical Africa. Within the next fourteen months, two governments were to be toppled by armed insurgents; two other countries were to be "stabilized" by army intervention; and the rallying of the army to the side of the President was to abort an attempted *coup d'état* in at least one other. President Sylvanus Olympio, who had refused on grounds of economy to expand his 250-man token army to find places for demobilized veterans of the French Army, was assassinated by a group of disgruntled ex-sergeants in January, 1963. When Zanzibar became independent in 1963, the new government turned down a defense agreement with Britain and postponed establishment of an army; a little more than a month later, an estimated 600 armed insurgents moved into the military vacuum, seized the police arsenal, and overthrew the government before sundown. In none of these instances of insurgency was the overthrow of the regime triggered by popular demonstrations. The military assumed a different role in Congo-Brazzaville and Dahomey: In Brazzaville in August and in Porto Novo in October, the army moved into a deteriorating political situation to impose a reformist solution midway between the conservative stance of the incumbent regime and a vocal popular demand for radical change. In Senegal in December, 1962, the loyalty of key units of the army to President Senghor was the decisive factor in the failure of Prime Minister Mamadou Dia's move to take over the government by force; a year later, the army again held firm when dissidents sought to incite the military to revolt during national elections. In Ghana, the essentially apolitical, British-trained army and police remained—through 1963, at least—one of the strongest pillars of the regime.

The lessons of these varied experiences were not lost on African leaders. By early 1964, every crowned and uncrowned head of state on the continent was warily reassessing the morale, loyalty, competence, and numerical adequacy of his security forces. Almost everywhere, African armies were certain to grow—and to grow more ambitious.

H. K.

PART ONE

The Independent States, Colonial Territories, and Surrounding Islands of Africa

A Country-by-Country Political Guide

Algeria*

Population: 10,300,000 (1963 est.).

Area: 919,519 square miles.

Capital: Algiers (population: 870,000).

Political Status: Independent republic.

Date of Independence: July 1, 1962.

Chief of State and Head of Government: President and Prime Minister Ahmad Ben Bella, elected directly (September, 1963) by universal suffrage for a 5-year term.

Political Party: Front de Libération Nationale (FLN).

Legislative Branch: Unicameral. National Assembly of 196 members elected by universal adult suffrage (September 20, 1962) from a single list of candidates prepared by the FLN. Indefinitely suspended in October, 1963.

Monetary Unit: 4.94 Algerian francs = US$1.00.

Principal Languages: Arabic, French, Berber.

External Affiliations: United Nations, Arab League, Organization of African Unity. Participates in franc-zone arrangements.

No sooner was Algeria independent in July, 1962, when conflict erupted within the ranks of those who had guided the seven-year revolution against French rule. Ahmad Ben Bella (one of the original leaders of the revolution, but imprisoned in France from 1956 to 1962) was supported by the army general staff, under the command of Colonel Houari Boumedienne; the Algerian "external" military forces, stationed in Morocco and Tunisia; and the population of the Arab-dominated west, southwest, and Saharan portions of Algeria. His principal rivals for power, Ben Youssef Ben Khedda and Belkacem Krim, respectively Premier and Vice-Premier of the Provisional Government (GPRA), which had negotiated terms with the French, rallied most of the "internal" army, intellectuals, and middle-class elements in north central and northeast Algeria and the modernized Berbers of the Kabylia

---

* Maps are located at the back of the book, pp. 315 ff.

9

mountains. As the nation stood on the brink of civil war, Ben Bella's group, in September, 1962, outmaneuvered its opponents and took control of the ruling FLN Political Bureau with a minimum of bloodshed.

The victors moved quickly to consolidate their power, isolate their enemies, and deal with Algeria's mounting economic crisis. A National Assembly was elected from among FLN-designated candidates, and a crackdown against opposition elements began in November. The Communist Party and the clandestine Kabylia-centered Front des Forces Socialistes were banned, and the powerful and rebellious FLN Fédération du France (which had grouped Algerians living in France and subsequently supported Ben Khedda in the post-independence struggle) was dissolved. Plans were announced in December to reorganize Colonel Buomedienne's contingents into a regular army, a step that involved the purge of at least half of the original force of 135,000. After an intense struggle, the labor union, Union Générale des Travailleurs Algériens (UGTA), lost its autonomy in January, 1963. In September, 1963, the new constitution presented to the nation established Algeria as a single-party state and ensured continued army influence in politics. Later the same month, the Ben Bella steamroller was overtly challenged for the first time when Berbers in the Tizi-Ouzou area of Kabylia revolted in force against the regime.

Although Algeria's French-built infrastructure, rich agriculture acreage, iron ore deposits near Tindouf, and oil and natural gas resources (estimated reserves for both: 500 million tons minimum) could render its economic future relatively promising, the immediate problems are grim. Immediately after independence, 90 per cent (900,000) of the European population migrated, removing vital technical skills, entrepreneurial talent, and investment capital. Factories were operating at 25–30 per cent of capacity in 1962, over 2 million were unemployed, and taxation revenue (60 per cent of which had heretofore been supplied by Europeans) dwindled. One-third of Algeria's most fertile, modernized land (2.7 million acres) was vacated in the mass exodus. To harvest the 1963 crop, workers' management committees were established under state control.

Emergency help has come from several sources. The Soviet Union has promised loans up to $100 million. France spent a billion dollars a year on the Algerian war and has been spending about one-third of this amount annually in assisting Algeria since independence. U.S. aid in the fiscal year 1963–64 may total $40 million. The continued flow of aid on this scale may depend in part on internal political trends. France initially appeared willing to accept Ben Bella's steady turn toward socialism, but the accelerated pace of nationalization of the economy and the press in the last half of 1963 put new strains on Franco-Algerian relations.

For the moment, Algeria remains dependent on the West for most financial assistance. On the other hand, revolutionary traditions within the FLN and increasing internal pressures from Ben Bella's left may force the regime to assert its independence of all blocs in the months ahead while consolidating lines of friendship with Africa south of the Sahara, the Middle East, and the Eastern bloc. However the Algerians choose to define their future, the country's internal peace will depend greatly on whether the army remains loyal and united behind the regime in power.

Angola

Population: 4,800,000 (1962 est., including 215,000 Portuguese settlers).

Area: 478,350 square miles (not including Cabinda, which is nonetheless governed as an integral part of Angola).

Capital: Luanda (population: 200,000).

Political Status: Overseas province of Portugal.

Local Head of Government: Governor-General, Lieutenant-Colonel Silvino Silveiro Marques, appointed by the Council of Ministers in Lisbon.

Major Political Parties: União Nacional is the governing party of Portugal and Mozambique. Principal African nationalist parties (banned) include the Frente de Libertação Nacional de Angola (FNLA), led by Holden Roberto; Democratic Front for the Liberation of Angola, incorporating one wing of the former Movimento Popular de Libertação de Angola (MPLA), led by Dr. Agostinho Neto; and the remnants of the MPLA, led by Viriato da Cruz.

Legislative Branch: Angola has 7 representatives in the Lisbon Assembleia Nacional, each elected for 4 years by restricted (i.e., literacy in Portuguese or income) male suffrage. A unicameral provincial Legislative Council (Conselho Legislativo), including both elected and appointed members, has very limited authority.

Monetary Unit: 28.75 overseas escudos = US$1.00.

Principal Languages: Portuguese, Umbundu, Kimbundu, Kikongo, Tchokwe, Kwanyama.

Angola was visited by Portuguese navigators in 1482 and has been claimed by Portugal for more than 400 years. Since 1951, it has been by law an overseas province, i.e., an integral part of Portugal. The avowed goal of Portuguese colonial policy, which has undergone only minor changes in four centuries, is cultural assimilation, which implicitly precludes preparation for self-rule as envisaged by African nationalism. Even within its own terms of reference, however, Portugal has made slim progress toward establishing Portuguese culture firmly in Angola; by 1962, only a small fraction of Angolans were legally recognized as *assimilado,* and illiteracy was 99 per cent.

In March, 1961, a nationalist-led military revolt was launched in northern Angola by the União das Populacões de Angola (UPA). In the first six months of the rebellion, according to unofficial reports, 2,000 Portuguese and 50,000 Africans were killed. Responding to this challenge, Portugal increased its armed forces in Angola to 43,000 by mid-1963. Even so, the increasingly better-equipped and better-trained guerrilla forces—now formally named the Angolan National Liberation Army (ALNA)—were readying themselves in late 1963 for new offensives aimed at forcing the Portuguese to negotiate a settlement based on no lesser goal than full independence. The main rebel training base is near Thysville in Congo-Leopoldville; many of the officers were previously trained in Algeria.

Although Portugal has made some gestures toward reform under pressure of world opinion—notably the abolition of *assimilado* status in favor of full Portuguese citizenship for all Africans living under the Portuguese flag, reforms in the labor code, some improvements in educational facilities and opportunities for Africans in the overseas territories, and (in October, 1963) an agreement to sit down under U.N. auspices with representatives of the independent African states to discuss differences—the gap between African aspirations and the reforms outlined in Portugal's new Organic Law of 1962 is so wide that prospects for an early peace in Angola appear dim.

Within the nationalist movement, 1963 was marked by the splintering of one of the two major rival groups (the Movimento Popular de Libertação de Angola, led by Dr. Agostinho Neto, Mario de Andrade, and Viriato da Cruz) and the clear emergence of Holden Roberto's Frente de Libertação Nacional de Angola (combining Roberto's original UPA and the Democratic Party of Emmanuel Kunzika) as *the* Angolan nationalist liberation movement. At the meeting of the Foreign Ministers of the Organization of African Unity at Dakar in August, 1963, the African states unanimously endorsed the FNLA, and its Leopoldville-based "Government of the Republic of Angola in Exile," as the only channels through which independent Africa's material support for the liberation movement would henceforth be channeled. Beginning with Congo-Leopoldville, a number of African states have now accorded formal recognition to the GRAE.*

Of all the African territories, Angola is the most important to Portugal economically. The four pillars of the economy are mining (especially iron and diamonds), oil, fishing, and plantation farming. Coffee accounts for 35 per cent of current exports. Exports were valued at $135,439,000 in 1962–63, as against only $114,239,000 in imports, leaving a favorable trade balance of more than $21 million. Even so, the territory's mineral, hydroelectric, and agricultural resources have still been only partially surveyed. Preliminary findings suggest that the long-term potential is formidable.

* See "The Angola Rebellion: Status Report," by John Marcum, *Africa Report,* January, 1964, p. 3.

Burundi

Population: 2,500,000 (1962 est.).

Area: 10,744 square miles.

Capital: Usumbura (population: 45,000).

Political Status: Independent constitutional monarchy.

Date of Independence: July 1, 1962.

Chief of State: Mwami (King) Mwambutsa IV, hereditary monarch, on the throne since 1915.

Head of Government: Premier Pierre Ngendandumwe, leader of majority UPRONA party, in office since June, 1963.

Major Political Parties: L'Union Nationale et du Progrès (UPRONA), governing party; Parti Démocrate Chrétien (PDC); Parti Démocrate Rural (PDR).

Legislative Branch: Bicameral. National Assembly of 65 members elected by universal adult suffrage for 6-year terms. Last election, September, 1961. Senate has not yet been established.

Monetary Unit: 50 Rwanda-Burundi francs = US$1.00.

Principal Languages: French, Kirundi.

External Affiliations: United Nations, Organization of African Unity, European Economic Community (associate).

When the Belgian trust territory of Ruanda-Urundi became independent in July, 1962, the territory split into two separate states of markedly different political complexion. In Burundi, power remains in the hands of the Nilo-Hamitic Batutsi aristocracy (14 per cent of the population). The Batutsi are presumed to have come to Ruanda-Urundi as a warrior people from the Galla country of Ethiopia more than 400 years ago, to become the rulers of the indigenous Bahutu majority. The social and political role of the Hutu has been progressively extended under recent constitutional reforms, however, and ministerial posts in the present government are divided between young Tutsi and Hutu graduates of Belgian universities or the Congo's Louvanium. The Mwami retains direct control of the police and army.

Burundi's bustling, easygoing capital city of Usumbura contrasts sharply with the austerity of Rwanda's Kigali. Located on Lake Tanganyika, Usumbura is a trading center of some importance with a number of small industries for the processing of coffee, cotton ginning, and the manufacture of cotton oil, soap, and cement. Relations with all friendly countries are welcomed, and the roster of embassies in Usumbura includes the Soviet Union.

Although Burundi and Rwanda have moved in different political directions, their basic economic problems remain almost identical. Both are small, poor, agricultural countries, with probably the highest population density in sub-Saharan Africa. Known mineral resources do not warrant large-scale development. Coffee is the only important cash export crop of their essentially subsistence economies; Burundi's production (19,308 metric tons in 1961) varies sharply from year to year and went into near-catastrophic decline after Belgian discipline of growers was relaxed at independence. About 90 per cent of Burundi's coffee is customarily purchased by the United States. Combined exports for Rwanda and Burundi totaled $27 million in 1961, with imports of $34 million.

Any economic and social development is heavily dependent on foreign aid. Burundi's major current sources of financial and technical assistance are Belgium, the European Economic Community, the United Nations, and West Germany.

Cabinda

Population: 58,631 (1960 est.).
Area: 2,895 square miles.
Capital: Cabinda.
Political Status: Administered as a district of Angola.
Monetary Unit: 28.75 overseas escudos = US$1.00.

Cabinda is a small timber-producing enclave tucked between the Congo republics on Africa's Atlantic coast, and administered as an integral part of Angola. It has been governed by Portugal since 1885, when treaties signed with local chiefs in Cabinda were formally recognized by the European powers at the Congress of Berlin.

The several small African nationalist parties active in Cabinda call for separate independence for the enclave, and have thus far rejected the efforts of Angolan nationalist parties (particularly Holden Roberto's União das Populacões de Angola) to establish working relationships and common goals. In August, 1963, representatives of three Cabinda parties—the Movement for the Cabinda Enclave (MLEC), Action Committee for Cabinda National Union (CAUNG), and the Mayumbe Alliance—met in Brazzaville as the "Cabinda Liberation Front" (FLC). The Front reportedly received financial as well as moral support from Congo-Brazzaville when former President Fulbert Youlou was in power, but the attitude of the present Brazzaville Government is not clear.

Federal Republic of Cameroun

Population: 4,100,000 (1963 est.).

Area: 178,368 square miles.

Capital: Yaoundé (population: 60,000).

Political Status: Independent federal republic.

Date of Independence: January 1, 1960 (East Cameroun); federation dates from October 1, 1961.

Chief of State and Head of Government: President Ahmadou Ahidjo, formerly President of Cameroun Republic; under special provisions of federal constitution became federal President until 1965, when the federal President is to be elected by universal adult suffrage for a 5-year term.

Major Political Parties: Union Camerounaise, led by Federal President Ahmadou Ahidjo (East Cameroun); Kamerun National Democratic Party, led by Federal Vice-President and West Cameroun Prime Minister John Ngu Foncha; Cameroon People's National Convention, led by Dr. Emmanuel L. M. Endeley; One Kamerun, led by Ndeh Ntumazah (West Cameroun).

Legislative Branch: Federal. Unicameral. Constitution calls for Federal Assembly of 50 members (40 from East Cameroun, 10 from West Cameroun) elected by universal adult suffrage for 5-year terms. Present Federal Assembly was selected in April, 1962, from the legislatures of East and West Cameroun, respectively, under the special provisions of the federal constitution.

East Cameroun: Unicameral. Legislative Assembly of 100 members elected by universal adult suffrage for 5-year terms. Last election, April, 1960.

West Cameroun: Bicameral. Legislative Assembly and House of Chiefs, both elected by universal adult suffrage for 5-year terms. Last election, December, 1961.

Monetary Unit: 247 CFA francs = US$1.00.

Principal Languages: French (East Cameroun) and English (West Cameroun). Others are Bamileke, Fulfulde, Bulu, Ewondo, Douala, and "Wes-kos" (pidgin English).

External Affiliations: United Nations, Organization of African Unity, Union Africaine et Malgache, European Economic Community (associate), common external tariff with Union Douanière Equatoriale, franc zone.

The Cameroun, the first successful bilingual federation on the African continent, represents the union of the former Cameroun

Republic (now the East Cameroun) and the former British-administered trust territory of Southern Cameroons. The Cameroun was a German protectorate from 1884 to 1916, but was split following World War I into two League of Nations mandates under British and French administration. These, in turn, were converted after World War II into United Nations trust territories. East Cameroun attained independence in 1960, and, following supervised plebiscites in the British Cameroons (February, 1961), the present federation was formed. The northern part of the British Cameroons, whose citizens rejected federation with the Cameroun Republic, became an integral part of the Northern Region of Nigeria in July, 1961.

The two states of the federation include remarkably heterogeneous populations; in the East Cameroun are to be found large numbers of Fulani and animists in the north and substantial groupings of Bamileke, Bulu, Beti, Ewondo, Bassa, and others in the south. In the West Cameroun there is ethnic cleavage between the large grassfields populations (Tikar and related groupings) and those of the coastal areas (southern Nigerians, particularly Ibos, Bakweri, Bakundu, and related groups). These ethnic differences inevitably generated social, economic, and political tensions. In the southern part of East Cameroun, for example, prolonged anti-government guerrilla activity—which began in 1955 and has only recently been contained—followed distinct ethnic lines.

The arrest, conviction, and imprisonment of the four principal opposition leaders in East Cameroun during 1962 had the effect of converting it into a *de facto* one-party state. West Cameroun continues to maintain a multiparty system, at least at this writing. Although some tentative steps were taken during 1962 and 1963 to fuse the governing party of the West, the Kamerun National Democratic Party, and the East Camerounian Union Camerounaise into a single national movement, the merger had not been effected by late 1963. The two states of the federation still maintain basically different—i.e., French-based and British-based—political systems, and national political activity embracing both units is in its infancy.

The economies of both states of the Cameroun are based almost exclusively on diversified agriculture, most of it at the subsistence level. Cocoa, coffee, bananas, cotton, palm products, and tropical woods are exported, but not in sufficient quantity to provide the capital required to finance the kind of development that Cameroun requires to become genuinely self-supporting. The bulk of East Cameroun exports go to protected franc-zone markets, but Commonwealth preferences for West Cameroun products ended in October, 1963. Current plans for economic development are based on the assumption that 40 to 45 per cent of the total scheduled costs will come from outside sources, of which France remains the most important. The several forms of French aid (technical assistance, military support, loans, capital grants, etc.) amounted to approximately $50 million during 1962 and again during 1963, well over half of all revenues available to the government in those years.

The major industrial enterprise in Cameroun is the French-owned aluminum plant of the Compagnie Camerounaise d'Aluminum Pechiney-Ugine (ALUCAM) at Edea, which began operations in 1957 and by 1963 had an annual capacity of 45,000 tons. It originally used alumina imported from France and Guinea, but work is now under way on a north-south railway axis that will eventually open up the extensive and high-grade bauxite deposits recently found in the Tibati area of East Cameroun and extending into the neighboring Central African Republic. Financing of the construction of the first 206 miles of the railway extension (Yaoundé to Goyom) has been undertaken by the European Economic Community, France, and the United States at an initial cost of about $32 million. Other development priorities are the extension of the electrical power emanating from Edea; improvement and extension of internal roads, especially the overland link between Yaoundé and the capital of West Cameroun, Buea; and construction of new schools and hospitals.*

* See "One-Party State for Cameroon?," *Africa Report,* November, 1962, p. 2; and "The New Cameroon Federation," by Victor T. LeVine, *Africa Report,* December, 1961, p. 7.

Cape Verde Islands

Population: 201,549 (1960 census).

Area: 1,557 square miles.

Capital: Praia.

Political Status: Overseas province of Portugal.

Local Head of Government: Governor responsible to the Minister for Overseas Territories in Lisbon. His functions are limited, however, for the islands are divided into 12 concelhos, or local self-governing administrative units.

Monetary Unit: 28.75 overseas escudos = US$1.00.

Principal Languages: Portuguese, Capeverdean Creole.

Cape Verde consists of a crescent-shaped formation of 10 islands and 5 islets of volcanic origin about 373 miles off the coast of Senegal. Apparently they were uninhabited until the Portuguese arrived on the two main islands (Santiago and Fogo) in the fifteenth century, and subsequently brought labor from the African mainland to work the land. Settlers came later from Italy and Spain as well. The largest single group in the population today— about 60 per cent—are the *mesticos* (mixed). Thus, in contrast to other Portuguese territories in Africa, there has never been a separate legal status for *indigenato;* all residents of Cape Verde were registered as full citizens of Portugal in the 1950 census and may vote in Portuguese elections.

Cape Verde has the highest rate of literacy of any Portuguese territory in Africa, and at one time was believed to have a greater percentage of literates than metropolitan Portugal; according to Portuguese sources, there were 1,165 students in secondary schools on the islands in 1960. There are variations in the composition of the population from island to island, as well as in the form of Portuguese Creole spoken, but the Capeverdeans as a group have a distinctive culture of their own, including a literature and songs.

The islands have few natural resources and even subsistence farming is uncertain because of frequent drought. On three of the nine inhabited islands, there is little but salt and sand; on most of the others, only part of the terrain is suitable for crops. Modest quantities of coffee, bananas, vegetable oils, peanuts, and canned fish are exported to Portugal, and salt is sold to countries on the African mainland. Locally grown corn is the staple diet, but much of the other food consumed must be imported.

Cape Verde's chief economic importance is as a refueling station for ships and aircraft. At one time, a significant amount of income came to the citizenry in remittances sent home by emigrants who had settled in the United States (sizable Capeverdean communities were built up in Massachusetts, Rhode Island, and California during the last century), but emigration is now restricted and the volume of remittances has reportedly decreased gradually over the years.

There are several African nationalist parties, all with headquarters on the mainland, which seek independence for Cape Verde and Portuguese Guinea and some form of union between the two. (See "Portuguese Guinea.") In addition, at least two political movements concerned primarily with the future of Cape Verde have been recently set up in Dakar: the Mouvement de Libération du Cap Vert (MLCV), led by Mendès Diaz, apparently an appendage of the Union des Populations de Guinée dite Portugaise (UPG), and the Union du Peuple des Iles du Cap Vert, a self-proclaimed Marxist-Leninist party, headed by José Laitão de Groca.

Central African Republic

Population: 1,229,000 (1962 est.).

Area: 238,000 square miles.

Capital: Bangui (population: 100,000).

Political Status: Independent republic.

Date of Independence: August 13, 1960.

Chief of State and Head of Government: President David Dacko, head of government since May, 1959, and invested (December, 1960) by the Assembly as first President; re-elected without opposition in national elections held on January 5, 1964. Legislation to extend presidential term from 5 to 7 years enacted by the National Assembly in November, 1963.

Political Parties: All political parties have been merged into the governing Mouvement d'Emancipation Sociale de l'Afrique Noire.

Legislative Branch: Unicameral. National Assembly of 50 members elected by universal adult suffrage for 5-year terms. Last election, 1959.

Monetary Unit: 247 CFA francs = US$1.00.

Principal Languages: French; each of the four principal ethnic groups (Mandijia-Baya, the Banda, the M'Baka, and the Zande) have languages of their own and also speak a common lingua franca known as sangho.

External Affiliations: United Nations, Organization of African Unity, Union Africaine et Malgache, Union Douanière Equatoriale, European Economic Community (associate), franc zone.

The Central African Republic, known as Ubangi-Shari when it was part of the federation of French Equatorial Africa, acquired its present name from its placement in the very center of Africa. This unique geographical location, a manageable terrain, and a network of partly navigable rivers enabled Ubangi to become a major crossroads and trading center early in its history; this role was enhanced in the present century by the addition of air facilities and the construction of the best system of north-south and east-west roads in Equatorial Africa. Access to the sea remains difficult and costly, however, for the republic has no railroads and is almost 900 miles from the nearest ocean port. Sparsely populated (1.7 persons per square mile), C.A.R. has only one town of more than 25,000 inhabitants—the capital and important river port of Bangui. The multiplicity of immigrant ethnic groups is a by-product of the country's historic crossroads function.

While the Central African Republic has no known major resources comparable to those of Gabon, its agricultural economy is well balanced if underdeveloped. Food crops, raised for subsistence and barter, include cassava, avocados, bananas, mangoes, pineapples, lemons, limes, millet, and rice. The export economy is based almost exclusively on cotton, coffee, and peanuts, though small quantities of diamonds, palm kernels, tobacco, sesame seed, and rubber are also exported. High incidence of sleeping sickness has thus far limited stock raising, and meat must be imported from Chad.

Total exports in 1961 were valued at $13.8 million, while imports totaled $21 million. The republic is a member of the franc zone and most of its trade is with France, which also supplies about $22 million a year in various forms of aid. Additional assistance has come in recent years from Israel.

The only political party is the Mouvement d'Emancipation Sociale de l'Afrique Noire. Although MESAN suffered a major set-back when its charismatic founder, Barthelemy Boganda, died in a plane crash in 1959, it recovered from momentary panic to win forty-eight of fifty National Assembly seats in national elections held later in the same year. After a bitter postelection power struggle within the party, Boganda's cousin and principal aide, David Dacko, was confirmed as the youngest head of government in Africa. He is now thirty-three.

In November, 1962, the Cabinet officially dissolved the several opposition parties (there were five) and decreed that the Central African Republic would henceforth be a one-party state. President Dacko, discussing this projected policy decision at a party congress earlier the same year, observed that the decision to establish a united political movement—"one shepherd and one flock"—was not a matter of dissolving legitimate parties, but of converting the "handful of discontented people which foreign organizations maintain and support, and which they dare to call 'opposition.'"

The sole objective of the new arrangement, it was pointed out, was to "save the Central African Republic from anarchy . . . the infant disease of all young independent states." He expressed confidence that the nation would now be spared the kind of crises which other African states had experienced, and emphasized that "no decision will be taken without first consulting a roundtable comprising representatives of trade unions, women's organizations, and other groups."

President Dacko has said that his government's domestic policies are based on "empiric socialism," and that the republic will avoid the "doctrinal or authoritarian socialism with which certain sister countries have already had an unfortunate experience." He has expressed regret that "foreign capital is little inclined to come and share the terrible handicap of our distance from the sea."

Ceuta and Melilla

Population: Ceuta, 73,000 (1959 est.); Melilla, 79,000 (1959 est.).

Area: Ceuta, 7.6 square miles; Melilla, 4.8 square miles.

Political Status: Plazas of Spain.

Principal Language: Spanish.

Ceuta and Melilla—two intensely Andalusian cities along Morocco's Mediterranean coast—came under Spanish jurisdiction in the fifteenth century. They remained under Spanish control under the terms of Moroccan independence in 1956, and are administered today as city-provinces of metropolitan Spain. Ceuta, opposite Gibraltar, and Melilla, roughly 200 miles east of Ceuta, have separate mayors, who both sit in the Cortes in Madrid. However, the Governor General for both entities is the chief of the Spanish Army in North Africa. The cities are African only in the geographic sense, since about 90 per cent of the inhabitants are Spanish.

Some fish is exported, with Ceuta's output going mostly to Spanish territories and Melilla's to non-Spanish areas. Melilla also transships iron ore mined in Morocco proper by Minas del Rif, a Spanish concessionaire. The main functions of Ceuta and Melilla, however, are to supply the Spanish troops customarily stationed there, and to service calling ships.

Chad

Population: 2,800,000 (1963 est.).

Area: 495,000 square miles.

Capital: Fort Lamy (population: 95,000).

Political Status: Independent republic.

Date of Independence: August 11, 1960.

Chief of State and Head of Government: President François Tombalbaye, elected for a 7-year term (March, 1962) by an electoral college composed of members of the National Assembly, mayors, municipal councilors, tribal chiefs, and councilors of rural communities.

Political Party: Parti Progressiste Tchadien.

Legislative Branch: Unicameral. National Assembly of 84 deputies elected (March, 1962) under a single-list system by universal adult suffrage. A new 75-seat Assembly elected (December 22, 1963) from a single list.

Monetary Unit: 247 CFA francs = US$1.00.

Principal Languages: French, Arabic, Sara.

External Affiliations: United Nations, Organization of African Unity, Union Africaine et Malgache, European Economic Community (associate), Union Douanière Equatoriale, franc zone.

The largest and most isolated of the four states of former French Equatorial Africa is the sparsely populated Republic of Chad, which stretches northward to the southern border of Libya, southward to the Central African Republic, and shares some 600 miles of western border with Sudan. The vast size of the country, the apparent lack of significant economic resources, poor transportation, and the sharp cleavages between the Arabized Moslem north and the Christian-led but largely animist south are the most significant barriers to education, nationhood, and political stability.

In the general elections of 1959, the southern-based Parti Progressiste Tchadien (PPT) won sixty-seven seats, as against ten for the northern-based Parti National Africain (PNA), and six for independents. Opposition to the regime was systematically whittled down in the next two years, and in March, 1961, the governing party was merged with the PNA. Formation of new opposition parties was banned by presidential decree in January, 1962, and the elections in March of that year (implementing a new constitution which greatly enhanced the power of the presidency) were held under a single-list system that returned only PPT candidates to the National Assembly. Legislation establishing Chad permanently and officially as a one-party state is pending.

In March, 1963, five prominent northern politicians were arrested and charged with "endangering the internal and external security of the state" by their effort to "turn the inhabitants of northern Chad against their brothers in the south and thus to sink Chad into chaos." Two were subsequently sentenced to death, the others to long prison sentences. In September, 1963, the entire country was placed under a temporary state of emergency after rioting erupted in the capital in protest against the attempted arrest of three other Moslem leaders charged with attempting to organize an opposition movement. President Tombalbaye subsequently called a series of meetings with traditional Islamic leaders in an effort to heal the rift between the government and Chad's Moslem population.

Agriculture and nomadic and seminomadic herding provide a livelihood—mostly at the subsistence level—for 96 per cent of the Chadian population. The major export is cotton (80 per cent of the total), but meat, livestock, animal and reptile hides and skins, fish (from Lake Chad), and gum arabic are also exported in modest quantities, largely to France at supported prices. Total exports in 1961 were $21.6 million.

At present, Chad has no railroads, its major river is navigable only in the rainy season, and less than 1,000 of the country's 18,600 miles of roads and trails are all-weather. A rail link to the sea (via Cameroun) is given highest priority in the government's development planning, for it is recognized that Chadian products will remain uncompetitive on world markets as long as they must be flown or shipped (at least 1,000 miles) overland by truck through Nigeria, Central African Republic and Congo-Brazzaville, or Cameroun. There are no known mineral resources.

French aid to Chad amounted to more than $95 million between 1960 and 1963, not including developmental assistance provided through le Fonds d'Investissements et de Developpment Economique et Social (i.e., another $50 million between 1948 and 1959). The number of French technicians working in Chad increased from 439 to 515 in 1964, and the roster of French teachers in Chadian schools rose from 60 to 167 in the same period. Expatriate administrators dropped, however, from 95 to 30.

Comoro Islands

Population: 183,000 (1960 est.).

Area: 863 square miles (approximate area of the four islands of Mayotte, Anjouan, Grande Comore, and Moheli).

Capital: Dzaoudzi, on the island of Mayotte. (Mayotte population: 23,000).

Political Status: Autonomous overseas territory of France.

Local Head of Government: French High Commissioner Henri Bernard, assisted by a Council of Government composed of 6 to 8 ministers and headed by President of the Council Said Mohamed Cheikh (elected by a two-thirds majority of the Territorial Assembly).

Local Legislative Branch: Unicameral. Territorial Assembly of 31 members elected (1961) by universal adult suffrage for 5-year terms.

Monetary Unit: 247 CFA francs = US$1.00.

Principal Languages: French, Arabic.

The Comoro Archipelago lies between the northern tip of Mozambique and the Malagasy Republic. Arabs form the dominant ethnic group of the largely Moslem population, which also includes peoples of African, Malagasy, and Asian origin.

The four islands, jointly administered with Madagascar from 1912 to 1946, attained the status of an autonomous territory of France under a reform law of December, 1961. The High Commissioner, who acts as the representative of the French Government, promulgates laws and decrees pertaining to internal affairs, supervises the legality of administrative acts, safeguards constitutional rights, and has responsibility for defense and external security. The Council of Government, whose members head the various administrative agencies, is the working executive. The Chamber of Deputies discusses a range of local problems and approves the budget. There are four District Assemblies on the principal islands, each composed of from six to twenty-two elected members. The deputies are elected to represent the Comoros in the French

National Assembly and there is one senator representing the Archipelago in the French Senate.

Food crops are grown in abundance on these mountainous tropical islands; copra, vanilla, spices, perfume plants, coffee, and sisal are cultivated for export. The Comoros' few industries are limited to processing these products for export and for local use. France, the United States, the Malagasy Republic, and Germany are the territory's chief customers in that order, while France and the Malagasy Republic supply the bulk of imports.

Congo-Brazzaville

Population: 845,000 (1960 est.).

Area: 132,046 square miles.

Capital: Brazzaville (population: 135,000).

Political Status: Independent republic.

Date of Independence: August 15, 1960.

Chief of State: President Alphonse Massamba-Debat, chosen by an electoral college consisting of members of the National Assembly and of prefectoral, subprefectoral, and municipal councils, December 20, 1963, for term of 5 years. To be assisted temporarily by a National Council of the Revolution.

Head of Government: Prime Minister Pascal Lissouba, also chosen by the above-cited electoral college, December 20, 1963, for an unspecified term.

Major Political Parties: Union Démocratique de Défense des Intérêts Africains (UDDIA), governing party during the regime of former President Fulbert Youlou; Mouvement Socialiste Africaine (MSA), led by Jacques Opangault; Parti Progressiste Congolaise (PPC), allied to the MSA in 1959 elections.

Legislative Branch: The unicameral 60-seat National Assembly elected in June, 1959, for a 5-year term was dissolved by Army decree on August 15, 1963. New elections for a 55-seat National Assembly were held on December 8, 1963, on the basis of a single "national list."

Monetary Unit: 247 CFA francs = US$1.00.

Principal Languages: French, Mboshi, Kongo, Teke-Yans, Mbete, Makaa.

External Affiliations: United Nations, Organization of African Unity, Union Africaine et Malgache, Union Douanière Equatoriale, European Economic Community (associate), franc zone.

French-speaking Africa's second *coup d'état* of 1963 took place in Brazzaville on August 15, when President Fulbert Youlou resigned "to prevent the shedding of Congolese blood." Youlou's resignation was preceded by three days of trade-union demonstrations protesting the arrest of two labor officials, a recent ban on public meetings, and the alleged inattention of the Youlou Government to economic problems acutely affecting labor. Press reports that the strike was in protest against recent legislation introducing one-party government (to have become effective on August 15, the third anniversary of Congolese independence) were subsequently denied. The trade unions, a spokesman said, were not unalterably opposed to a single political party but "were only opposed to the kind of party Youlou had in mind . . . run by the same old politicians."

After a night-long conference between trade-union leaders and senior officers of the Congolese Army, an eight-man Provisional Government "composed of technicians" was announced. There were no labor or military representatives among the ministerial appointments, all of whom were university trained and/or had held specialized public or private posts. Alphonse Massamba-Debat, forty-two, Speaker of the National Assembly from 1959 to 1961 and Minister of Development from 1961 to July, 1963, was named Prime Minister and Minister of National Defense. Mr. Massamba-Debat emphasized that the ministerial team would "remain conscious of their status as technicians," eschewing any supplementary compensation beyond their civil-service salaries and remaining in "lodgings appropriate to civil servants of a poor country." He reaffirmed the "friendship between the Congolese and French peoples" and expressed special appreciation that the "French Army did not lose its head" during the events of August 13–15. In the course of the *coup d'état*, 500 French troops maintained in Congo-Brazzaville under the terms of a 1960 defense agreement were deployed to protect vital government offices and installations, reinforced by an airlift of several hundred additional troops from Senegal and the Central African Republic.

A national referendum and general elections were held on December 8, 1963, to invite popular approval of a new draft constitution and to elect a new National Assembly. The new constitution, which sharply reduces the powers accorded to the President in the 1960 constitution, is officially described as "half-presidential, half-parliamentary." On December 20, Mr. Massamba-Debat was elected as President for a five-year term, by an electoral college consisting of members of the reconstituted National Assembly and of the prefectoral, subprefectoral, and municipal councils. Dr. Pascal Lissouba was named Prime Minister. They will be assisted, for a time, by a "National Council of the Revolution."

Labor's predominant role in the recent political changes in Brazzaville was not unexpected. More than a seventh of the republic's population is concentrated in its three major towns, and the Congo has long had the strongest trade-union movement in Equatorial Africa. Significantly, it also has an acute urban unemployment and rural labor shortage problem, a relatively impressive literacy rate, and a higher ratio of wage earners to population than any equatorial state except Gabon.

In their classic study *The Emerging States of French Equatorial Africa,* Virginia Thompson and Richard Adloff observed that Congo-Brazzaville "is the least favored by nature and the best equipped by man" of the four territories which once comprised France's equatorial federation. Its dense forests contain few of the okoumé trees that are the source of so much of Gabon's wealth, and cover no known mineral resources except some newly discovered potash. Only a small section of the southern part of the country can be described as first-class farming land.

Congo-Brazzaville owes its relatively high level of development primarily to its geographical location. Bordered by the Congo River on one side and the Atlantic Ocean on another, it was uniquely suited for development as a transit area to world markets. During the colonial period, Brazzaville was established as the federal capital (and supplied with infrastructure suitable to this role). Pointe-Noire was provided with a man-made port unequaled in the area, and the only railroad in the equatorial region was built to connect Brazzaville to the coast. As a result of French financial support and missionary zeal, 65 per cent of school-age children were attending school by independence in 1960.

Although imports still far outweigh the modest exports of lumber, coffee, palm products, bananas, peanuts, lead, and a few other items, a genuine effort is being made to attract industries and expand agricultural production. More importantly, Congo-Brazzaville is beginning to benefit from the new economic boom in Gabon. The volume of merchandise passing through the port of

Pointe-Noire in the first quarter of 1963, just after Gabon's new manganese mine at Moanda went into production, totaled 214,-000 tons—more than three times that of the corresponding period in 1962. Even so, the economy will continue to be crucially dependent for some years on the external financial and technical aid supplied largely by France and the European Economic Community.

Congo-Leopoldville

Population: 14,000,000 (1963 est.).

Area: 905,378 square miles.

Capital: Leopoldville (population: 700,000).

Political Status: Independent republic.

Date of Independence: June 30, 1960.

Chief of State: President Joseph Kasavubu, elected (June, 1960) by Parliament for a 4-year term (or until adoption of a definitive constitution).

Head of Government: Prime Minister Cyrille Adoula, appointed by President Kasavubu and unanimously confirmed by Parliament, August, 1961.

Major Political Parties: Mouvement National Congolais-Lumumba (MNC-L); Parti Solidaire Africaine (PSA), Kamitatu and Gizenga wings; Balubakat (Cartel Katangais); Alliance des Bakongo (ABAKO); Parti de l'Unité Nationale Africaine (PUNA); Union des Mongo (UNIMO); Mouvement National Congolais-Kalonji (MNC-K); Centre de Regroupement Africain (CEREA).

Legislative Branch: Bicameral. Under provisions of the temporary Loi Fondamentale, the Parliament elected in May, 1960, consisted of a Chamber of Deputies of 137 members and a Senate of 84 members. At least 3 senators from each of the 6 original provinces were traditional chiefs, elected by special traditional "electoral colleges" in each province. Both houses were prorogued by President Kasavubu on September 29, 1963, pending a popular referendum on a new constitution to be drafted by a special commission.

Monetary Unit: 180 Congolese francs = US$1.00 (since devaluation of the currency on November 9, 1963).

Principal Languages: French, Swahili, Kikongo, Lingala, Tshiluba.

External Affiliations: United Nations, Organization of African Unity, European Economic Community (associate).

Even as late as 1955, it was regarded a radical heresy when a Belgian professor proposed self-government for the Congo in thirty years. Under the system of paternalistic rule that was in force until the very eve of independence, neither the Congo's educational system nor its political institutions was designed to produce or train personnel for leadership positions. Literacy was 40 per cent (high for Africa), facilities for technical education were among the best on the continent, and Africans shared many material benefits of Congolese economic prosperity, but there were few university graduates and the training available was not directed toward development of political or administrative responsibility.

When Brussels abruptly decided in January, 1960, to get in the forefront of the "wind of change" and accede to the Congolese demands for political freedom, the new representative institutions hastily constructed and manned did not have time to grow steadying roots. The collapse of the country less than a fortnight after independence was triggered by rebellion within the Belgian-officered Force Publique, which in turn panicked the European population, and provoked the secession of the country's richest province, Katanga. On July 12, 1960, President Kasavubu and the late Prime Minister Patrice Lumumba requested the "urgent dispatch" of U.N. military assistance "to protect the national territory of the Congo against the present external aggression which is a threat to international peace."

More than three turbulent years later, there is now cautious hope that the U.N. force may have nearly completed its mission. With the collapse of Katanga secession in January, 1963, the Congo became a single political entity again and ceased to be a major Cold War issue. In October, the General Assembly authorized U.N. troops to remain for one final six-month transitional period—until June 30, 1964—and then return the task of maintaining public order to the Armée National Congolais, now a force of 30,000 men being retrained under General Joseph Mobutu with Belgian, Israeli, and other outside technical assistance.

During the next few years at least, the army is likely to be the uncertain linchpin of Congolese stability. For the competence of the military inevitably takes on particular significance in a country that still lacks any mass party or parties, a charismatic national leader, a real sense of national identity, or even a constitutional base for its governmental structure, and in which the psychological gap has steadily widened between the population as a whole and the new political elite.

On September 29, 1963, after prolonged stalemate within the unwieldy Parliament on approval of a new draft constitution to replace the temporary Loi Fondamentale of 1960, President Joseph Kasavubu prorogued both houses indefinitely and appointed a special constituent commission of leading Congolese to prepare a new organic law for submission to popular referendum "within 100 days." In the interim, the Congo was to be governed by decree.

Meanwhile, with elections mandatory after adoption of a new constitution, diverse efforts are being made ·by persons in the Adoula Administration to organize some sort of a national political movement. The Prime Minister came to politics directly from the labor movement, and has never had a party base. His impressive abilities are in the field of compromise and arbitration among competing elite groups rather than in building popular support at the grass-roots level. The initiative in developing a party representative of the administration has been taken primarily by the "Binza group" (a loose caucus of major officials, including Minister of Justice Justin Bomboko; Albert Ndele, presumptive president of the National Bank; General Mobutu; and Sûreté chief Victor Nendaka). Defense Minister Jerome Anany, not in the Binza group, also seems increasingly determined to play a major role.*

While the Congo's present economic situation remains critical, its long-term potential is impressive. Sixty per cent of the world's cobalt, 70 per cent of its industrial diamonds, and 10 per cent of its copper and tin came from the Congo before independence. And though minerals accounted for three-fifths of the country's exports in 1959, the variety of exports was greater than that of any African country except South Africa. Besides many locally consumed agricultural products produced within the northern and southern savannah areas, there were, in more peaceful times, exportable surpluses of palm oil, rubber, coffee, bananas, tea, and cotton. The gross national product in 1958—more than a billion dollars—was exceeded in Africa south of the Sahara only by Nigeria and South Africa.

* See "The Congo Begins to Stir" by M. Crawford Young, *Africa Report*, October, 1963, p. 9.

Dahomey

Population: 2,003,000 (1962 est.).

Area: 44,290 square miles.

Capital: Porto Novo (population: 65,000); may be moved to Cotonou.

Political Status: Independent republic.

Date of Independence: August 1, 1960.

Chief of State: President Mignan Apithy, elected by universal adult suffrage, January 19, 1964, for a term of 5 years.

Head of Government: Vice-President Justin Ahomadegbé, elected by universal adult suffrage, January 19, 1964, for a term of 5 years. Under the new constitution, the Vice-President will determine the nation's policies and will be responsible for national defense.

Major Political Parties: Three major political parties participating in the 1960 election were the Rassemblement Démocratique Dahoméen (RDD), led by Hubert Maga; the Parti des Nationalistes du Dahomey (PND), led by Sourou Mignan Apithy; and the Union Démocratique Dahoméen (UDD), led by Justin Ahomadegbé. Between 1961 and 1963, the Parti Dahoméen de l'Unité papered over the divisions between the PND and the UDD (since neither was strong enough to govern alone), and the resulting government proscribed the UDD. Following the military intervention of October, 1963, a new "national party" was formed, to be called the *Parti Démocratique Dahoméen.*

Legislative Branch: Under the 1960 constitution, Dahomey's National Assembly consisted of 60 members to be elected every 5 years by universal adult suffrage. The mandate of the Assembly elected in December, 1960, was terminated following the military intervention of October, 1963, and a special commission was appointed to draft a new constitution that would establish a compromise between an "orthodox presidential and a classic parliamentary regime." A new 42-seat Assembly was elected on January 19, 1964, by universal adult suffrage, for a term of 5 years.

Monetary Unit: 247 CFA francs = US$1.00.

Principal Languages: French, Fon, Yoruba, Hausa, Bariba.

External Affiliations: United Nations, Organization of African Unity, Union Africaine et Malgache, Conseil de l'Entente (with Ivory Coast, Upper Volta, and Niger), European Economic Community (associate), franc zone.

The change of government that occurred in Dahomey in October, 1963, was reported by the press as tropical Africa's third military *coup d'état* of the year, but a second look at the results suggests that the army's initial objectives were not very revolutionary. Although President Hubert Maga stepped down as head of state (to be replaced by a "provisional" soldier-administrator, Colonel Christophe Soglo, Chief of Staff of the 1,000-man Dahomean Army), he temporarily assigned five key portfolios in the provisional cabinet—Foreign Affairs, Justice, Tourism, Public Works, and Posts, Telegraphs, and Transport. Former Vice-President Mignan Apithy took over the ministries of Finance, Economic Affairs and Planning, and Agriculture. Most of the remaining portfolios—Education, Health, Labor, Civil Service, and Social Affairs—went to Justin Ahomadegbé, a third major political leader of Dahomey whose party was banned in 1960. Thus the first "provisional government" was, in fact, a "national government" in which the major rival power centers of Dahomey were carefully balanced—Mr. Maga's north, Mr. Apithy's Porto Novo stronghold in the southeast, and Mr. Ahomadegbé's constituency in the southwest.

The history of Dahomey politics since 1946, when France introduced the constitutional reforms that were to set the territories of French West Africa on the road to independence, has been characterized by a struggle for position among these three leaders and the ethnic groups and regional areas they represent. In short, the solution imposed by the military in October would seem to have resolved none of the country's complex ethnic and political quarrels, only placed them in suspended animation. Dahomey's trade unions—which touched off the October street demonstrations and riots, partly to protest the governing party's failure to prosecute one of its own deputies on a murder charge—were not directly represented in the new provisional government, although they won their key point: an all-party caretaker government pending new elections. In the longer run, however, the 1963 crisis may turn out to have been a major event in Dahomean history: The army and the labor unions discovered for the first time that they possessed the power to shape political events. The subsequent dismissal and house arrest of former President Maga in December, and Colonel Soglo's continuing role as political arbiter, suggested that this power would be used.

Other signs that major social upheaval may lie ahead in Dahomey include the continued stagnation of the economy and a growing imbalance between restless, educated Dahomeans and available white-collar jobs. (For many years, the enterprising Dahomeans were much in demand to fill white-collar and professional positions in the bureaucracies of other French-speaking West and Equatorial African territories. The demand for their services has waned sharply in the period of heightened nationalism since independence, thus adding to the already serious pressure on available jobs at home.)

There is no room, moreover, for these restless young men to "go west." A long narrow strip of land 415 miles long and barely 77 miles wide, Dahomey has the highest population density in West Africa (45 persons per square mile). Virtually everyone who does not work for the government is employed in agriculture, much of it at the subsistence level. Palm products (oil, kernels, and nuts) account for 65 per cent of the exports each year, though coffee, peanuts, and fish are also important; France remains the principal market. Ways of improving the range, quality, and yield of the food and export crops are under constant study, and several research centers are operated with French technical and financial assistance. In 1962, an intense drive was launched by the government to expand the land under cultivation by 20 per cent, largely through establishment of village collective farms. While production has indeed increased in recent years as a result of these and other efforts, imports nonetheless outweigh exports by several million dollars a year, and Dahomey could not make ends meet without the budgetary and developmental aid supplied by France.

Ethiopia

Population: 22,000,000 (1962 est.).

Area: 400,000 square miles.

Capital: Addis Ababa (population: 450,000).

Political Status: Independent monarchy.

Date of Independence: c.1040.

Chief of State and Head of Government: Emperor Haile Selassie I, hereditary.

Major Political Parties: None.

Legislative Branch: Bicameral. Chamber of Deputies of 251 seats elected by universal adult suffrage for 4-year terms. Last election, 1959. Senate, not to exceed one-half the number of seats in the Chamber of Deputies, appointed by the Emperor for 6-year terms.

Monetary Unit: 1 Ethiopian dollar = US$.4025.

Principal Languages: Amharic, English, Tigriniya, Tigre, Harari, Kaficho, Walamo, Kambata, Sidamo.

External Affiliations: United Nations, Organization of African Unity.

There are no political parties in Ethiopia, and all political power remains centralized in Emperor Haile Selassie. Since the abortive *coup d'état* of December, 1960, when a section of the Imperial Guard revolted during the Emperor's absence from the country and attempted to install the Crown Prince on the throne, security precautions have increased, but the Emperor has also sought to deal affirmatively with the discontent uncovered by the revolt. He has reconstituted his administration to include younger and more progressive men in some key ministerial posts, and has placed new emphasis on expansion of educational facilities and opportunities and other reforms. While these gestures are not likely to satisfy the critics of his regime, most observers doubt that the disparate opposition will again mobilize itself to try to seize power in the natural lifetime of the Emperor. He is now in his seventies, however, and an orderly succession is not at all certain

—especially since no designated successor had been named by 1963.

When Haile Selassie passes from the scene, four major political forces are likely to be involved in the ensuing struggle for power —the traditional Amharic aristocracy, the clergy of the powerful Ethiopian Coptic Church, elements of the armed forces, and the new intelligentsia. This does not mean that the institution of the monarchy will necessarily be eliminated—its deeply rooted traditions are perhaps indispensable to the continued unity of this ethnically and geographically diverse country—but only that there seems no potential royal successor on the horizon capable of governing Ethiopia in quite the manner of Haile Selassie.*

Although the country is now overdependent on the export of a few cash crops—coffee was largely responsible for the increase in exports from about $12 million to $171 million between 1942 and 1960—the Ethiopian highlands are among the most fertile and potentially versatile farming areas of Africa. Even so, coffee is likely to remain the mainstay; indeed, the word "coffee" is said to be derived from the Kaffa region in the southwestern part of the country, where much of the annual export production of some 33,000 metric tons grows wild. The decline in world coffee prices during 1959 gave impetus to plans for broadening the agricultural base, notably a projected Gezira-type irrigation scheme in the Awash River valley, expected to open up 250,000 acres for cultivation. Some 75,000 acres of the new development will be reserved for cotton.

The Emperor has been successful in obtaining developmental aid from remarkably diverse sources since the end of the Italian occupation. From 1946 to 1960, for example, Ethiopia received about $100 million in direct economic, military, and technical assistance from the United States; $23.5 million from the World Bank (mostly for improvement of internal communications), and about $120 million in credit from the Soviet Bloc.

* See "Reshaping an Autocracy," by A. Castagno, *Africa Report,* October, 1963, p. 3.

Gabon

Population: 450,000 (1961 est.).

Area: 102,317 square miles.

Capital: Libreville (population: 31,000).

Political Status: Independent republic.

Date of Independence: August 17, 1960.

Chief of State and Head of Government: President Leon M'Ba, elected (February, 1961) by universal adult suffrage for a 7-year term.

Political Parties: Bloc Démocratique Gabonais (BDG), led by President M'Ba; the Union Démocratique et Sociale Gabonaise (UDSG), led by Jean-Hilaire Aubame.

Legislative Branch: Unicameral. National Assembly of 67 members elected by universal adult suffrage for 5-year terms. Last election, February 12, 1961. Assembly dissolved by President M'Ba on January 21, 1964, pending new elections.

Monetary Unit: 247 CFA francs = US$1.00.

Principal Languages: French, Fang, various Bantu languages.

External Affiliations: United Nations, Organization of African Unity, Union Africaine et Malgache, Union Douanière Equatoriale, European Economic Community (associate), franc zone.

The Republic of Gabon is the smallest, least populated, and most prosperous of the states of French-speaking Equatorial Africa. Situated on the western coast of the continent, astride the equator, it is heavily forested with valuable woods and well endowed with subsoil mineral resources. Until 1950, when Ghana took the lead, Gabonese exports of forestry products (especially *okoumé*) were greater than those of any other African country; in 1962, they reached a total of 668,000 tons. In the southeast, perhaps the most important high-grade manganese deposit in the world (estimated reserves: at least 200 million tons) is being developed by an international concern combining European and American enterprise. In the northeast, another American-European group is beginning to exploit one of the world's richest deposits of high-

44

quality iron ore (estimated at 1 billion tons). Oil production from known reserves along the coast totaled 816,000 tons in 1962. Uranium deposits are estimated to contain 25 million tons of ore, capable of yielding about 5,000 tons of uranium metal. Between 1956 and 1961, Gabon's gross national product rose from $53 million to $122.5 million, even though exploitation of known mineral resources was barely under way.

The country's current Interim Three Year Development Plan (1963–65) emphasizes major improvements in internal transportation, diversification of agriculture to ensure a more balanced food supply for the population, education and training of the citizenry, health and sanitation, development of forestry-based industries, and attention to the hydroelectric potential of the country. A large part of the needed funds will come from rising domestic revenues, but external financial assistance is also being provided by the French Fonds d'Aide et de Coopération, the European Economic Community, United Nations agencies, and various Western nations. Government policy—like that of President M'Ba's early political mentor, Ivory Coast President Felix Houphouet-Boigny —has been conscientiously directed toward establishing a favorable environment for foreign business. The liberal investment code enacted in 1961 was designed to encourage additional foreign private investment and protect present investors.

In political affairs, the position of President M'Ba has been progressively consolidated by various means since independence. The last elections, held in 1961 under a new presidential constitution, resulted in a sweeping victory for the single list of sixty-seven candidates put forth jointly by the Bloc Démocratique Gabonais and the handicapped opposition party, Jean-Hilaire Aubame's Union Démocratique et Sociale Gabonaise. President M'Ba reportedly planned to announce the official merger of the two parties in the latter half of 1963, but the decree was shelved after the fall of President Fulbert Youlou from power in neighboring Congo-Brazzaville (shortly after announcing plans to establish a one-party government).

Although Gabon is a member of the Union Africaine et Malgache, the equatorial customs union (Union Douanière Equatoriale), and other institutions of regional cooperation, the government remains cool toward various schemes for political federation with the other French-speaking equatorial states (Chad, Congo-Brazzaville, Central African Republic). Several bilateral accords with France were signed at independence, and 75 per cent of Gabon's exports go to its associates in the EEC.

Gambia

Population: 320,000 (1963 est.).

Area: 4,000 square miles.

Capital: Bathurst (population: 28,000).

Political Status: Self-governing British colony and protectorate.

Chief of State: Queen Elizabeth II, represented locally by Governor Sir John W. Paul.

Head of Government: Prime Minister David K. Jawara, leader of government since May, 1962.

Major Political Parties: People's Progressive Party, led by David K. Jawara; United Party, led by former Chief Minister P. S. N'Jie; Democratic Congress Alliance, led by Garba-Jahumpa.

Legislative Branch: Unicameral. House of Representatives of 2 appointed members and 36 elected by universal adult suffrage for a 5-year term. Last election, May, 1962.

Monetary Unit: 1 West African pound = US$2.80.

Principal Languages: English, Wollof, Mandinga, Fula.

Britain's oldest, smallest, and last possession in West Africa, Gambia achieved the status of full internal self-government on October 4, 1963. By an Order-in-Council signed by Her Majesty Queen Elizabeth II, this constitutional change places the government of Prime Minister David Jawara in full control of all internal matters except foreign affairs, defense, and internal security, which remains a residual responsibility of the Governor. Independence is likely in 1964.

The territory consists of a small colony at the mouth of the Gambia River, which has been under British authority since 1783, and a long narrow inland protectorate extending some 300 miles upstream along either side of the river (from which the country derives its name) into the heart of Senegal.

Surrounded by Senegal on its three landward sides and bound to it by ethnic, economic, and Islamic ties of long standing, Gambia would seem to be a logical candidate for some sort of "Senegambian" federation. The idea of association has been approached with caution on both sides, however, for the two territories were subject to very different conditioning during the colonial era— e.g., the elite language is French in Senegal and English in Gambia, and the administrative and judicial systems are not parallel —and Gambians are wary of being Gallicized. Senegal, on its part, has pressed the case for union gently, letting economic logic speak for itself. At the request of the two governments, the United Nations appointed a four-man team of experts (two Swiss and two Dutch) in 1962 to study the economic and political problems of various forms of future association. The team's report, due early in 1964, will not be binding on either country.

On the occasion of self-government in October, 1963, Prime Minister Jawara stated that Gambia wanted the closest possible association with Senegal, but that it "intended to retain its distinct personality and its own culture." Earlier in the same month, however, he condemned existing boundaries in Africa as the "most harmful heritage of the colonial era." The position of the opposition party has also been ambivalent.

Peanuts—largely raised by peasant farmers of the protectorate, with the assistance of itinerant Senegalese—provide about 90 per cent of Gambia's small export earnings. Other exports include beeswax, hides and skins, cotton, and palm oil. The search for petroleum in the river bed continues.

Ghana

Population: 7,148,000 (1962 est.).

Area: 92,100 square miles.

Capital: Accra (population: 400,000).

Political Status: Independent republic.

Date of Independence: March 6, 1957 (became a republic on July 1, 1960).

Chief of State and Head of Government: President Kwame Nkrumah, head of government since 1951; elected (1960) for his first presidential term by universal adult suffrage. However, the 1960 constitution stipulates that subsequent Presidents will be chosen by the National Assembly.

Political Parties: President Nkrumah's Convention People's Party held 108 of the 114 seats in the National Assembly in 1963; the opposition United Party had 6. In a popular referendum held in January, 1964, Ghana's voters approved the establishment of a one-party state.

Legislative Branch: Unicameral. National Assembly of 104 deputies elected by universal adult suffrage in 1956 for a maximum of 5 years, plus 10 "specially elected" women's representatives. Its life was renewed for another 5 years when the new republican constitution was adopted in 1960. The Assembly can be dissolved by the President at any time, whereupon elections must follow within 2 months.

Monetary Unit: 1 Ghana pound = US$2.80.

Principal Languages: English, Twi, Ewe, Ga.

External Affiliations: United Nations, Organization of African Unity, Commonwealth.

Ghana, the former British colony of the Gold Coast, became independent in 1957, incorporating the U.N. trust territory of British Togoland. The few years since independence have wrought striking political changes. Ashanti separatism, which threatened in 1957 to split the nation, has been largely dissipated. The state has not merely held together but has been consolidated by a single radical socialist party whose web of authority now extends over the entire country, embracing farmer, youth, and labor movements. On July 1, 1960, following a national plebiscite, a new re-

49

publican constitution came into force which assigns broad powers to President Nkrumah as both head of state and head of government. The opposition United Party, the successor to the regional political parties that challenged the regime in the mid-1950's, has steadily dwindled, and a number of its leaders are now in exile.

Dr. Nkrumah is a strong advocate of pan-African unity. In 1958, he sponsored the first Conference of Independent African States and the first All-African People's Conference, both in Accra. In 1961, Ghana was a prime mover in the formation of the Casablanca Group (with Guinea, Mali, Morocco, the U.A.R., and the then Provisional Government of the Algerian Republic) and in drafting the foreign policy sections of the Casablanca Charter —i.e., nonalignment, elimination of foreign bases in Africa, rapid liberation of all remaining colonial territories, and closer working relationships in all fields among African states. Although the Casablanca Group disintegrated in 1963, Ghana continues to pursue these goals within the framework of the broader Organization of African Unity, established at Addis Ababa in May, 1963. President Nkrumah has made it clear that Ghana regards the OAU approach as merely a first step toward a genuine African political union, and not an end in itself.

Economically, Ghana is one of Africa's wealthier and more dynamic countries. The per capita income—$199 in 1961—is among the highest in independent Africa. Ghana is a major producer of cocoa (35 per cent of world production in 1962–63), which remains the principal export and source of foreign exchange. The government is seeking to diversify the economy by developing other export crops and is speeding industrialization; production of new food crops to meet basic nutritional requirements is also being encouraged. Ghana's mineral exports include gold, diamonds, manganese, and bauxite. The latter will provide the raw material for an aluminum-smelting plant to be built as the second stage of the $200 million Volta River hydroelectric project, now under construction (with the financial assistance of the World Bank, the United States, and the United Kingdom).

President Nkrumah's political and economic goals for Ghana have long been avowedly socialist, and he has developed cordial relations with a number of Communist countries in his militant pursuit of a policy of independence and nonalignment. However, Ghana's historic overseas ties with the West—especially in trade and education—remained strong through 1963, and the Nkrumah brand of African socialism has to date explicitly provided for a private sector. In 1963, the private sector was still the most important part of the Ghanaian economy, and 90 per cent of the country's trade was with the West. The total British investment in the Ghana economy was estimated by *New Commonwealth* in October, 1963, at $544 million.

Ghana has had three major internal political crises since independence. In September, 1961, a strike of railway, harbor, and bus workers was touched off by the announcement of an austerity budget that included a compulsory savings scheme. The strike was soon brought to an end, and a number of opposition leaders and minor figures in the governing party were subsequently detained for alleged complicity. In August, 1962, an unsuccessful attempt to assassinate Dr. Nkrumah led to the imposition of a state of emergency in the capital and to the arrest of several leading figures within the governing party. In late 1963, Ghana entered a new period of uncertainty when President Nkrumah (1) was empowered by new legislation (November 4, 1963) to extend Preventive Detention almost indefinitely; (2) dismissed the highly respected Justice of the Supreme Court (December 11, 1963) after he rendered a judgment of acquittal against two Cabinet officers tried on charges of complicity in the alleged 1962 assassination plot; (3) announced (December 31) that a national referendum would be held early in 1964 on a constitutional amendment establishing a one-party state; and (4) began a purge of the Ghana Police after a young constable made another unsuccessful attempt (January 2, 1964) on the President's life.

These developments, reinforced by a constant and ever more strident attack in the semiofficial press against all Western-oriented elements in the country, raised new speculation that Ghana's "pendulum" period was over, and that Dr. Nkrumah was deliberately moving—or, alternatively, being propelled by the Marxist militants in his entourage—toward an early and total break with what the Accra weekly *Spark* calls the "backward-looking intellectual elite." If this turning point was, indeed, soon approaching, the role of the heretofore nonpolitical Ghana Army was likely to become decisive. As of early 1964, Ghana's Marxist "vanguard militants" controlled the press, radio, most "educational" posts in the governing party, and many key trade-union positions. But, despite the heightening tempo of political indoctrination, it seemed evident that they were still a numerical minority in the civil service, the Convention People's Party, the security forces, and the country at large.

Guinea

Population: 3,000,000 (1963 est.).

Area: 95,000 square miles.

Capital: Conakry (population: 78,000).

Political Status: Independent republic.

Date of Independence: October 2, 1958.

Chief of State and Head of Government: President Sékou Touré, invested as Prime Minister in 1958, and elected (January 27, 1961) President of the Republic by universal adult suffrage for a 7-year term.

Political Party: Parti Démocratique de Guinée.

Legislative Branch: Unicameral. National Assembly of 75 members elected by universal adult suffrage from a single list for a 5-year term. Last election, October, 1963.

Monetary Unit: 247 Guinean francs = US$1.00 (but non-convertible).

Principal Languages: French, Fulani, Malinke, Soussou.

External Affiliations: United Nations, Organization of African Unity.

In the September, 1958, French constitutional referendum, Guinea—alone among France's African territories—opted to become a fully independent republic rather than self-governing within the new French Community. In retaliation for this defection, France quickly withdrew virtually all its administrative staff (almost three-quarters of Guinea's bureaucracy at the time), as well as technical and military personnel and all movable capital equipment. During the first weeks of independence, there were many who believed that complete economic and administrative collapse was inevitable.

Under the determined leadership of President Sékou Touré, whose rise to political prominence had been through the West African labor movement, the country miraculously survived and consolidated its independence—with the help of a $28 million emergency loan from Ghana, temporary assistance from Senegalese teachers in keeping schools operating, and, eventually, large-scale infusions of Soviet Bloc financial and technical assistance. In December, 1958, the position of the Parti Démocratique de Guinée as the power center of the country was given legal status when the opposition parties fused with the governing party and Guinea became officially a one-party state. The Guinea experiment became the touchstone of radical young Africans throughout the continent.

Sékou Touré's stated goal was total "decolonization" to "destroy the habits, conceptions, and ways of conduct" built up during sixty years of French colonial rule, and to make of Guinea as African a country as Kwame Nkrumah had made of Ghana. Toward this end, most institutions of national life were drastically reshaped to speed the burial of internal ethnic and cultural differences and build a new sense of Guinean nationhood.

The new elite came to power strongly influenced by Marxist economic ideas and steeped in Marxist phraseology, but subsequent events have demonstrated that there was no intent to deliver Guinea into subservience to yet another non-African power. The emphasis on the teaching of African history, languages, and cultural values in Guinean schools is one of many manifestations of the PDG's concern with giving its socialism a uniquely African personality. Moreover, rejection of the colonial past never went to the extreme of replacing French as the language of instruction in Guinean schools or revamping the French-based judicial system. Even when relations between Paris and Conakry were at their lowest ebb—in 1960—more Guineans went to France than to any other country for higher education, and French newspapers circulated freely in Conakry.

The one area in which the new government initially attempted —with near-disastrous results—to employ a doctrinaire approach was in reorganizing the economy. With the assistance of a corps of newly engaged technical experts, most of them drawn from the Soviet Bloc, the government rapidly took over all import and export trade, all wholesale trade, and much of the retail trade. It adopted a new currency, nationalized banks and insurance companies, and put most expatriate-owned business under government control. (The only major exception to the sweep of nationalization was the FRIA aluminum plant, operated by a consortium of American and European firms about 100 miles from Conakry, which accounted for almost 50 per cent of the value of Guinea's exports in 1962.) Agricultural productivity—crucial in a country where 90 per cent of the population is directly or indirectly dependent on the soil—declined sharply, and with it the volume of internal trading. Shortages of food and consumer goods were chronic during 1960 and 1961, and dwindling foreign exchange hampered importation of necessary replacement equipment and operating supplies.

In November, 1961, after an outbreak of teachers' strikes and other manifestations of popular dissatisfaction, the government took a new look at its economic policies. Both Bloc embassies and "colonialist elements" were accused of fomenting the unrest, but the subsequent turn of Guinean policy reflected particular disenchantment with the economic and political results of over-dependence on Soviet financial assistance and technical advice. With the Algerian cease-fire in March, 1962—a major turning point in Guinea's relations with France and the West—Sékou Touré shifted to a more flexible policy aimed at restoring Guinea to economic health.

Accordingly, the government has actively sought aid from a wider ideological spectrum; revised its Investment Code to encourage private investment (particularly in the development of bauxite and iron ore reserves); joined the World Bank and the International Monetary Fund; undertaken new measures to strengthen its currency; settled many of the outstanding differences with France; turned domestic retail trade back to independent dealers, except in those regions of the country where no private outlets exist; relaxed internal price controls; denationalized diamond mining; taken firm steps to reduce extravagance in the bureaucracy; and launched a nationwide campaign to "educate the people and encourage them to increase and diversify their agricultural production." ("It is really unthinkable," President Touré told the National Assembly in October, 1963, "for an agricultural country such as Guinea to be obliged to import 1.9 billion francs worth of rice yearly." To change this, he said, would require a new attitude on the part of the Guinean peasant, who now "works only five months in a year and rests the remaining seven," and of civil servants and artisans, "who believe that 40 or 42 hours of work weekly is enough to make them worthy of the Guinean revolution.")

Under President Touré, Guinea continues to play a dynamic role in intra-African politics. A founding member of the Casablanca Group, Touré in 1962 and 1963 was a prime mover in breaking down the sharp divisions between the Casablanca and Monrovia-Brazzaville "blocs," and in the establishment of a single Organization of African Unity in Addis Ababa in May, 1963. In its relations with the rest of the world, Guinea has mended its fences toward the West, but without departing from its basic commitment to a policy of "positive nonalignment."

The High Commission Territories

The three High Commission Territories of southern Africa—Basutoland, Bechuanaland, and Swaziland—have been wards of Britain since the late nineteenth century. When the Union of South Africa was being formed in 1909, it was first assumed that the territories would become integral parts of the new state. The local tribal authorities clung tenaciously to their treaties with Britain, however, and were finally allowed to remain under U.K. colonial administration. In view of the location of the three territories within the frontiers of the Union, Britain agreed that the Union of South Africa Act should contain a section setting out the conditions under which they might one day be incorporated —if and when the governments of the Union and the United Kingdom should agree, and if certain specified conditions were met pertaining to land and other rights for the indigenous population. For some fifty years thereafter, Britain gave Basutoland, Bechuanaland, and Swaziland what has been described elsewhere as a "passive kind of protection," based on the implicit assumption that incorporation in South Africa would be their ultimate choice and that their economic well-being was a function of South Africa's growth. With the development of political consciousness in Britain and in Africa, and the extremist turn of South African racial policies, it has become increasingly evident in recent years that incorporation would not be accepted willingly. Responding to this new situation, Britain began in the 1950's to give belated attention to the internal economic development of the three states and to give each of them representative governing institutions suited to their varying aspirations. But the longer-term policy dilemma confronting Britain in the High Commission Territories remains unresolved.

In September, 1963, Prime Minister Hendrik Verwoerd reopened the sensitive issue of the relationship between the High Commission Territories and the Republic when he challenged

Britain to allow his government to "give full information to the inhabitants of these territories . . . on the advantages that would accrue to them if they . . . chose to accept the Republic as their aide or guide or guardian to independence and prosperity." Contending that South Africa had "no territorial ambitions," he offered them instead the opportunity to become "fully Bantu-governed states" on the pattern of the Transkei. There are no indications that this solution would be accepted willingly either by London or the African populations involved as long as the present government of South Africa is in power.

1. Basutoland

Population: 800,000 (1963 est.).

Area: 11,716 square miles.

Capital: Maseru.

Political Status: British High Commission Territory.

Chief of State: Queen Elizabeth II, represented locally by Sir Hugh Stephenson, High Commissioner for Basutoland, the Bechuanaland Protectorate, and Swaziland, with headquarters in Pretoria; and in Basutoland by the Queen's Commissioner (formerly Resident Commissioner), A. F. Giles.

Head of Government: Under the 1960 constitution, the Executive Council consists of 4 senior officials (including the Queen's Commissioner) and 4 elected members of the Basutoland National Council. Important executive functions are also vested in the Paramount Chief of the Basuto people, Motlotlehi Moshoeshoe II, especially in regard to the land of Basutoland. The Executive Council is advisory both to the High Commissioner and the Paramount Chief.

Major Political Parties: Basutoland Congress Party; the Basutoland Freedom Party; the Basutoland National Party; Marema Tlou; the Basutoland Labor Party, favoring cooperation with South Africa; and the Communist Party of Lesotho. Exiled members of South Africa's two major nationalist movements, the African National Congress and the Pan-Africanist Congress, are also active.

Legislative Branch: Forty of the 80 seats in the Basutoland National Council (established under the terms of the 1960 constitution) are chosen indirectly by popularly elected district councils. The Paramount Chief of the Basutos nominates 14 members, and 22 Senior Chiefs are automatically members. The remaining 4 members are appointed by the U.K. Veto power over the Council rests with the Queen's Commissioner. Last elections, January, 1960.

Monetary Unit: 1 South African Rand = US$1.40.

Principal Languages: English, Sesotho.

The three High Commission Territories are strikingly different, bound together only by their common plight. The least viable economically and the most advanced politically is Basutoland. It consists of a dramatically beautiful 5,000-foot plateau studded by jagged mountains that rise to 11,000 feet. Although Basutoland is about the size of Belgium, the mountains are suitable only for grazing and 80 per cent of the population lives in a narrow lowland strip representing only a quarter of the total area.

Everywhere the overriding problem is erosion, for overgrazing has denuded much of the highlands of grass cover and has led to gully erosion in the arable land below. The lowland soils suffer further from having been cropped continuously for eighty years without the administration of fertilizers; because the enclave is virtually treeless, animal manure is used for fuel instead of being returned to the land. Up to two-thirds of the male population may work in South Africa at one time, and most of the cultivation is done by women using primitive methods. Most of the cash income comes from remittances from family members working in the neighboring Republic and from exports of wool, mohair, and a few agricultural products—also chiefly to South Africa.

Basutoland's revenue in 1961–62 was $8.4 million, which included a $3.22 million grant-in-aid from the U.K. and $2.38 million in customs and excise duties from the Republic of South Africa in accordance with a scale established in the 1909 Agreement. In 1962–63, expenditures were estimated at $8.82 million and revenue at $5.32 million, leaving a shortfall of $3.5 million to be met by the U.K. Present modest development projects—underwritten by U.K. Colonial Development and Welfare Acts grants and voluntary organizations (especially the Oxford Committee for Famine Relief)—place major emphasis on increasing the productivity of lands already under cultivation. This undertaking is complicated by the land-tenure system of the Basuto. Although grazing rights in the highlands are communal, all arable land is allocated by chiefs and is nonalienable. An estimated 150,000 of the 160,000 families have small individual holdings.

One resource that Basutoland possesses in abundance is water, and several schemes are being studied that would develop this hydroelectric potential and perhaps market some of the millions of gallons of pure mountain water now wasted annually in run-off. There are no known mineral resources, except, possibly, some exploitable diamond deposits in the north.

Despite the fact that Basutoland's day-to-day existence is crucially dependent on policy decisions in Pretoria, this uncertainty is not reflected in the country's robust political life. The two major parties are Ntsu Mokhehle's pan-Africanist Basutoland Congress Party (which won twenty-nine of the forty elected seats in the 1960 elections, but sits in militant opposition to the territory's Executive Council) and its more moderate 1961 offshoot, the Basutoland Freedom Party, discreetly supported by the Oxford-educated, twenty-five-year-old Paramount Chief of the Basutos, Motlotlehi Moshoeshoe II. Completing the ideological spectrum are the Marema Tlou, led by Chief S. S. Matete; the Catholic-supported Basutoland National Party, led by Chief Leabua Jonathan; a small but active Communist Party, established in May, 1962, under the leadership of John Motloheloa, an African deported from the Republic; and the Basutoland Labor Party, which favors a Transkei-type relationship with South Africa.

An all-party Constitutional Commission, established by the Basuto National Council in 1961 with Professor D. V. Cowen as adviser, unanimously proposed in October, 1963, that Basutoland be granted self-government in 1964 and full independence in 1965. Preliminary indications were that Britain had grave doubts about the prudence of this timetable. Moreover, the Commission's recommendations ran into unexpected opposition on the floor of the Legislative Council when debate began in December, 1963.

Some of the factors contributing to the relative sophistication of political life in Basutoland include the ethnic and linguistic unity of the Basuto population, the concentration of much of the population in a relatively limited area, the infusion of a growing number of political exiles from South Africa, and the availability of educational opportunities. Primary education is free, and it is estimated that 95 per cent of Basuto children attend state-aided mission schools at some time in their lives. In addition to twenty secondary schools, Basutoland also has the only accredited university in southern Africa offering equal academic facilities for all races. Established in 1945 by the Catholic Church as the University College of Pius XII, with a staff eventually drawn from fourteen different countries, it was secularized (and renamed the University of Basutoland, Bechuanaland, and Swaziland) in January, 1964.

2. Bechuanaland Protectorate

Population: 337,000 (1963 est.).

Area: 275,000 square miles.

Capital: Mafeking, South Africa (population: 9,000).

Political Status: British protectorate since 1885; High Commission Territory since 1909.

Chief of State: Queen Elizabeth II, represented locally by Sir Hugh Stephenson, High Commissioner for Basutoland, the Bechuanaland Protectorate, and Swaziland, with headquarters in Pretoria; and in Bechuanaland by the Queen's Commissioner (formerly Resident Commissioner), R. P. Fawcus.

Head of Government: The Queen's Commissioner for Bechuanaland Protectorate, assisted by an Executive Council composed of the Queen's Commissioner ex-officio, 5 officials (the Government Secretary, the Financial Secretary, the Legislative Secretary and 2 others appointed by the Queen's Commissioner), and 4 unofficial members (2 European and 2 African) appointed by the Queen's Commissioner from among the elected members of the Legislative Council.

Major Political Parties: The Bechuanaland Democratic Party, 2 factions of the Bechuanaland People's Party, and the multiracial Bechuanaland Liberal Party.

Legislative Branch: Unicameral. Legislative Council of 31 to 35 members chaired by the Queen's Commissioner and made up of 3 ex-officio members (the Government Secretary, the Financial Secretary, and the Legislative Secretary); 7 nominated official members; up to 4 unofficial members appointed by the Queen's Commissioner (equally balanced between Europeans and Africans); and 21 elected members (10 Europeans, 10 Africans, and 1 Asian). The European members are elected by European voters, and the Asian member by votes of his own racial group. The African members are elected by an African Council (consisting of the Queen's Commissioner and not more than 7 other official members, chiefs of the 8 principal tribes, 32 African members appointed or elected from the divisions of the protectorate, and not more than 2 other appointed members) acting as an electoral college. The African Council and an 8-member European Advisory Council (both established in 1920) also advise the Queen's Commissioner on matters relating to their respective communities.

Monetary Unit: 1 South African Rand = US$1.40.

Principal Languages: English, Tswana, Afrikaans.

In November, 1963, the leaders of all political factions in Bechuanaland sat down together to exchange views on the next stage of constitutional development. At the end of two days, they unanimously and "in a cooperative and harmonious spirit" agreed on a set of principles that would transform Bechuanaland into a self-governing multiracial state by 1964. September or October, 1964, were set as target dates for general elections by universal adult suffrage of a new Legislative Assembly. The proposals call for a Prime Minister and a Cabinet system, but would leave responsibility for defense, external affairs, internal security, finance, public service, and certain other matters to the Queen's Commissioner.

Political groups represented at the meeting included the Bechuanaland Democratic Party, led by Seretse Khama; the two factions of the Bechuanaland People's Party; and white and Asian members of the Legislative Council. Most observers believe that forty-two-year-old Seretse Khama—who made world headlines when he was temporarily exiled and permanently relieved of his Bamangwato chieftaincy in 1950 because of his marriage to an English woman—will be Bechuanaland's first Prime Minister. He won more votes than any other candidate in the 1961 elections and his Bamangwato tribe comprises one-third of the total population. In April, 1963, moreover, the multiracial Bechuanaland Liberal Party, which commands much of the European and moderate African support in the south, allied formally with the Democratic Party. The other major grouping is the Bechuanaland People's Party, based largely in Francistown in the north and Lobatsi in the south. It is a militant pan-Africanist nationalist movement, which would have Bechuanaland become the launching pad for the assault on South Africa. In 1962, the party split into two factions—one affiliated with the South African Pan-Africanist Congress and the other linked to the Republic's African National Congress.

Of the three High Commission Territories, Bechuanaland would seem to be the most unlikely political pace-setter. The protectorate is a vast and sparsely populated pastoral tableland; almost two-thirds of the land area is occupied by the Kalahari

Desert (last refuge of the aboriginal Bushmen) and the northwest is largely uninhabited swampland. Most of the people—both the African majority and some 3,000 Europeans—live in the east, near the railway that runs from South Africa through 394 miles of landlocked Bechuanaland to Southern Rhodesia. In contrast to the ethnic unity of Basutoland, there are eight autonomous Bechuana tribes (besides the Bushmen) who have only recently begun to think in terms of supratribal loyalties.

Bechuanaland is, moreover, bound to South Africa by a web of relationships that reach back to the last century. The present protectorate is only the northern part of a larger British entity established in 1885; its other half was incorporated into Cape Colony in 1895 and is now an integral part of the Republic. Even today, Bechuanaland's capital remains located in South Africa, though a new administrative center is now under construction at Gaberones. South Africa is the direct source of a quarter of Bechuanaland's annual revenue of about $2.8 million (i.e., the protectorate's share of customs and excise taxes under terms of the 1909 Act), and buys most of Bechuanaland's modest exports of beef, corn, beans and pulses, manganese, and asbestos.

British grants-in-aid take up the shortfall in the budget—which runs about $1.4 million annually. Current development projects, financed by the Colonial Development Corporation and the Colonial Development and Welfare Acts, place major emphasis on expansion and improvement of the livestock industry through better pasture management, improved breeding, and animal husbandry; water conservation; and modernization of transport facilities. Some 400 million tons of medium-grade bituminous coal, fortuitously located near the railway, await exploitation, as do extensive salt deposits in the north central sector. Expansion of educational facilities at all levels is also a priority goal for the 1963–68 period.

If Bechuanaland succeeds in becoming the first multiracial state on South Africa's border, it is likely to play a role in the unfolding history of the continent out of all proportion to its intrinsic importance. Seretse Khama sees this role as one of proving to South African whites, by example, that races can work together effectively on a basis of equality without harm to the interests of either. Other political elements in Bechuanaland, less optimistic about the prospects for changing white attitudes in the Republic, would make maximum use of Bechuanaland's strategic military position as a corridor between independent Africa and the heartland of apartheid.

Taking note in November, 1963, of the increasingly stringent controls being applied by the South African Government to regulate movement in and out of the High Commission territories, Queen's Commissioner R. P. Fawcus reaffirmed that the protectorate would continue to give shelter to refugees arriving from South Africa. He counseled the Legislative Council that the territory must pursue a policy of "caution but not timidity" toward those "neighboring countries who are so much stronger than ourselves but with whom we must trade to live."

3. Swaziland

Population: 282,000, including 10,000 Europeans (1963 est.).

Area: 6,704 square miles.

Capital: Mbabane (population: 6,000).

Political Status: British High Commission Territory.

Chief of State: Queen Elizabeth II, represented locally by Sir Hugh Stephenson, High Commissioner for Basutoland, the Bechuanaland Protectorate, and Swaziland, with headquarters in Pretoria; and in Swaziland by the Queen's Commissioner (formerly Resident Commissioner), Brian A. Marwick.

Head of Government: The Queen's Commissioner, assisted by two advisory groups that meet separately. The European Advisory Council, formed in 1921, is consulted on questions involving Europeans; the Paramount Chief of the Swazi people (the Ngwenyama, Sobhuza II) and, through him, the appointive Swazi National Council, is consulted on matters affecting Africans. Under the new constitution scheduled to become effective early in 1964 (see below), the Queen's Commissioner will chair an Executive Council consisting of 3 civil-service directors of law, administration, and finance, and 4 representatives of the new Legislative Council.

Major Political Parties: Swaziland Progressive Party, Ngwane National Liberatory Congress (NNLB), Swaziland Democratic Party.

Legislative Branch: At present, none. Under the new constitution introduced by British Colonial Secretary Duncan Sandys in May, 1963, due to become effective in 1964, Swaziland will have a Legislative Council consisting of 24—8 whites (4 elected by Europeans, 4 elected by all voters), 8 Africans to be certified by the Paramount Chief after election by traditional methods, and 8 other members of any race elected by universal adult suffrage.

Monetary Unit: 1 South African Rand = US$1.40.

Principal Languages: English, Afrikaans, Swazi.

Swaziland is the smallest and most prosperous of the High Commission Territories. Entirely surrounded by South Africa, except for a seventy-mile border with Mozambique, it has been for the past half-century a classic example of energetic white entrepreneurship operating in a sympathetic tribal setting.

During the 1880's, the Paramount Chief of the Swazis granted Europeans mineral and land concessions covering the entire territory. Britain subsequently (beginning in 1907) took steps to reduce these concessions, setting aside 1,639,000 acres (about one-third of the territory) for the exclusive use of Africans. A further 1,115,000 acres were taken over as Crown land, though some of this was later sold or reassigned. Swazi holdings have been further extended during the past half-century through direct purchase from Europeans (about 258,000 acres); Colonial Development and Welfare Act purchases of over 200,000 acres for redistribution to Africans; and an allotment of over 100,000 acres from the Crown lands. At present, Europeans control about 43 per cent of the land area, 1 per cent is Crown land, and the remainder is now under Swazi control. Significantly, the white and Swazi holdings alternate throughout the country, and partition would appear impracticable.

The bulk of the African population is engaged in the traditional Swazi pastoral way of life or low-yield subsistence agriculture. The territory's consistently favorable trade balance is largely accounted for by the large-scale agricultural projects, mining operations, and developing industries organized by the 10,000 European residents. Principal export crops include sugar (annual exports of over $8 million), timber, tobacco, and butter. Exports from the Havelock asbestos mine in the northwestern part of the country total nearly $6 million annually, and the first shipments of a promised 12 million tons of high-grade iron ore to Japan (from deposits just outside the capital city of Mbabane) are expected in 1964. In 1964, too, three major pre-industrial development projects costing $36.4 million will be brought to completion: a 140-mile railway giving Swaziland access to the sea via Mozambique; an all-weather $7.7 million black-top highway through the heart of the country; and the first stage of a three-stage hydroelectric scheme that will ultimately generate 30,000 kw. The highway is being partly financed by the International Development Association and the hydroelectric scheme by a World Bank loan, but Swaziland's principal source of developmental assistance has been Britain's Colonial Development Corporation, which had invested or committed $51.8 million for large-scale mineral, afforestation, and irrigation schemes by the middle of 1963.

Like Britain's other territories in southern Africa, Swaziland is closely bound economically to South Africa. It uses the same currency as the Republic and is treated as part of South Africa for customs purposes, receiving a fixed percentage of all duties collected in the Republic. About two-thirds of Swazi exports go to South African markets, and 10,000 Swazi males work in South African mines and industries. Much of the European-owned land is held by owners resident in the Republic and many of the European residents of Swaziland also have businesses in South Africa.

Development of popular political movements has been impeded by the combined opposition of two powerful conservative forces: the Ngwenyama—Chief Sobhuza II, the traditional tribal leader of this virtually one-tribe country—and the white settlers. Working together, the European and traditionalist delegations succeeded in stalemating a constitutional conference convened in London at British initiative early in 1963 to develop a more representative form of government.* In May, 1963, Colonial Secretary Duncan Sandys took note of the apparently irreconcilable gap between the conservative and modernist positions, and announced that a compromise constitution of Britain's own making would be introduced by early 1964. The Sandys constitution was promptly attacked as "too radical" by European settlers and dismissed as "reactionary and racist" by Swazi nationalist parties. At year's end, all political groups were digging in their heels to fight its implementation.

The three nationalist parties include: the Swaziland Progressive Party, under the leadership of J. J. Nquku, now sharply reduced in size and influence by fission; the stronger breakaway Ngwane National Liberatory Congress (NNLB) under Swaziland's first medical doctor, Dr. Ambrose P. Zwane; and the multiracial Swaziland Democratic Party, with ties to the Liberal Party in South Africa, led by Simon Nxumalo. The Mbandzeni National Convention Party (MNCP) has reportedly been dissolved. All

---

* See "Constitutional Confusion in Swaziland," by Claude Welch, Jr., *Africa Report,* April, 1963, p. 7.

existing parties favor adult suffrage (including women), resistance to any kind of inclusion in South Africa, state control of land and mineral rights, and more openings for Swazis in the administration and industry.

Their principal objection to the Sandys constitution concerns the proposed breakdown of the twenty-four elected seats (see above). This formula, they argue with rare unanimity, would enable traditionalists and European settlers to dominate the legislative body.

Ifni

Population: 52,995 (1960 census).

Area: Officially 791 square miles, though Spain has relinquished much of the hinterland to Morocco.

Capital: Sidi Ifni (population: 13,000).

Political Status: Province of Spain.

Local Head of Government: Governor-General Adolfo Artalejo Campos.

Monetary Unit: 60 pesetas = US$1.00.

Principal Languages: Spanish, Arabic, Berber.

Although the Spanish claim to Ifni dates back to 1476, and is referred to in the 1860 Treaty of Tetuan, the enclave has been governed by Spain only since 1934. In 1958, following Moroccan efforts to annex the territory, Ifni was accorded full juridical status as a province of the motherland and the military garrison was reinforced. The enclave has no significant resources, and its present value to Spain is chiefly as a military base and political pawn.

Ifni's nearly 8,500 Europeans—occupied largely with commerce, administration, or military activity—reside almost exclusively in Sidi Ifni, the capital city, where they make up about half the population. Nomadic Berbers inhabit the remainder of the province. Due to the ethnic unity and at least nominal Islamic faith of the Berber element, Hispanization of the hinterland has progressed slowly, and most of the area outside Sidi Ifni is, for all practical purposes, Moroccan. However, July, 1963, newspaper reports that Ifni had been officially taken over by Morocco were subsequently denied in both Rabat and Madrid.

The Governor-General of Ifni, who is responsible directly to the Director-General of African Provinces in Madrid, is also the commanding officer of the provincial armed forces. Although the Ifnians, as full Spanish citizens since 1958, have the right to elect representatives to the Spanish Cortes, these elections have not been held to date.

Ivory Coast

Population: 3,400,000 (1962 est.).

Area: 125,000 square miles.

Capital: Abidjan (population: 180,000).

Political Status: Independent republic.

Date of Independence: August 7, 1960.

Chief of State and Head of Government: President Félix Houphouet-Boigny, head of government since 1959; elected (November 27, 1960) President under terms of new presidential constitution for a 5-year term, by universal adult suffrage.

Major Political Party: Parti Démocratique de la Côte d'Ivoire.

Legislative Branch: Unicameral. National Assembly of 70 members elected by universal adult suffrage from a single list containing only representatives of the Parti Démocratique de la Côte d'Ivoire, for 5-year terms. Last election, November 27, 1960.

Monetary Unit: 247 CFA francs = US$1.00.

Principal Languages: French, and more than 60 variations of local tribal languages. The most important are Agni, various Kru languages, Malinke and related Mende languages, and various Kova-Kova languages.

External Affiliations: United Nations, Organization of African Unity, Union Africaine et Malgache, Conseil de l'Entente (with Dahomey, Niger, and Upper Volta), European Economic Community (associate), franc zone.

The Ivory Coast was the nursery of the nationalist movement in French West and Equatorial Africa, and many of the present-day governing parties in these states derive from the interterritorial Rassemblement Démocratique Africaine founded by Félix Houphouet-Boigny in 1946. After four years as the fiery *enfant terrible* of French-African politics, Houphouet abruptly changed course in 1950, dropped his tactical alliance with the French Communist Party, and embarked on a new policy of Franco-African cooperation and free-enterprise economic development.

Until 1959, the Ivory Coast stood back from the race for independence, favoring instead the idea of an Afro-French community. Strongly opposed to those schemes for African unity that involved

71

devolution of national authority, Houphouet in 1959 fathered the Conseil de l'Entente, a loose grouping of the Ivory Coast and three of its less prosperous neighbors, as a holding action against the efforts of the Mali Federation to proselytize new members. With France's decision to grant independence to the Mali Federation in June, 1960, Houphouet concluded that the Community as originally conceived by President Charles de Gaulle was ended as an effective institution, and promptly set all four Entente states on the road to independence.

In October, 1960, Houphouet convened in Abidjan a meeting that was to lead to the establishment of a formal political and economic association of twelve French-speaking states in the Union Africaine et Malgache. The form taken by the UAM at its founding meeting at Yaoundé, Cameroun, in 1961 reflected the ideas of Houphouet more than those of any other African leader —i.e., the principle of national sovereignty was maintained, non-interference in the internal affairs of member states was pledged, and the powers of the organization's secretary-general were strictly limited.

Although Houphouet's unabashed Francophilia and free-enterprise economic policies are ideologically unfashionable in the Africa of the 1960's, he rests his case on the telling point that the Ivory Coast has the most rapidly expanding economy of any state in French-speaking Africa. Agriculture remains the source of most of the country's wealth, and coffee, wood products, cocoa, bananas, and palm nuts account for the bulk of exports ($178 million in 1961, as against $155 million in imports). Diamonds and manganese are also exported, and the search for other minerals continues. Generous incentives offered to foreign investors are attracting an increasing range of industries, including an automobile assembly plant, aluminum factory, soap factory, match factory, two shipyards, food-processing plants, and lumber mills. Abidjan is now one of the busiest and most modern ports in Africa. Although French aid is still vital to all ongoing development plans, it is the stated goal of the Ivory Coast to achieve self-sustained growth by 1970. The gross national product is currently estimated at $520 million.

Despite these impressive economic statistics, Houphouet's enduring charisma, and increasingly firm security measures, there were tangible signs during 1963 that pressures for change are festering below the calm surface of Ivoirien politics. In January and again in August, the government announced that plots to overthrow the regime by force had been frustrated. Writing from Abidjan just before the first attempted *coup d'état,* Victor Du Bois summarized the mood of the dissidents: "The long-range policy of economic development for the nation which the government has drawn up, though eminently sound, has failed to satisfy the yearnings of Ivoirien youth and of Ivoirien intellectuals for a political philosophy sufficiently 'revolutionary' in spirit and content to allow them to feel that they are keeping pace with other nationalist movements in Africa. However much Houphouet himself may disdain nationalism, the youth of the country are very much aware of its existence and want to be a part of it. . . . The absence of such a philosophy has, in the eyes of many of these young Ivoiriens, robbed their nation's political party of the dynamism which, they feel, exists in Guinea and Ghana. Precisely what such a national philosophy should be or what it should contain has yet to be defined, but the hunger for it is there."

Kenya

Population: 8,676,000 (1962 est.).

Area: 224,960 square miles.

Capital: Nairobi (population: 250,800).

Political Status: Independent dominion in the Commonwealth.

Date of Independence: December 12, 1963.

Chief of State: Queen Elizabeth II, represented locally by Governor-General Malcolm MacDonald.

Head of Government: Prime Minister Jomo Kenyatta, leader of the majority party, invested as Prime Minister with self-government in May, 1963.

Major Political Parties: Kenya African National Union (KANU), Kenya African Democratic Union (KADU).

Legislative Branch: Bicameral. National Assembly consisting of House of Representatives composed of 129 members (117 constituency-elected and 12 specially elected), and Senate of 41 members, both elected for 5-year terms. Last election, May, 1963.

Monetary Unit: 1 East African shilling = US$0.14.

Principal Languages: Swahili, English.

External Affiliations: United Nations, Organization of African Unity, Commonwealth, East African Common Services Organization.

The seven months of internal self-government that preceded Kenya's independence on December 12, 1963, were characterized by three outstanding features: (1) the crucial role of Prime Minister Jomo Kenyatta as the most important single symbol of national identification for the Kenyan population, as the indispensable keystone holding together the disparate segments of the governing Kenya African National Union, and as the one authoritative voice capable of reassuring the country's remaining 55,000 European settlers that independence would not usher in "another Congo"; (2) the trend toward consolidation of power and authority at the center instead of in the regions, a reversal of the course set at the 1962 constitutional conference in London;

and (3) continued study of the political implications of the anomaly that the money sector of independent Kenya's economy will be largely controlled by immigrant communities (European and Asian) comprising less than 3 per cent of the population.

Tribalism has received more than its share of the blame for the divided character of the Kenya nationalist movement during the past decade. After the paralyzing Mau Mau rebellion (1952 to 1956), the colonial regime exercised the extraordinary powers available to it under emergency regulations to restrict African political organization to the local (i.e., tribal) level. For another three years, until the ban on mass political parties was lifted in 1960, the growing force of African nationalism was diverted into parochial movements built around a dozen different personalities, held together only by the common objective of African self-determination and the symbolism of Jomo Kenyatta's past and promised leadership.

With the 1960 agreement that African majority rule would be the basis of future constitutional developments, these various local parties coalesced into two national movements of strikingly different character—the Kenya African National Union, representing urban nationalism and those majority tribes (Kikuyu, Luo, and Kamba) most affected by the social changes that postwar industrialization had brought to Kenya; and the Kenya African Democratic Union, primarily an alliance of agrarian minority tribes which favored a loose federal state that would grant a high degree of autonomy to local authorities. In Kenya's first elections, held in February, 1961, KANU won nineteen Legislative Council seats to KADU's eleven, but refused to form a government unless Kenyatta was immediately released from detention to serve as Chief Minister. The colonial administration refused, and a minority government was formed by KADU in cooperation with some European, Asian, and government-appointed members. This interim solution, and the subsequent establishment in April, 1962, of a nonproductive KADU-KANU coalition government, further delayed the development of a stable political framework for Kenya. The long, complex constitution drawn up in March, 1963, as the basis for self-government provided for a central parliamentary government "with sufficient power to hold the country together" but also established seven regional governments with a high degree of autonomy regarding land rights, tribal matters, and local law and order.

After KANU's sweeping victory in the May, 1963, elections, and the establishment of a KANU government under the leadership of Prime Minister Jomo Kenyatta, Britain convened a final pre-independence constitutional conference in London. Over the strong protests of KADU's representatives, some of the powers given to the regional governments in 1962 were transferred to the central government (e.g., the independent regional judiciary was abolished, a unified and centrally controlled police force was authorized, and the amendment machinery was simplified). It seems likely that the new constitution to be drafted when Kenya becomes a republic, an early KANU objective, will carry the shift from regionalism to centralism even further.

Kenya, like Uganda and Tanganyika, is primarily an agricultural country, with no known mineral resources of importance. However, its agricultural potential is far more developed—exports for the first six months of 1963 totaled more than $63 million—and industrialization has progressed to the point where 10 per cent of Kenya's gross domestic product now comes from manufacturing. The number of persons employed in industry is equal to the combined total for Uganda and Tanganyika. A new land policy, adopted by the Kenya Government in 1960, aimed at the progressive disappearance of racial barriers to land ownership and use. Resettlement schemes now under way are placing landless Africans on subdivided farms bought by the government from departing Europeans. African farmers have begun to produce cash as well as subsistence crops, but they still make comparatively little contribution to Kenya's export trade. A World Bank report on the Kenya economy, published in 1963, observes that the "Asian and European communities will remain the dominant financial factor for some time" and advises the new government that its "principal need is to create conditions for them to regain confidence to use their savings in Kenya and to lend funds to the government." This advice, while economically sound, poses serious political problems for an African government in the 1960's.

Critically linked to Kenya's economic problems and aspirations is the necessity of maintaining the present East African common market. Having a far more advanced economic and social infrastructure than Uganda and Tanganyika, Kenya also has far more to lose from a possible disruption of the East African common market and the consequent economic dislocation and loss of confidence by internal and overseas capital. As the most industrialized of the East African countries, and the one with the most acute unemployment problems, Kenya cannot afford to lose—and, indeed, must expand—its present markets in Uganda and Tanganyika.

For these pressing economic reasons, as well as a genuine commitment to the creation of a political association of the peoples of East Africa, KANU regards the achievement of an East African Federation as an essential objective.*

* See also "Independent Kenya: Problems and Prospects," by Carl G. Rosberg, Jr., *Africa Report,* December, 1963, p. 3.

Liberia

Population: 1,000,000 to 2,000,000 (est.; census under way).

Area: 42,990 square miles.

Capital: Monrovia (population: 60,000).

Political Status: Independent republic.

Date of Independence: July 26, 1847.

Chief of State and Head of Government: President William V. S. Tubman, elected (May, 1963) for fifth term of 4 years by universal adult suffrage.

Major Political Parties: True Whig Party, and various ephemeral opposition parties.

Legislative Branch: Bicameral. Senate of 10 members elected by universal suffrage for 6-year terms (5 elected in 1961; next election in 1965). House of Representatives of 39 members elected for 4-year terms. Last election, 1963.

Monetary Unit: 1 Liberian dollar = US$1.00 (U.S. coins and currency also circulate.)

Principal Languages: English, Vai, Kru, Kpelle, Brebo, Bassa.

External Affiliations: United Nations, Organization of African Unity.

The Republic of Liberia evolved from settlements for freed slaves established early in the nineteenth century by American philanthropic societies. Liberia's first 100 years, often called the "century of survival," were principally taken up with the struggle, not always successful, to stay solvent and maintain the integrity of the national territory. With neither domestic capital nor foreign investment to exploit the country's natural riches, little social or economic development was possible. In 1945, government revenues were only $1 million, and the Firestone rubber plantations, begun in 1926, were the only sizable economic enterprise.

The election of William V. S. Tubman to the presidency in 1943 opened a new era, for he immediately announced an "open-door policy" toward foreign investment. More than twenty major agricultural, forestry, and mining concessions have resulted, the most significant being those for development of Liberia's huge deposits of unusually rich iron ore. One mine is in full production, two others have begun producing, another is being developed, and further possibilities are being explored. The current annual increase in GNP is estimated at 15 per cent, and government revenues rose to $35 million in 1962. With reserves estimated in millions of tons, Liberia's economic outlook is very promising; current estimates indicate that revenues may reach $75 million by 1975.

At the moment, however, Liberia is experiencing an embarrassing financial squeeze. Because of the necessity to make up accumulated deficiencies in transportation, communications, power, education, and social services, the government has been spending money faster than it has been coming in. To finance the needed construction, President Tubman optimistically resorted to expensive short-term loans, agreeing to repay about $125 million in the period 1963–66. Owing to unexpected delays in getting the new iron mines into full production, plus a decline in the price of rubber on world markets, the government was unable to meet the 1963 obligations on these loans. A standby credit of $5.7 million from the International Monetary Fund has taken the immediate pressure off, however, and Liberia is meanwhile negotiating with its principal creditors a rescheduling of debts to allow repayment over a longer period. To prevent repetition of the 1963 crisis, planning and fiscal management procedures are being reorganized with U.S. technical assistance.

President Tubman was re-elected for a fifth term in a landslide victory in May, 1963, and his True Whig Party has no serious rival. Although the constitution is similar in language to that of the United States, in practice President Tubman has far more personal power than his American counterpart. A major objective of his administration has been the National Unification Program, dedicated to raising the economic and social level of the people of the interior and opening opportunities for them to participate in national affairs on equal terms with the descendants of the early settlers, who heretofore have formed the political and social elite. A major effort is also being made to bring Liberia's educational system up to the standard existing in the more developed countries of West Africa, for the government recognizes that the serious deficiencies of Liberian schools act as a brake on full development of the country's potential.

Integration of the hinterland, rapid development of the economy, and expanding educational horizons are inevitably introducing a greater dynamism into Liberian society. Overt, if short-lived, protests at the conservative stance of Liberian domestic and foreign policy have occurred among labor, students, the military, and frustrated members of the elite in recent years, but President Tubman's remarkable political skill has thus far enabled him to remain firmly in control. Most of the control mechanisms of his administration are highly personal in nature, however, and any successor will have to develop new institutions to deal with a new set of political problems.

Libya

Population: 1,244,000 (1962 est.).

Area: 680,000 square miles.

Capital: Tripoli (population: 196,000) and Benghazi (population: 83,200). Beida is the planned future capital.

Political Status: Independent monarchy.

Date of Independence: December 24, 1951.

Chief of State: King Muhammad Idris al-Mahdi al-Sanusi, hereditary.

Head of Government: Prime Minister Mohammad Muntasir, appointed (January 23, 1964) by the king.

Major Political Parties: None.

Legislative Branch: Bicameral. House of Representatives of 55 members elected by universal adult suffrage for 4-year terms. Last election, 1960. Senate of 24 members nominated by the king as of April, 1963, for 8-year terms.

Monetary Unit: 1 Libyan pound = US$2.80.

Principal Languages: Arabic, English, Italian.

External Affiliations: United Nations, Arab League, Organization of African Unity, participates in sterling area arrangements.

With an area over one-half the size of India, Libya is one of the four largest countries of Africa. Nine-tenths of its vast extent is desert, however, and only 2.5 per cent of the land (17,300 square miles) is presently arable. Eighty per cent of the population, concentrated on a productive strip along the coast and in oases, still depends on agriculture and animal husbandry for a meager living.

When Libya became independent in 1951 from Italian control and United Nations tutelage, it seemed hopelessly doomed to economic backwardness. Various forms of aid plus rental on United States and United Kingdom military bases established in the desert paid for half of Libya's public expenditures in the decade after independence. With the discovery of oil in 1959, however, the country's prospects changed dramatically, and Libya, though facing mounting inflationary pressures, could become economically self-supporting within the near future. Oil production was expected to reach 340,000 barrels per day in 1963; 470,000 in 1964; and 500,000 in 1965. Between 1962 and 1965, oil revenues should exceed $400 million. Seventy-five per cent of this income, or $300 million (which will average over $120 per capita by 1964, double the Saudi Arabia average) has been earmarked for the country's Five-Year Plan by 1965.

King Idris I, though ill and aging, remains the supreme head of state and commander of the armed forces. Political power is concentrated in the Palace and in a small group representing the conservative aristocracy, merchants, and tribal chiefs. Political parties have been banned since independence, and opposition to the regime or any specific government policy must be expressed clandestinely. Education and oil prosperity are making inroads on the old order, however. Ideologically, many members of Libya's growing new middle class are attracted to the socialist and radical nationalist ideas of the Ba'thists (Arab Resurrection Party), and pressures for institutions based on some new form of consensus are increasing.

Steps have recently been taken to unify the three federal provinces (Tripolitania, Cyrenaica, and Fezzan) into a single system with a simplified administrative structure. Such moves should reduce high budgetary costs, streamline the bureaucracy, and further national unity.

Malagasy Republic

Population: 6,000,000 (1963 est.).

Area: 227,900 square miles.

Capital: Tananarive (population: 247,917).

Political Status: Independent republic.

Date of Independence: June 26, 1960.

Chief of State and Head of Government: President Philibert Tsiranana, elected (1959) for a 7-year term by electoral college consisting of members of both houses of the legislature, provincial councils, and representatives of municipal and rural assemblies.

Major Political Parties: Parti Sociale Démocrate de Madagascar et Comores, led by President Tsiranana; Parti de la Rénovation Nationale Malgache; Ankoton'ny Kongresi'ny Fahaleovantenan Madagasikara (AKFM); Union Démocratique et Sociale de Madagascar (UDSM); Parti Chrétien (PC); Rassemblement National Malgache (RNM).

Legislative Branch: Bicameral. National Assembly of 107 members elected by universal suffrage for 5-year terms. Senate of 54 members (36 elected for 6-year terms by provincial councils and representatives of municipal and rural assemblies, 18 appointed). Last election, September, 1960.

Monetary Unit: 247 CFA francs = US$1.00.

Principal Languages: French, Malagasy.

External Affiliations: United Nations, Organization of African Unity, Union Africaine et Malgache, European Economic Community (associate), franc zone.

Annexed by France in 1896, Madagascar became the independent Malagasy Republic in 1960. Its precolonial political history was highlighted by the rise and fall of several large coastal states before 1800 and by the emergence of the Imerina Kingdom in the nineteenth century—the first deliberate attempt to unify the island into a single state.

The island of Madagascar, fourth largest in the world, is something of a paradox. While geographically close to Africa, its original inhabitants came from the distant Malay Archipelago some twenty centuries ago. Subsequent arrivals from Africa fused with earlier populations and it is no longer possible for most Malagasy to discern where Asia stops and Africa begins, although endogamous minorities exist on both sides.

Topography and climate match the human variety, but in language and culture the Malagasy are one people. The cultural and linguistic base is Malayo-Indonesian. Nearly half of the population is literate. There are 22 newspapers, and some 500,000 listen daily to Radio Tananarive. The University of Madagascar in Tananarive has a student body of 1,000. Catholic and Protestant missions play a major role in secular as well as religious life.

About 85 per cent of the Malagasy live in rural communities of less than 2,000, and agriculture—much of it small-scale—is the economic pillar of the island. Coffee, sugar cane, vanilla, cloves, and rice are major cash crops, and exports earn some $75 million annually on the average. There are 600,000 wage earners on the island, and Madagascar has a strong trade-union movement. Europeans, Indians, and Chinese account for 3,000 out of 3,600 private employers; only 11 establishments employ more than 1,000 persons.

The Malagasy Republic is a member of the Union Africaine et Malgache and maintains close economic and cultural ties with France. The cumulative total of French assistance since 1949 is in the neighborhood of $500 million. Nearly 1,000 Malagasy students attend French universities on full scholarships each year.

The moderate Parti Sociale Démocrate, led by President Philibert Tsiranana, was returned to power by a sweeping majority in general elections of September, 1960, taking 82 out of 107 National Assembly seats. The pro-Communist Ankoton'ny Kongresi'ny Fahaleoyantenan Madagasikara (AKFM), strongest group standing in opposition to Tsiranana's moderate policies, gained only three seats.*

* See "Madagascar Emerges from Isolation," by Raymond Kent, *Africa Report,* August, 1963, p. 3.

Mali

Population: 4,500,000 (1963 est.).

Area: 463,500 square miles.

Capital: Bamako (population: 120,000).

Political Status: Independent republic.

Date of Independence: September 22, 1960.

Chief of State and Head of Government: President Modibo Keita, elected (1959) by majority vote of the National Assembly.

Political Party: Union Soudanaise-Rassemblement Démocratique Africain (US-RDA).

Legislative Branch: Unicameral. National Assembly of 80 members elected by universal adult suffrage for 5-year terms. Last election, March, 1959.

Monetary Unit: 245 Malian francs = US$1.00 (but nonconvertible).

Principal Languages: French, Bambara, Fulani, Songhai, other African languages.

External Affiliations: United Nations, Organization of African Unity, European Economic Community (associate), negotiations in progress regarding membership in franc zone.

Perhaps nowhere in Africa has the political leadership been more precise in setting forth its objectives and more steadfast in pursuing them than in Mali. Although the *militants* of the US-RDA are deeply influenced by Marxist ideas, their tactics and goals are tempered by a pragmatism that is consciously African. Thus, Mali has placed priority emphasis on (1) effecting a radical break with colonial (i.e., French) rule; (2) reorganizing the economy on a Marxist pattern, with development and growing prosperity as the goal; (3) consolidating Mali's nationhood through a dynamic, disciplined mass-party organization; and (4) pursuing a militant policy of nonalignment in the Cold War by welcoming trade and diplomatic relations with all friendly states. Differences over the first three of these policy objectives, as well as personality conflicts at the leadership level, were responsible for the short life

85

and acrimonious end of Mali's postindependence federation with neighboring Senegal (January 17, 1959, to August 19, 1960).

The US-RDA is the sole repository of political authority in Mali, and the party directly controls the government, press and radio, labor unions, youth and women's organizations, and most other aspects of public life. Party leaders travel constantly in an endeavor to perfect an organization of interlocking local units reaching into the most remote villages and down to the humblest peasant. At the top, the Political Bureau of the party—a collegial body of twenty whose membership has been carefully shaped to cut across tribal and regional loyalties—establishes policy by consensus and persuasion. Modibo Keita, as leader of the party and chief of state, is first among equals; the party exploits but is not totally dependent on his personal prestige. Ranking very close to Modibo in the hierarchy are Jean-Marie Kone, Minister of State for Planning and Economic and Financial Affairs; Barema Bocoum, Minister charged with Foreign Affairs; and Mahamane Alassane Haidara, President of the National Assembly.

Mali has weathered three major crises since independence. When the federation with Senegal floundered in August, 1960, the railroad linking landlocked Mali to the Senegalese port of Dakar was abruptly closed—and remained cut off for almost three years. Because Mali is agriculturally self-sufficient, at least at the subsistence level, the government was spared a panic solution. In 1961 and 1962, the peanut crop—the country's major export—was moved to the port of Abidjan, Ivory Coast (and thus to the new markets in the Soviet Bloc) by a rail-and-road link. Although the price of many imported items went up as a result of the route change, the predicted dramatic worsening of Mali's economy never materialized; any losses incurred were more than balanced, in the Malian view, by the psychological reassurance that Mali was not as isolated or as dependent on a single neighbor as had been assumed. In June, 1963, the Dakar-Niger railroad was reopened and a beginning was made toward re-establishing the historic ties between Mali and Senegal—but this time on a new footing of equality.

Factions within the party posed another threat to the Malian experiment. A radical wing led by Minister of Interior Madeira

Keita, supported by a militant youth organization, wanted the party to move farther and faster to the left. This group encouraged a more militant anti-Western policy and sought to tie Mali more closely to the Soviet Bloc. At the party congress in 1962, however, Madeira Keita was demoted, the autonomous youth organization was decentralized, and Henri Corenthin, who had dominated the Youth Executive, was dropped from the Political Bureau. Mali has since pursued a more genuine policy of non-alignment.

The establishment of the Mali franc in July, 1962, touched off a third crisis. Two persons were killed and 250 arrested when Mali merchants, fearing personal economic disaster, rioted against the government in Bamako. In the subsequent trial, leaders of the pre-independence opposition party were convicted of plotting to overthrow the government. The principals received life sentences, thus further consolidating the party's control.

In the economic field, the US-RDA has found the issues more inchoate and the going more difficult. Although corruption is minimal and the leadership industrious, there is no escaping the fact that Mali is a poor country with enormous social and economic problems. The literacy rate is among the lowest in Africa, and per capita income is estimated at $53 per year. Ninety-five per cent of the people are farmers or pastoralists, and it will take time for state-controlled developmental projects (such as the Office du Niger), education, and an improved infrastructure, to touch the lives of the rural masses. Agricultural surpluses—peanuts, rice, millet, cattle, and fish—offer hope that food-processing industries can be developed locally, and known deposits of manganese, bauxite, and other minerals may in time prove economically exploitable.

If it is to rise much above the subsistence level, however, Mali knows that it will continue to need help from many sources. Relations between France and Mali have generally remained cordial, even during the bitter days following the break-up of the Mali Federation, and France continues to supply much financial assistance, plus technicians and teachers. The Soviet Bloc and Communist China had provided credits totaling approximately $80 million by 1963, and lesser amounts have come from the

United States and West Germany, among others. The government affirms that it will accept developmental aid from any source, public or private, domestic or international, bilateral or multilateral, so long as the terms are adaptable to Mali's clearly enunciated socialist framework. On this, says Mali, there can be no compromise.

Mauritania

Population: 1,000,000 (1963 est.).

Area: 418,000 square miles.

Capital: Nouakchott (population: 8,000).

Political Status: Independent Islamic republic.

Date of Independence: November 28, 1960.

Chief of State and Head of Government: President Moktar Ould Daddah, head of government since 1959; elected (August 20, 1961) first President by universal adult suffrage. Under a new presidential constitution adopted in May, 1961, his term is 5 years.

Major Political Parties: All parties merged into the Parti du Peuple (PDP) in 1961.

Legislative Branch: Unicameral. National Assembly of 40 members elected by universal adult suffrage for 5-year terms. Last election, May, 1959.

Monetary Unit: 247 CFA francs = US$1.00.

Principal Languages: Arabic (Hassaniya dialect), French.

External Affiliations: United Nations, Union Africaine et Malgache, Organization of African Unity, European Economic Community (associate), franc zone.

When the Islamic Republic of Mauritania acquired its independence in November, 1960, its assets seemed so meager and its liabilities so great that a question mark hung over its very survival as an independent state. Most of the republic is a barren flatland, sparsely inhabited by nomadic tribesmen who move with the seasons in search of grass and water for their flocks. Settled agriculture is confined to scattered oases and to the northern banks of the Senegal River, where millet, dates, fruits, grains, and vegetables are grown and small amounts of salt, gum arabic, and fish are produced. Of the 20,000 estimated wage-earners in the country at the time of independence, all but 2,000 were civil servants or military personnel.

There were political problems as well. The vastness of the country, as well as the historic cleavage between the Arabized

Moors of the north and the *Noirs sédentaires* near the Senegal and Mali borders in the south, militated against national cohesion. Without French financial aid, technical assistance, diplomatic support, and even military protection, Mauritania was unlikely to be able to operate as a state, much less withstand Moroccan threats of annexation; yet President Moktar Ould Daddah recognized that he must somehow assert Mauritania's independence in meaningful terms to contain the centrifugal forces that pulled its north toward Morocco and its southern Negroes toward Mali and Senegal.

At the end of three years of independence, Mauritania's prospects must be reassessed. French policy, by combining helpfulness with restraint, has enabled Moktar to govern in fact as well as in name. In the face of incredible odds, a gradual improvement has been made in the educational facilities and administrative apparatus required to knit the country into some semblance of nationhood. Morocco's failure to win support for its claim to Mauritania among the main body of African states eased the external threat, and separatist pressures in the south declined after the break-up of the Mali Federation in 1960. The discovery of a major deposit of high-grade iron ore (estimated reserves: 145 million tons) as well as a sizable deposit of low-grade copper, both in the north, dramatically changed the economic outlook. In President Ould Daddah, moreover, Mauritania has a leader of stature who, though a Sorbonne-educated lawyer, also remains remarkably representative of his constituents and respectful of traditional means of achieving consensus.*

After independence in 1960, Moktar undertook a series of tactical moves aimed at consolidating the segmented elements of the Mauritanian body politic. As a first step, he deliberately broke with the more committed pro-French elements in the governing group, carrying with him many of their followers as well as his own. Having divested himself of the image of a French puppet, he was able to form a coalition embracing the bulk of the opposition Nahda al-Watain, which had heretofore looked to Rabat for guidance and support. This political realignment was formalized

* See "Mauritania: Problems and Prospects," by J. H. A. Watson, *Africa Report*, February, 1963, p. 3.

in the creation of a single national movement, the Parti du Peuple, and the institution of a presidential regime in 1961. The new presidential constitution greatly enhanced the authority of the chief of state, thus enabling Moktar to deal firmly in 1962 with a new subversive threat allegedly inspired from Morocco. Meanwhile, Moktar has employed every technique of modern political organization adaptable to Mauritania—radio, reorganization of the education system to make it the "crucible in which the soul of the nation is forged," development of cadres of local party militants, etc.—to make the PDP a genuine mass political party. The carrot rather than the stick has been used to encourage the integration of the southern Negroes, whose representatives are now found at every level of administration. The amicable border settlement with Mali reflects the new situation in the south.*

* See "A Disputed Frontier Is Settled," by I. William Zartman, *Africa Report*, August, 1963, p. 13.

Mauritius

Population: 680,305 (1962 est., including 440,000 Indians, 23,500 Chinese, remainder African, European, and persons of mixed origins).

Area: 720 square miles.

Capital: Port-Louis (population: 113,000).

Political Status: French colony until 1810, when ceded to England; British crown colony since 1814.

Local Head of Government: Governor Sir John Rennie; Dr. S. Ramgoolam, leader of majority party in Legislative Council is Chief Minister.

Political Parties: Mauritian Labor Party, Muslim Committee of Action, Independent Forward Bloc, Parti Mauriten, Independent Party.

Local Legislative Branch: Legislative Council of 55 seats (40 elected by universal adult suffrage, 3 ex-officio, and 12 Official Members appointed by Governor). Last election, October, 1963.

Monetary Unit: 1 Mauritian rupee = US$.20.

Principal Languages: English, French, Creole (patois), Hindi.

Mauritius lies in the Indian Ocean about 550 miles east of the Malagasy Republic. All available arable land is devoted to the intensive cultivation of sugar and tea: Cane sugar and its by-products account for 99 per cent of the island's exports. Sugar and tea plantations, processing plants, even local branches of international companies are almost universally owned by members of the indigenous population.

Under constitutional reforms adopted in 1961, Mauritius is moving rapidly toward internal self-government. Dr. S. Ramgoolam, leader of the Hindu-based majority Mauritius Labor Party, serves as Chief Minister and advises the Governor on the appointment and removal of Ministers and the summoning, proroguing, and dissolution of the Legislative Council. Whether or not further steps toward independence should be taken in the near future is a matter of some controversy among Mauritians.

Minority groups fear that their liberties will not be safeguarded, but Dr. Ramgoolam's party won nineteen of forty elected seats in the 1963 elections, campaigning on a platform of early independence; it is allied in the Legislative Council with the Muslim Committee of Action (four seats). Opposition parties represented in the Council are the Independent Forward Bloc (seven seats), the Parti Mauritien (eight), and the Independent Party (two).

A Development Plan introduced in 1961 emphasizes social-welfare projects. Construction of low-cost housing, extension of water and electric facilities, and sewage improvement are given priority, as well as construction of a truck road and harbor improvements in Port-Louis. The need to decrease the disparity in incomes was stressed by Ramgoolam in the October, 1963, campaign.

Morocco

Population: 12,300,000 (1963 est.).

Area: 171,305 square miles.

Capital: Rabat (population: 250,000).

Political Status: Independent monarchy.

Date of Independence: March 2, 1956.

Chief of State: King Hassan II, hereditary.

Head of Government: Premier Ahmad Bahnini, appointed by the king in November, 1963.

Major Political Parties: Front pour la Défense des Institutions Constitutionnelles (FDIC), led by Ahmad Rheda Guedira; Istiqlal (Independence Party) led by Allal al-Fassi; Union Nationale des Forces Populaires (UNFP), led by El Mehdi Ben Barka and Abderrahim Bouabid (formerly allied to the Union Marocaine du Travail, the politically oriented trade union led by Mahjub Ben Seddiq and Abdullah Ibrahim); Mouvement Populaire (within the FDIC), led by Mahjubi Aherdane and Dr. Abd al-Karim Khatib.

Legislative Branch: Bicameral. Chamber of Representatives of 144 members elected by universal adult suffrage for 4-year terms for the first time in May, 1963. Chamber of Counselors of 120 members, two-thirds elected in each prefecture and province by colleges composed of members of prefectoral and provincial assemblies; one-third elected by Chambers of Agriculture, Commerce, and Industry, Handicraftsmen, and representatives of labor unions, for 6-year terms, for the first time in October, 1963.

Monetary Unit: 1 Dirham = US$.20.

Principal Languages: Arabic, French, Spanish, Berber.

External Affiliations: United Nations, Arab League, Organization of African Unity, participates in franc zone arrangements.

Despite the centuries of independence it knew prior to 1912, when the French and Spanish established protectorates that were to last until independence in 1956, Morocco remains a country still in the process of establishing its national identity. During the protectorate period, Morocco was administered as four separate regions—a French zone, two Spanish zones, and internationally controlled Tangier. This, together with other historical and geographical factors, has produced a heterogeneous population of different loyalties, elites, languages, outlooks, and standards of living.

Since succeeding his father as King of Morocco in February, 1961, Hassan II has become the arbiter of the country's complex political life. By a series of remarkable political maneuvers, Hassan capitalized on divisions within the principal opposition movements to his right and left—the old-line nationalist party, Istiqlal, and the radical socialist Union Nationale des Forces Populaires—and promulgated a new constitution that extends the bases of the monarchy's legitimacy. As of 1963, Hassan was chief of state, head of government, the nation's principal religious leader, commander in chief of the highly modernized and mobile armed forces and national police (estimated combined strength, 45,000), and the initiator of most legislation introduced before the newly created Moroccan Parliament. The present government, formed in January, 1963, after a massive referendum victory for the new constitution, contains no representatives of either of Morocco's mass parties. An attempt to establish a Palace-oriented popular political movement—the Front pour la Défense des Institutions Constitutionnelles—has had only limited success.

Though King Hassan's approach to kingly politics is somewhat unique in the twentieth century, he nonetheless appears to be committed to the modernization of Morocco's economy and to the task of giving his 12 million subjects a better way of life. This would seem to require mobilization of the Moroccan population behind a consistent program of development, and it remains an open question whether the necessary popular commitment can be obtained without the help of the country's most dynamic parties. Some observers believe that the Moroccan army might eventually be called into political play on behalf of the Palace if the first Parliament elected in May, 1963, is too divided to operate constructively.

In foreign policy, postindependence Morocco's initiatives have not prospered. The Casablanca Group alliance, a pet project of the late King Mohammed V, was finally buried at the Addis Ababa conference. Morocco's claims to Mauritania, never warmly endorsed by other African states, appear to have been unofficially dropped. The border dispute with Algeria still festers. Threats to take over nearby Spanish territories—Ifni and Spanish Sahara —have been quietly shelved in the face of a Spanish diplomatic and military counteroffensive.

Morocco is primarily an agricultural country with nearly 25 per cent of its arable land divided into mechanized high-yield estates; however, wide yearly fluctuations in rainfall and the use of archaic techniques on the other three-quarters of the land under cultivation make for a high degree of uncertainty about the harvest. About 35,000 miners, or 1.1 per cent of the Moroccan work force, supply 40 per cent of the total value of exports. The most important mining enterprise is phosphate (operated as a state monopoly), which accounts for one-half of the total value of mining production. Indeed, Morocco is the world's largest exporter of phosphate (more than 8 million tons in 1962), and has reserves estimated at 21 billion tons.

Despite these resources, and some $80 million in developmental aid from France and the United States yearly since independence, Morocco still has far to go before it can close the gap between exports and imports or provide adequate jobs for its growing army of unemployed and underemployed.

Mozambique

Population: 7,000,000 (1963 est.).

Area: 297,731 square miles.

Capital: Lourenço Marques (population: 100,000).

Political Status: Overseas province of Portugal.

Local Head of Government: Governor-General, Rear Admiral Manuel Maria Sarmiento Rodrigues, appointed by the Council of Ministers in Lisbon.

Major Political Parties: União Nacional is the governing party of Portugal and Mozambique. Mozambique African nationalist movements (banned) include Frente de Libertação de Moçambique (FRELIMO), União Democrática Nacional de Moçambique (UDENAMO), and the Mozambique African United Front.

Legislative Branch: As a Portuguese province, Mozambique has 7 representatives in the Lisbon Assembleia Nacional, each elected for 4 years by restricted (i.e., literacy in Portuguese or income) male suffrage. The Provincial Legislative Council (Conselho Legislativo), partly elected and partly appointed, has very limited authority.

Monetary Unit: 28.75 overseas escudos = US$1.00.

Principal Languages: Portuguese, Thonga.

Mozambique, on the east coast of Africa, was visited by Vasco da Gama on his voyage to India in 1498, and the Portuguese founded their first settlements there early in the sixteenth century. Like Angola, it has been ruled as an overseas province of Portugal since 1951. The avowed goal of Portuguese colonial policy, which has undergone only minor changes in four centuries, is cultural assimilation, which implicitly precludes preparation for self-rule as envisaged by African nationalism.

Even within its own terms of reference, however, Portugal has made slim progress toward establishing Portuguese culture firmly in Mozambique: By 1962, only a small fraction of Mozambicans were legally recognized as *assimilado,* and illiteracy was 99 per cent. The widely heralded reform of the "Organic Law of the

Portuguese territories," announced in August, 1961 and promulgated in 1963, gave the African full Portuguese citizenship for the first time, but its practical effect has so far been largely limited to improvements in the conditions of labor.

The major African nationalist organization in the territory is the Frente de Libertação de Moçambique (FRELIMO), founded in July, 1962, in Dar es Salaam, Tanganyika, under the leadership of Dr. Eduardo Mondlane. Both FRELIMO and its rivals, the União Democrática Nacionale de Moçambique (UDENAMO), led by Paul Gumane, and the Mozambique African United Front, led by Mathew Mmole and Adelino Gwambe, demand an independence commitment from Portugal—barring which they threaten to organize a guerrilla war similar to those already under way in Angola and Portuguese Guinea.

The African states of the Organization of African Unity (OAU) undertook in May, 1963, to give substantial financial and technical assistance to the Mozambican nationalists in their campaign for independence. FRELIMO was designated as the official OAU channel at the Dakar Foreign Ministers' Conference in August, 1963. As a precautionary measure, the Portuguese Government has brought in military reinforcements, estimated at 17,000, and has strengthened its military installations along the Tanganyikan border in the north.

Mozambique is a primarily agricultural country. Six crops—cotton, sugar, copra, cashew nuts, tea, and sisal—account for about 80 per cent of exports by value. Exports were valued at $88 million in 1962, but the foreign-trade deficit nonetheless exceeded $49 million. Although an estimated one-third of the total land area is said to be suitable for cultivation, only about 1 per cent is now farmed under a plantation system; African field hands earn 15 to 20 cents per day.

Mineral resources do not, so far at least, appear to be impressive, though sixty-eight small mines produce marketable quantities of diamonds, iron, manganese, asphalt, rock salt, and other minerals. After fifteen years of exploration, there is as yet no hard evidence that oil exists in commercial quantities. Industrial development includes a cement plant, an oil refinery (using some local and imported crude oil), a flour mill, and a few small light industries.

The well-developed ports of Beira and Lourenço Marques, which provide a crucial outlet to the sea for Mozambique's land-locked neighbors (especially Northern Rhodesia's copperbelt) account for nearly half of the province's income. A six-year development program initiated by Portugal in 1959 called for expenditures of about $125 million, over half of which has gone for colonization projects for settling white Portuguese, and for expansion of road and railway facilities. As elsewhere in Portuguese Africa, the fate of these economic plans and projects depends upon political developments.

Niger

Population: 2,600,000 (1962 est.).

Area: 459,000 square miles.

Capital: Niamey (population: 20,000).

Political Status: Independent republic.

Date of Independence: August 3, 1960.

Chief of State and Head of Government: President Hamani Diori, invested by the Legislative Assembly as Prime Minister, and unanimously elected Niger's first president by the same body in November, 1960. A new presidential constitution adopted in 1960 calls for direct election of the president by universal adult suffrage for a term of 5 years, but the elections scheduled for that year were postponed and the mandate of the existing government extended.

Major Political Parties: Parti Progressiste Nigerien, governing party led by President of the National Assembly Boubou Hama; opposition Sawaba Party (banned), led by exiled former Prime Minister Djibo Bakary.

Legislative Branch: Legislative Assembly of 60 members; according to the 1960 constitution, elections are to be held every 5 years by universal suffrage. Last election, 1958.

Monetary Unit: 247 CFA francs = US$1.00.

Principal Languages: French, Arabic, Hausa.

External Affiliations: United Nations, Organization of African Unity, Union Africaine et Malgache, Conseil de L'Entente (with Dahomey, Ivory Coast, and Upper Volta), European Economic Community (associate), franc zone.

Although the Niger Republic is almost two and a half times as large as France, only 2 per cent of the total land area has sufficient water to be cultivated on a regular basis. Most of the settled population lives in a narrow strip along the southern border between the Niger River and Lake Chad, or in a few farming settlements in the north central Air Massif, whose peaks rise to almost 6,000 feet. Away from the watered areas of the south, vegetation becomes progressively more scarce, and nomad tribes roam with their flocks over the vast plateau of central Niger in a constant search for grazing land and water. In the far north, the shifting sands of the Sahara Desert are empty of life. The population, about 80 per cent Moslem and most of the rest animist, is composed of four principal ethnic groups: Hausa (est. 1,350,000), sedentary farmers in the southeast; Djerma-Songhai (600,000), sedentary farmers in the southwest; and nomadic Peuls (440,000) and Touaregs (300,000) farther north.

Between 1949 and 1960, France invested almost $26 million (through FIDES), mostly in projects designed to increase food production and develop crops suitable for export. Of the latter, the most successful has been peanuts, which now constitute 85 per cent of Niger's modest exports (total exports: about $12 million annually). Stock-raising is the second most important industry, but the Peul nomads regard their flocks primarily as a prestige item rather than as an economic asset. All of Niger's peanuts are customarily sold to France or the European Common Market at supported prices; however, a serious effort is being made to reduce internal marketing costs so that the nuts eventually can be sold on world markets at more competitive prices. Access to the sea is a special problem, for Niger is located in the heart of Africa and its immediate neighbors on the east and west—Chad and Mali —are also underdeveloped and landlocked. The Sahara constitutes an effective barrier in the north. Exports must move south, usually through Nigeria, or Upper Volta and the Ivory Coast.

The current Five Year Plan emphasizes detailed study and investigation of Niger's resources and every possible means by which they might be maximized. There is particular interest in schemes that involve cooperative undertakings with neighboring states (e.g., development of the Niger River). Unless oil or other valuable minerals are discovered beneath Niger's desert sands, however, any real economic development beyond the present subsistence level will require a continuing flow of French or other foreign capital and extensive technical assistance.

President Hamani Diori, a French-educated Hausa schoolmaster before he entered politics in 1946, came to power in 1958. His Parti Progressiste Nigerien, campaigning in favor of a "yes" vote in the 1958 referendum on the new French Constitution, won fifty-four seats against six for the radical predecessor regime, which had advocated that Niger join Guinea in voting for immediate independence. Since then, President Diori has consolidated his party's position by (1) allying himself with Niger's powerful Moslem traditional chiefs; (2) exiling former Prime Minister Dijbo Bakary and banning his radical Sawaba Party (1959); (3) associating Niger in a customs union and other forms of political and economic cooperation with its neighbors; (4) signing a regional defense agreement with France and the Ivory Coast (which permits 1,000 French troops to be stationed in the country); and (5) introducing a strong presidential constitution greatly enhancing the power of the executive branch.

Even so, political views sharply different from those of the regime continue to be heard in Niamey, especially frustration at Niger's heavy reliance on France and admiration for the more revolutionary approach to nation-building being employed in neighboring Mali.

7

Nigeria

Population: 55,653,000 (1963 census).

Area: 356,669 square miles.

Capital: Lagos (population: 500,000).

Political Status: Federal republic.

Date of Independence: October 1, 1960; became a republic on October 1, 1963.

Chief of State: President Nnamdi Azikiwe; served as Governor-General from October, 1960, until October, 1963, when he was elected first President by the federal Parliament for a 5-year term.

Head of Government: Prime Minister Alhaji Sir Abubakar Tafawa Balewa, leader of government in the federal House of Representatives from 1957 to 1959, and federal Prime Minister since then, leading NPC-NCNC coalition.

Major Political Parties: Northern Peoples Congress (NPC), governing party of Northern Nigeria, led by the Northern premier, Alhaji Sir Ahmadu Bello, Sardauna of Sokoto; National Convention of Nigerian Citizens (NCNC), governing party of Eastern Nigeria and coalition partner in Western Nigeria and the federal government, led by Eastern Region premier, Michael I. Okpara; Action Group (AG), former federal Opposition and former governing party of Western Nigeria, led by Chief Obafemi Awolowo; United Peoples Party (UPP), AG breakoff, coalition partner in Western Nigeria, led by Western Region premier, Samuel L. Akintola; Nigerian Elements Progressive Union (NEPU), only significant Northern opposition, generally in alliance with the NCNC, led by Alhaji Aminu Kano; Nigerian Youth Congress (NYC), radical protoparty, formed in 1960 by Dr. Olatunji Otegbeye.

Legislative Branch: Bicameral. Federal House of Representatives of 319 members elected by universal adult suffrage for 5-year terms. Last election, December, 1959. Appointive Senate of 44 members (12 from each region, 4 from Lagos, 4 specially nominated by the Prime Minister). The Senate's membership will increase from 44 to 56 when the new Mid-West region elects its representatives. Regional Houses of Assembly directly elected for maximum of 4 years or life of houses. Last elections in North (1962), East (1962), and West (1961). Regional Houses of Chiefs appointed.

Monetary Unit: 1 Nigerian pound = US$2.80.

Principal Languages: English, Hausa (North), Yoruba (West), Ibo (East).

External Affiliations: United Nations, Organization of African Unity, Commonwealth.

Since independence in October, 1960, the Nigerian Government has been preoccupied with three major concerns: the establishment of a position in intra-African politics appropriate to the continent's most populous nation; the introduction and financing of the most ambitious economic development plan in tropical Africa; and the search for internal political stability.

Initially, the coalition government headed by Prime Minister Balewa (see above) took an openly pro-Western position on most Cold War issues and a relatively conservative stance within the African community. Responding to growing dissatisfaction from Nigerian intellectuals, articulated in the press and Parliament largely by the opposition Action Group, the government gradually shifted toward a more central position in the African ideological spectrum. Thus, the 1960 Anglo-Nigerian Defense Pact was abrogated; the U.S.S.R. was permitted to establish an embassy in Lagos; Foreign Minister Jaja Wachuku became a pivotal figure in United Nations affairs (especially on the Congo); and Nigeria took the initiative in organizing the series of conferences that eventually resulted in the melding of the Casablanca and Monrovia blocs into the Organization of African Unity in May, 1963.

Nigeria's ambitious 1962–68 Development Plan calls for the expenditure of some $1,895,000,000. Even at the Plan's outset, the gross national product was around $3 billion, and the balance of trade generally favorable. Natural resources (especially iron, tin, columbite ores, coal, limestone, petroleum, hydroelectrical potential, and diversified agriculture) rate Nigeria's economy among the most promising in Africa. In development of its human resources, too, Nigeria is already in the vanguard: universal primary education, supported by taxation at the regional level, has existed in the Western and Eastern Regions since before independence, and is now a goal in the North; five universities were already functioning in 1963, and even these were incapable of absorbing all of the qualified applicants coming out of the secondary schools.

Although significant pledges of developmental assistance have come from abroad since 1962—$120 million (in loans) from the World Bank, $224 million (in loans and grants) from the United

States, $28 million (in loans) from Britain, $25 million (in loans and grants) from West Germany—the total now available for the Plan falls short of the target of about $675 million from external sources, and it now seems unlikely that all of the goals set forth in 1962 will be attained by the end of the six-year period. The Plan, designed as a first step toward the creation of a self-generating economy, calls for a three-pronged attack on shortcomings in agriculture, industry, and education. The largest single item—for which about $190 million has been earmarked—is the construction of a major dam on the Niger River comparable to the Rhodesias' Kariba and Ghana's Volta.*

At the time of independence, Nigeria's apparent political equilibrium derived from a delicately contrived balance among its three major regionally based political parties: The Northern People's Congress ruled in the conservative, Moslem Northern Region, and was a partner in the governing coalition at the federal level; the NCNC, founded by Nigeria's Governor-General (now President) Nnamdi Azikiwe, was dominant in the East and also a coalition partner at the center; and the Action Group, led by Chief Awolowo, governed the Western Region and held sufficient seats in the federal parliament to make its role as the loyal Opposition one of considerable power.

Between late 1959 and 1962, the Action Group increasingly phrased its opposition to the government in populist, mildly socialist terms. Moreover, it was evident that Chief Awolowo was no longer thinking of the Action Group as simply the "party of the Western Region," but rather as a national party drawing into its fold all Nigerians to the left of the government. Chief Awolowo's challenge to the established structure of the Nigerian political scene earned him some powerful enemies. Within the Action Group itself, a quarrel developed between those who endorsed party chieftain Awolowo's new radicalism and an "old guard" faction headed by the Western Premier, Chief Akintola.

Although patched up several times in 1962, the Awolowo-Akintola split came to a head in May, 1962, when Akintola was ousted as both premier and deputy chief of the party. A special

---

* See "The Nigerian Six Year Plan," *Africa Report*, June, 1962, p. 10.

session of the Western House of Assembly called to endorse the Awolowo-supported successor was broken up by the federal police after violent counterdemonstrations within the chamber, and the federal legislature subsequently abolished the new government, declared a state of emergency in the West, and appointed an interim regional administration under federal control.

In September, 1962, after publication of a damning report by a special commission on allegedly irregular relationships between the Action Group leadership and various statutory development corporations in the Western Region, Awolowo and other opposition leaders were arrested on charges of treasonable felony. During a prolonged and intricate trial, the federal government pressed its claim that a plot existed to overthrow the central government of Nigeria. In August, 1963, Awolowo was convicted and sentenced to ten years' imprisonment. A fragile coalition government combining Akintola's newly created United Peoples Party and some NCNC elements with uncertain popular base, took power in the West in January, 1963 following the suspension of emergency regulations.

As events of 1963 indicate, Nigeria's search for political stability is still unfinished. The specter of Northern secession cannot yet be entirely discounted. The growing body of the young and underemployed intelligentsia will eventually doubtless find another spokesman to replace the imprisoned Awolowo. The creation of a new Mid-West Region in May, 1963, may encourage still further efforts to unhinge and reshape the Federation. The 1963 census—which showed some dramatic changes in the population placement and thus necessitated shifts in the seating arrangement in the federal House of Representatives—opened up a new and critical phase in Nigeria's nearly unique attempt to make multiparty government work in an African setting.

Northern Rhodesia

Population: 3,496,000 (1963 census, including 76,000 Europeans and 8,700 Asians).

Area: 290,323 square miles.

Capital: Lusaka (population: 113,000).

Political Status: Self-governing British protectorate.

Chief of State: Queen Elizabeth II, represented locally by Governor Sir Evelyn Hone.

Head of Government: Prime Minister Kenneth Kaunda, invested January 22, 1964, when Northern Rhodesia became self-governing.

Major Political Parties: United National Independence Party, led by Kenneth Kaunda; African National Congress, led by Harry Nkumbula; Peoples Democratic Congress, led by Job Michello; National Progress Party, led by John Roberts.

Legislative Branch: Unicameral. Legislative Assembly of 75 elected members (of which 10 are reserved for Europeans).

Monetary Unit: 1 Federal pound = US$2.80. (To be replaced by a local currency in 1964.)

Principal Languages: English, Bemba, Lozi, Tonga, Nyanja, Lunda.

External Affiliations: Federation of Rhodesia and Nyasaland dissolved in December, 1963. Northern Rhodesia looks toward economic if not political ties with East Africa. Likely to remain a member of the Commonwealth upon independence.

With the dissolution of the Federation of Rhodesia and Nyasaland in December, 1963, followed in January, 1964, by elections under a revised constitution, Northern Rhodesia began the traditional last preparatory step of British dependencies toward independence—full internal self-government under an African Prime Minister. When the territory becomes fully independent, probably in late 1964, it will be renamed Zambia.

In the January, 1964, elections, Prime Minister Kaunda's United National Independence Party won fifty-five of the seventy-five elected seats; of the remainder, ten went to the African National Congress and ten reserved (i.e., white) seats were filled by candidates put forth by the National Progress Party. Mr. Kaunda campaigned vigorously for European as well as African support, and expressed disappointment at the rejection by white voters of all UNIP candidates put forth for the ten reserved seats. From the African majority, however, Mr. Kaunda's UNIP now had the clear mandate required to replace the unhappy coalition that had emerged from the last elections in October-December 1962.

Although UNIP won a sweeping popular endorsement from African voters in 1962, the cumbersome triple-roll electoral machinery employed at that time produced an unexpected result. Eight of fourteen "national roll" seats were left unfilled, and the final composition of the Legislative Council was UNIP, fourteen; the European-based United Federal Party (now NPP), fifteen; and ANC, seven. In the bargaining that followed, Nkumbula wavered between the European party and UNIP, finally agreed to join in a UNIP-ANC coalition only if ministerial positions were equally shared. Recurrent bickering at the ministerial level, and interparty violence at the local level (particularly on the Copperbelt), complicated the tasks of political transition during 1963.

In the 1964 elections preceding self-government, the complexities of a third "national roll" were eliminated and the seats reserved for Europeans decreased to ten out of a total legislature of seventy-five. Moreover, the ANC went into the campaign very much weaker than in 1962, for a breakaway group bolted the party in mid-1963 (to form the Peoples Democratic Congress under Job Michello) and the ANC's principal financial supporters of 1962 could no longer be relied on.

Economically, Northern Rhodesia will enter on independence with advantages not shared by many African countries. The gross national product of the cash economy in 1962 was $555 million, of which half came from mining (chiefly copper, but also cobalt, lead and zinc, manganese, etc.). This figure, moreover, does not take account of the production for subsistence of perhaps 2 million Africans outside the cash economy.

While much outside technical assistance is likely to be required to augment the very thin layer of trained Africans, Northern

Rhodesia would seem to have most of the other ingredients for rapid economic and social development—a sophisticated and hard-working political elite, adequate capital from internal sources, underpopulated agricultural land that could prosper with the application of modern farming methods, good communications, a pleasant climate, and impressive tourist attractions. Prime Minister Kaunda, 1963 president of the Pan-African Freedom Movement for East, Central, and Southern Africa, shows promise of becoming one of Africa's most respected statesmen.

Nyasaland

Population: 3,500,000 (1963 est.).

Area: 49,000 square miles.

Capital: Zomba (population: 14,000).

Political Status: Self-governing British protectorate; to become independent in July, 1964.

Chief of State: Queen Elizabeth II, represented locally by Governor Sir Glyn Jones.

Head of Government: Prime Minister Hastings Kamuzu Banda, invested February 1, 1963.

Major Political Party: Malawi Congress Party, led by Dr. Hastings Kamuzu Banda.

Legislative Branch: Unicameral. Legislative Assembly of 29 members (20 elected on a lower roll, 8 on a higher roll, with the Minister of Finance serving as an Official Member). Last elected, August, 1961.

Monetary Unit: 1 Federal pound = US$2.80.

Principal Languages: English, Nyanja, Tumbuka.

External Affiliations: Federation of Rhodesia and Nyasaland dissolved in December, 1963. Likely to remain in Commonwealth after independence.

Nyasaland—to be renamed Malawi when it becomes independent in July, 1964—is the most beautiful, albeit the most burdened with economic problems, of the three territories joined for a decade in the recently dissolved Federation of Rhodesia and Nyasaland.

In 1958, Dr. Banda was brought home (after forty-three years of exile in South Africa, the United States, Great Britain, and Ghana) to lead the growing nationalist movement. Stressing the rural areas and strong party organization at the village level, Dr. Banda and his militant younger lieutenants promptly "set the country on fire." Amid rumors of a plot to murder all whites, the Banda-led Nyasaland African Congress was banned in March, 1959, and most of its leadership was imprisoned. Six months later —in September, 1959—the Malawi Congress Party was organized, and Dr. Banda emerged from prison in April, 1960, to reassume the presidency of an even stronger movement.

In August, 1961, under a constitution introduced as part of a major shift in British policy toward Nyasaland in 1960, Malawi candidates swept all twenty of the lower-roll seats and two of the eight upper-roll seats in the Legislative Assembly. In November, 1962, Malawi leaders and the British Government agreed on the terms of a new two-stage constitution designed to lead the country to early self-government; a month later, Nyasaland was given official permission to secede from the Federation. In keeping with the timetable established in November, the executive council was replaced by a cabinet system, and, in February, 1963, Dr. Banda became Prime Minister of a self-governing Nyasaland. Independence is set for July 6, 1964.

There are some exceptions to the widespread grass-roots support for Dr. Banda's regime—for example, chiefs resentful of the loss of power and prestige to the party, Asian merchants who fear the effect of the new taxation policies, and the few minor opposition parties that speak with increasingly weak voices against the trend toward authoritarian government. For all practical purposes, however, the African population is thoroughly united within the Malawi Congress Party, and convinced of its doctrine that "nationalism, properly channeled, can perform feats which defy imagination and current economic theory." Hard work is the prescription dispensed by Dr. Banda wherever he goes, and the party leadership is expected to set an example by working harder than anybody else. A pragmatist rather than an ideologist, Dr. Banda nonetheless regards Ghana, where he practiced medicine for five years, as a model for much that has to be done in Nyasaland.

Since the political kingdom was won in 1961, the Malawi leadership has given increasing attention to the more difficult economic battle. The stark facts are that (1) more than 80 per cent of the population exists on subsistence agriculture; (2) only a small portion of the country is available for agricultural expansion, because much of the terrain is mountainous and Lake Nyasa occupies one-fifth of the total area (about 11,000 square miles); (3) what cash economy there is has been largely dominated by the

European and Asian population (20,000 total); (4) the income derived from wages sent home by several thousand Nyasas employed in the mines or on farms in the Rhodesias and South Africa is in danger of being cut off or reduced after independence; (5) the subsidy which Nyasaland has received for the past decade from the federal government—estimated anywhere from $4.2 million to $16.8 million annually, depending on the political orientation of the source—ends with independence; (6) no significant mineral resources have yet been discovered; (7) no development of the country's hydroelectric possibilities has yet taken place; and (8) industrialization is further inhibited by the limited internal market.

The government is concentrating on three immediate economic objectives. Party-directed re-education of the rural Nyasa to accept new methods of cultivation calculated to expand and diversify agricultural output resulted in an increase of about $3 million in the gross domestic product in 1962, and agricultural exports for the year (approximately $30 million) set a new record. Tea, sun-dried tobacco, peanuts, and maize are the main cash crops in order of importance, but experimentation with new crops is everywhere being assisted. Nyasaland's potential for diversification is far greater than many African countries, because the soil is good, rainfall is more than adequate, and differences in elevation make it possible to grow crops suitable for both temperate and tropical climates. Prospects for further development of commercial fishing are being studied.

Belt-tightening is a second major priority. Self-help schemes, higher taxes, retrenchment of some services, and salary reductions (including a flat 10 per cent reduction in ministerial salaries) were undertaken in 1962 and 1963 in anticipation of the approaching end of the federal subsidy.

Meanwhile, armed with these concrete examples of their own ingenuity, determination, and industriousness, government leaders are engaged in a campaign to woo the volume of technical and financial assistance from abroad that will be required for some time to come if any meaningful development of the economy is to be effected.

Portuguese Guinea

Population: 565,000 (1963 est.).

Area: 13,944 square miles.

Capital: Bissau (population: 22,000).

Political Status: Overseas province of Portugal.

Local Head of Government: Governor responsible to the Minister of Overseas Territories in Lisbon; assisted by an advisory Government Council comprised of various representatives of the provincial military and civilian administration plus three members of the provincial Legislative Council.

Major Political Parties: União Nacional is the governing party of Portugal and Portuguese Guinea. African political movements include Partido Africano da Independencia da Guine e Cabo Verde, led by Amilcar Cabral; Fronte pour la Libération et l'Indépendence Nationale de la Guinée Dite Portugaise (see below); Union des Ressortissants de la Guinée Portugaise.

Monetary Unit: 28.75 overseas escudos = US$1.00.

Principal Languages: Portuguese, Balanta, Fulani.

Besides its mainland territory, located on the west coast of Africa between the Republics of Guinea and Senegal, Portuguese Guinea includes, nearby, a group of small islands, the Bijagos Archipelago. The area was first visited by Portuguese ships in 1446 and settlers came soon thereafter.

Despite Lisbon's diligent efforts to insulate the territory from the nationalism that swept its neighbors on either side to independence, Guinea's Africans have been inevitably affected by political changes across its borders. Indeed, it is in this small, economically backward province that the most immediate threat to Portuguese rule in Africa now exists.

The largest, most active, and most radical of the three major African political movements is the Conakry-based Partido Africano da Independencia da Guine e Cabo Verde (PAIGC), which draws its support largely from the Balantes in the south. Led by a Cape Verde agronomist, Amilcar Cabral, the PAIGC has been responsible for most of the guerrilla activity carried out against

Portuguese barracks, administrative posts, and lines of communication since 1962. More than 15 per cent of Guinea's 14,000 square miles was reportedly occupied by rebel forces by mid-1963.*

The PAIGC operates clandestinely within the country, using an organizational framework that gives considerable autonomy to local cells. "Aid bureaus" are reportedly maintained in Algiers, Accra, Rabat, and Dakar, but party leaders claim that most of their arms and equipment have been stolen from Portuguese installations. Like the nationalist movements in Angola and Mozambique, PAIGC emphasizes that it seeks a negotiated rather than a military solution, but that it will continue to prosecute the guerrilla war *à l'Algérienne* until the Portuguese are forced to the bargaining table. As an ultimate goal, the PAIGC favors full independence for Portuguese Guinea (in some form of union with the Cape Verde Islands) and not amalgamation with either of its mainland neighbors.

The relatively moderate Fronte pour la Libération et l'Indépendence Nationale de la Guinée Dite Portugaise (FLING) is a loose-knit organization composed of at least four smaller groups; its headquarters are in Dakar. The largest of its components is the Mouvement de Libération de la Guinée Dite Portugaise (MLG) led by François Mendy, University of Dakar. MLG draws its strength mainly from the Manjak tribe, which straddles the border between Senegal and Portuguese Guinea. It has carried out sporadic raids against Portuguese authorities in the northern part of Guinea. Another subgroup of FLING is the Union des Populations de Guinée Dite Portugaise (UPG), led by Henri Labéry, a mulatto of French, Senegalese, and Cape Verdean origin.

A third principal political movement, the Union des Ressortissants de la Guinée Portugaise is headed by Benjamin Pinto-Bull, a teacher of Portuguese in a Dakar *lycée*. It favors cooperation with Portugal in exchange for increased African participation in the structure of political power.

The PAIGC has majority backing within the Liberation Com-

* See "Africa's Quiet War," by I. William Zartman, *Africa Report*, February, 1964, p. 8.

mittee of the Organization of African Unity, and would have been designated as the official channel for OAU aid at the August Foreign Ministers' meeting in Dakar except for Senegalese objections. Although Senegal has been a staging ground for both parties' rebel activities, it favors the policies of the more moderate FLING.

The revision of the Organic Law for the overseas territories promulgated in June, 1963, calls for the establishment of a territorial council in Portuguese Guinea for the first time, and enlarged Guinea participation in the national government in Portugal. In July, 1963, Lisbon appointed an African, James Pinto-Bull (brother of Benjamin) to the second most important position in the civil government. These reforms are not likely to be an effective answer to African nationalism, since they imply no change in the central principle of Portuguese colonial rule— that each of the African territories is an integral province of the motherland, with no prospect of moving toward self-rule.

Economically, Guinea is a net drain on Portugal, and it has little prospect for viability as an independent state without substantial external assistance. Imports in 1961 totaled $10,236,000, as opposed to $7,238,000 worth of exports, leaving a net trade deficit of $2,998,000. The Portuguese Government invested $2.8 million in the first five-year plan (1953–58) and $6.3 million in the current plan. Most development funds are allocated for the expansion of agriculture and the development of communications.

Guinea's economy is predominantly based on subsistence agriculture. Rice is the most important food crop, with annual production exceeding 100,000 tons. Millet, sorghum, manioc, yams, sweet potatoes, and beans are also grown. In 1962, Guinea exported some 30,000 tons of peanuts, representing approximately 43 per cent of total exports. The production of palm oil (16 per cent of exports) could be greatly expanded. Hides, wood, coconuts, and beeswax are also sold abroad.

Traces of bauxite, gold, and other minerals have been discovered, but apparently not in sufficient quantity to warrant commercial exploitation. The search for oil has thus far produced no tangible results. The country has some hydroelectric potential.

Réunion

Population: 349,908 (1962 est.).

Area: 969 square miles.

Capital: Saint-Denis (population: 65,275).

Political Status: Overseas department of France.

Local Head of Government: Prefect Alfred Diefenbacker, assisted by a Secretary-General.

Local Legislative Branch: General Council of 36 members elected by universal adult suffrage.

Monetary Unit: 247 CFA francs = US$1.00.

Principal Language: French.

Réunion, about 420 miles east of Madagascar in the Indian Ocean, was discovered in 1528 by the Portuguese navigator Pedro de Mascarenhas, but was not settled until French colonization began in the seventeenth century. Later, the French settlers were joined by Africans, Malays, Annamese, Chinese, and Malabar Indians.

Under the French constitution of 1946, Réunion became an Overseas Department of France, giving it juridical equality with the departments of metropolitan France. The highest resident authority in the island, a Prefect appointed by the French Minister of the Interior, is assisted by a Secretary-General and various administrative services. In April, 1960, the powers of the General Council were broadened by decree to provide for greater administrative decentralization. The Council approves the budget and must be consulted on all legislation and statutory measures concerning the department, and it has the right to propose measures to the government on specific local issues. Three deputies are elected to the French National Assembly from Réunion and two Senators to the Senate.

The population—mainly concentrated on the coast and in the high interior plains—is exceptionally young. Due to a high birth rate, 52 per cent of the people are under 20 years of age. Sugar cane, occupying about 70 per cent of the entire cultivated area of Réunion, is the major source of revenue, followed by rum and geranium and vetiver (plants from which perfume is extracted). The 1960 sugar cane yield was 1,877,000 metric tons. Food crops grown for local consumption include corn, potatoes, beans, coffee, and tropical fruits. Of the 1,240 miles of main and secondary roads on Réunion, about one-third are hard-surfaced.

There is telephone and telegraph communication with Mauritius, the Malagasy Republic, and (via the latter) metropolitan France. Air France maintains a thrice-weekly service, and cargo ships frequent Réunion's three ports—Saint-Pierre, Saint-Paul, and Pointe-des-Galets.

Rwanda

Population: 2,690,000 (1962 est.).

Area: 10,169 square miles.

Capital: Kigali (population 4,000).

Political Status: Independent republic.

Date of Independence: July 1, 1962.

Chief of State and Head of Government: Grégoire Kayibanda, formerly Prime Minister, elected first President of the Republic in October, 1961, by Legislative Assembly for a 4-year term.

Major Political Parties: Parti Républicain du Mouvement de l'Emancipation d'Hutu (PARMEHUTU), governing party; Union Nationale Rwandaise (UNAR); Association pour la Promotion de la Masse (APROSOMA).

Legislative Branch: Unicameral. National Assembly of 44 members elected by direct universal adult suffrage for 4-year terms. Last election, September, 1961.

Monetary Unit: 50 Rwanda-Burundi francs = US$1.00.

Principal Languages: French, Kinyarwanda.

External Affiliations: United Nations, Organization of African Unity, Union Africaine et Malgache, European Economic Community (associate).

When the Belgian trust territory of Ruanda-Urundi became independent in July, 1962, the territory split into two separate states of markedly different political complexion. In Rwanda, the Vermont-sized northern half of the trust territory, a nationalist political movement of the long-oppressed Bahutu majority revolted against the traditional Batutsi aristocracy in 1959, establishing a republican government and forcing the Mwami (king) into exile. An estimated 80,000 other Tutsis also fled the country, and are still living in camps in the Congo, Tanganyika, and Uganda, or working for the Tutsi-led government of neighboring Burundi.

President Kayibanda heads a revolutionary austerity regime in which Ministers receive low salaries and few amenities, the presidential car is a Volkswagen, and the official motto of the government is *"Liberté, Coopération, Progrès."* Rwanda takes pride in the fact that Kigali, with a population of 4,000 and with one paved street, is probably the smallest capital city in the world.

The influence of the Roman Catholic Church is strong among the governing group, and it is said that the 1959 revolution was sparked by a circular letter from the Archbishop describing the inequalities between the Tutsi aristocracy and the Hutu as incompatible with Christian precepts. Communist activity is explicitly prohibited in the constitution, though Rwanda is planning to establish diplomatic relations with the Soviet Union. Canadian Dominicans will operate the new University of Butare, which opened its doors in 1963; the government has given high priority to establishment of this institution, in part because of the desire to educate young Rwandans away from the "fleshpots" of Brussels, Paris, and Usumbura.

President Kayibanda's puritanism is keyed to some hard economic realities. Rwanda is a poor country with meager resources and probably the highest population density (265 per square mile) in sub-Saharan Africa. Coffee is the only important cash export crop of an essentially subsistence economy. Production was 14,321 metric tons in 1961, but has fallen sharply since the relaxation of Belgian discipline of growers; 90 per cent of the output is sold to the United States. In 1961, the combined exports of Rwanda and Burundi totaled $27 million.

Any economic and social development is heavily dependent on foreign aid. Major current sources of financial and technical assistance are Belgium, the European Economic Community, the United Nations, France, and Israel.

São Tomé and Principe

Population: 63,676 (1960 census).

Area: 372 square miles.

Capital: São Tomé (population: 7,817).

Political Status: Overseas province of Portugal.

Local Head of Government: Governor Dr. Manuel Marques de Abrantes Amaral.

Monetary Unit: 28.75 overseas escudos = US$1.00.

Principal Languages: Portuguese, Creole.

The islands of São Tomé and Principe, about 125 miles off the coast in the Gulf of Guinea, were discovered by Portuguese explorers in 1471 and have been governed by the Portuguese since 1522. The province includes Pedras Tinhosas and Rolas islands, and formerly the mainland fort of St. Jean Baptiste d'Ajuda, which was annexed by Dahomey in 1961.

The rich volcanic soil of the islands produces excellent-quality cocoa, coffee, copra, and cinchona. Production is organized on a plantation system, with much of the labor supplied by workers brought in from Angola and Mozambique. The entire product is exported to Portugal.

Senegal

Population: 3,100,000 (1962 est.).

Area: 76,084 square miles.

Capital: Dakar (population: 375,000).

Political Status: Independent republic.

Date of Independence: August 25, 1960.

Chief of State and Head of Government: President Léopold Sédar Senghor, first elected President in September, 1960; re-elected in December, 1963, for a 4-year term. A new constitution adopted in March, 1963, by popular referendum, after the abortive *coup d'état* by former Prime Minister Mamadou Dia, establishes a strong presidential regime in place of the previous dual-executive arrangement.

Major Political Parties: The governing Union Progressiste Sénégalaise, which was merged with the former opposition party Bloc des Masses Sénégalaises in September, 1963, won all 80 seats in the National Assembly in elections held in December, 1963, on a single-list system. The opposition Parti du Régroupement Africain also presented a list of 80 candidates for the 1963 elections. The Parti Africaine de l'Indépendence has been banned since August, 1960. The September, 1962, issue of the World Marxist Review describes the PAI as a "Marxist-Leninist Party" with which the French Communist Party expresses "its complete solidarity."

Legislative Branch: Unicameral. National Assembly of 80 members elected by universal adult suffrage for a 4-year term on a single-list system. All seats filled by the governing UPS. Last elections, December 1, 1963.

Monetary Unit: 247 CFA francs = US$1.00.

Principal Languages: French, Wolof, Pular.

External Affiliations: United Nations, Organization of African Unity, Union Africaine et Malgache, European Economic Community (associate), franc zone.

Dakar was the administrative center and showpiece of France's West African Federation, and Senegal thereby fell heir to a range of infrastructure not usually available to newly-independent states. Included were the foremost port in West Africa, a fully functioning university, an international airport, a good rail and road system linked to all of Senegal's neighbors, a powerful radio network, and the most elaborate economic planning machinery in West Africa.

In terms of political experience, too, Senegal came to independence better prepared than many of its neighbors. Part of the country first began choosing deputies to the French Parliament in 1871, and the local Territorial Assembly had been the center of Senegalese political life since 1952. The sizable educated elite has a strong literary bent, and Senegal boasts more internationally recognized writers than any other single African country. Of these, the most notable is President Senghor, whose poetry has long been read and admired in Europe by those who know nothing of his political importance.

The Senghor government has undergone two damaging crises since independence. The first was the collapse in August, 1960, of the short-lived political federation with neighboring Mali. In retrospect, the federation was doomed from the beginning, for each partner entered it with different expectations and neither was prepared to compromise cherished political viewpoints. The Senegalese assumed that they were entering a kind of common-law marriage that would leave each spouse a good deal of freedom in ordering its private affairs. Long experience in Western parliamentary politics led Senegal to take for granted that both territories would retain a measure of internal autonomy, surrender limited authority to the federal government, and adjust their differences in the same pragmatic way that internal political problems were settled in Senegal. Mali (then called Soudan) dreamed of a mystical union within which each partner would lose its separate personality in a highly centralized socialist state on the Soudanese pattern.

The end came when Federation Prime Minister Modibo Keita of Soudan upset the delicate Lebanese-style balance of political power at the center by appointing a Soudanese (i.e., Malien) as head of the federal armed forces over a previously agreed-upon Senegalese candidate, and then fired Senegalese Prime Minister Mamadou Dia from his post as Federal Minister of Defense for protesting the appointment. Senegalese authorities, suspecting an imminent Soudanese *coup d'état,* arrested Modibo Keita and twenty other Soudanese in Dakar, expelled them from the country, and sealed the border. It was to remain sealed to traffic for almost three years.

Although loss of its traditional exit to the sea posed an obvious problem for landlocked Soudan (see "Mali"), the closing of the border also caused serious dislocations in the Senegalese economy. Victor Du Bois has summarized the repercussions of the break in Senegal in a recent American Universities Field Staff Report (VDB-4-63): "Prior to the events of August 1960, Senegal exported 50 per cent of its sugar, 35 per cent of its matches, 30 per cent of its tobacco, 20 per cent of its shoe manufactures, and 15 per cent of its cement to Mali. This market was lost. . . . Prior to the breakup, Senegalese dockers at Dakar handled annually some 244,000 tons of goods destined for Mali. The rupture in relations between the two nations brought this traffic to a halt, causing a loss of revenue of $32,000,000 a year to the port of Dakar. Also hard hit was the interior port of Kaolack, through which nine-tenths of Mali's peanuts were shipped to the outside world. This represented 95 per cent of that inland port's activity. . . . Before the split, Senegal's Cap Vert textile mills had brought 80 per cent of their cotton from Mali and exported 40 per cent of their finished goods to that country. . . . The Senegalese section of the railroad also suffered sharp losses. Passenger traffic declined by 33 per cent and freight by 61 per cent, costing the line some $8,000,000 per year in lost revenues."

It was not until June 22, 1963, that relations were officially restored between the two countries. The new accords call for a free flow of rail traffic, restoration of Mali's port rights at Dakar and Kaolack, and re-establishment of favorable terms for interstate trade. Mali had developed alternate routes to the sea during the three-year emergency, however, and it is not expected that traffic between the countries will return to its previous volume.

Senegal's second debilitating crisis was a traumatic split in the governing Union Progressiste Sénégalaise, which resulted in the arrest in December, 1962, and subsequent conviction of Prime Minister Mamadou Dia on charges of attempting to upset the dual executive by *coup d'état*. Although Senegal had given the appearance of being one of Africa's most stable states, the compromise between radicalism and conservatism embodied in the governing party and in the institutions of the central government gradually deteriorated into a factional quarrel. The year 1962 was marked by increasing friction between a "Dia party" and a "Senghor party." This party strife was not based on any fundamental ideological or personal conflict between Prime Minister Dia and President Senghor—indeed, their views on the kind of "African socialism" suitable for Senegal were similar and they had been close friends for many years. The differences between the two leaders seem to have developed primarily from the conflicts inherent in a system of divided authority, their divergent views on the need for controls over expatriate business and on the relationship with France, and the kind of followers each tended to attract.

Senghor, a Catholic, was favored by those who rejected change: (1) the traditionalist Moslem elements, who were deeply suspicious of Mamadou Dia's economic policies and of the new regulatory practices required to implement the government's development plan; (2) most of the National Assembly, a body composed largely of senior members of the party; (3) the business community, closely tied to France; and (4) rural Senegal, where Senghor is a strong father figure. Paradoxically, Mamadou Dia—a Moslem economist—seemed to embody the aspirations of the urban Christian militants. This younger group, yearning for change, regarded Dia's economic-reform program as the minimal first step toward disengaging Senegal from its financial dependence on France, and chafed at the widening gap between their own views and those heard from senior citizens on the floor of the National Assembly.

The crisis peaked on December 14, 1962, when forty-one deputies tabled a censure motion against the government of Prime Minister Dia and a supporting statement denouncing the "fetters to the free exercise of parliamentary prerogatives" allegedly imposed by Dia under the terms of the state of emergency maintained since the break-up of the Mali Federation two years earlier. The Political Bureau of the Union Progressiste Sénégalaise, supported by President Senghor, subsequently ordered the deputies to withdraw their censure motion, but the deputies defied the party executive and refused. In an effort to prevent a vote on the censure motion on December 17, Dia sent units of the police and gendarmerie loyal to him to surround the National Assembly and evict the legislators. Forty-eight of the deputies subsequently convened at the home of Speaker Lamine Gueye, from whence they solicited from President Senghor (as "guardian of the Constitution") the authority to convene a special parliamentary session at the Speaker's home. Faced with the choice of supporting the Prime Minister or the Assembly, Senghor decided on the latter. On the same afternoon, while Dia forces held Radio Senegal and the Administrative Building, the deputies convened to pass the motion of censure and invite President Senghor to submit an amended presidential constitution to a popular referendum. Once the issues became clear, the security forces threw in their lot with the President, thus ensuring the outcome. No shots were fired.

On March 3, 1963, Senegalese voters went to the polls to approve a new constitution establishing a presidential system of government. Elections held in December, 1963, resulted in the election of President Senghor (he was the only candidate), and of UPS deputies to all eighty seats in the National Assembly. The opposition Parti du Régroupement Africain also entered candidates for all 80 Assembly seats and was reportedly allowed to campaign freely, but could win no representation because use of the "single list" system required that voters opt for the entire list of a party rather than individual candidates. The PRA list included a mixture of former Dia supporters, dissident members of the Bloc des Masses Sénégalaises who declined to follow the party into its merger with the Union Progressiste Sénégalaise in September, 1963, and some representatives of the banned Parti Africaine de l'Indépendence. At least twelve persons were killed and sixty injured during the elections when antigovernment demonstrators of still-undetermined affiliations attempted to incite security forces to mutiny in Dakar and other towns.

Senegal's economy remains largely agricultural, with peanuts accounting for 80 to 90 per cent of exports. A number of processing industries are being developed in Dakar, however, and phosphate production is capable of being increased from present annual output of 100,000 tons to 400,000 tons. In addition,

Senegal produces limestone for making cement (currently 200,000 tons a year), 30,000 tons of ilmenite, 1,000 tons of rutile, and 7,000 tons of zirconium. Systematic exploration for petroleum has been going on since 1952, but with minimal results thus far. A new oil refinery, with a capacity of 2 million tons of crude oil, was recently completed in Dakar.

Because of its weak economic base, and the dislocations created by the dispute with Mali, Senegal still remains crucially dependent on French financial assistance. This takes the form of subsidized prices for the peanut crop (to be gradually reduced beginning in 1964), an annual grant to take up the slack in the budget, and various forms of development aid. In his independence anniversary address on April 3, 1963, President Senghor warned that the budget deficit for 1963–64 would total more than $39 million unless the country gave its support to new austerity measures aimed at reducing waste and revitalizing the "stagnated economy."

Seychelles

Population: 42,936 (1961 est.).

Area: 156 square miles.

Capital: Port Victoria (population: 10,500).

Political Status: British colony.

Local Head of Government: British Governor (the Earl of Oxford and Asquith), assisted by an advisory Executive Council, consisting of 4 Official Members and "such other persons, at least one of which must be unofficial, as the Governor may, from time to time, appoint."

Legislative Branch: Legislative Council, chaired by the Governor (as President), including 5 official Members, 2 unofficial appointed members, and 5 elected (1963) by suffrage with a minimal literacy qualification.

Political Parties: Taxpayers' and Producers' Association (TAPA); Seychelles Islanders' United Party (SIUP).

Monetary Unit: 1 Seychelles rupee = US$0.20.

Principal Languages: English, Creole.

The Seychelles are a group of 99 islands—45 granite islands and 44 coral atolls—situated in the equatorial zone of the Indian Ocean approximately 970 miles east of Mombasa, Kenya. They were uninhabited until the French explored and settled them in 1768. The islands changed hands several times during the Napoleonic Wars; in 1814, the Treaty of Paris established their status as a colony of Great Britain. The present population includes descendants of the early French settlers, African emigrés from the mainland, Creoles, Indians, Chinese, and a few Europeans.

The main occupation is agriculture, mostly the growing of coconuts. Indeed, the price of copra is the most important economic barometer of the colony. Cinnamon, patchouli oil, vanilla, and fish are also produced for export, but are of minor importance. Breadfruit, bananas, cassava, and sweet potatoes are grown for local consumption, but additional food must nonetheless be imported. The only industries are connected with copra and the distillation of essential oils. A Minister for Tourism and Information was appointed in 1959, with the hope that tourists might bring a new source of revenue.

Because of their location in relation to existing United States satellite tracking stations, the Seychelles were chosen as the site for a new American installation which became operational in July, 1963. About ninety Seychellois will obtain permanent employment at the installation. Electricity has been extended to La Misère and Grand'Anse, where the transmitters will be located.

During the August, 1963, general election campaign, the Taxpayers' and Planters' Association (TAPA) campaigned, for the first time, on a platform calling for the replacement of the British Governor by a Commissioner, the early establishment of internal self-government, and several measures designed to raise the standard of living. The Seychelles Islanders' United Party (SIUP), a new political grouping, advocated "protection of the present constitutional status of the Seychelles," stricter measures to control the flight of capital, and a wide range of welfare measures. Final results gave two Legislative Council seats to TAPA, one to SIUP, one to an independent, and the fifth seat to a candidate supported by both parties.

Sierra Leone

Population: 2,183,000 (1963 census).

Area: 27,924 square miles.

Capital: Freetown (population: 125,000).

Political Status: Independent dominion in the Commonwealth.

Date of Independence: April 27, 1961.

Chief of State: Queen Elizabeth II, represented by Governor-General Sir Henry Lightfoot Boston.

Head of Government: Prime Minister Sir Milton A. S. Margai, leader of government since 1954.

Major Political Parties: Sierra Leone People's Party (SLPP), majority party, led by Sir Milton Margai; opposition All People's Congress (APC), led by Siaka Stevens.

Legislative Branch: Unicameral. House of Representatives consisting of 74 members—12 paramount chiefs and 62 ordinary members elected by universal adult suffrage for a term of up to 5 years. Last election, May, 1962.

Monetary Unit: 1 Sierra Leone pound = US$2.80.

Principal Languages: English, Creole (Krio), Mende, Temme.

External Affiliations: United Nations, Organization of African Unity, Commonwealth.

Sierra Leone's political history, like that of neighboring Liberia, is interwoven with the skeins of the American past. In 1787, British philanthropists chose Freetown as the site on which to establish a colony for a number of freed slaves from America and England. Later, the Freetown harbor was the base from which Her Majesty's frigates and gunboats moved out to intercept the slave ships and eventually put down the trade.

The small coastal colony was augmented in 1895, when a British protectorate was established over some 27,000 square miles of the surrounding hinterland to forestall French encroachment from the east. There was little political communication between the two sectors of Sierra Leone until almost the middle of this century, however. The Creoles of the colony were detribalized, deeply Anglicized, politically sophisticated, and relatively prosperous. They had little in common with the "native peoples" of the hinterland, where Britain ruled indirectly through about 150 small chieftaincies.

Economic development created the first bridges between the two areas, for it became apparent by the 1930's that the major resources of the country—both mineral and agricultural—were located in the interior. The discovery of diamonds, iron ore, cobalt, and other minerals, together with the introduction of new export crops (palm kernels, cocoa, coffee, ginger, piassava, kola nuts, etc.), began a transformation of the protectorate that was inevitably to become political and social as well as economic.

In 1951, a distinguished protectorate-born physician, Dr. Milton Margai, formed the Sierra Leone Peoples' Party to assert the voice of the more populous interior against the monopoly of power by the coastal aristocracy. Britain subsequently acquiesced in a series of constitutional changes which integrated the two sectors into a single political unit and broadened the electoral base by extending the franchise to all citizens. Dr. Margai became first Chief Minister when self-government was granted in 1954.

While the SLPP was initially a protest movement against the old order, Dr. Margai accomplished a remarkable political feat by transforming it into a national party embracing major political elements in both the protectorate and the colony. In 1960, a "government of national union" was established in cooperation with the principal opposition group (the People's National Party, headed by Sir Milton's brother, Albert) and the two parties were officially merged into the SLPP just before independence in 1961. Some critics of the present shape of things in Sierra Leone note ironically that integration of the elites of the country's two geographical sectors has been so successful that the protectorate leaders of the SLPP have taken on many of the Creole attitudes they once censured—notably Anglophilia, conservatism, and a somewhat aristocratic approach to the masses.

The chief spokesman for this point of view is the All Peoples' Congress, an opposition party formed in 1960 by Siaka Stevens. The APC won an unexpected twenty out of sixty-two elected seats in the May, 1962, elections by openly challenging both major sources of political power in the country—the Creole aristocracy and the powerful chiefs of the hinterland. Carpet-crossing since 1962 has increased the SLPP's parliamentary strength to forty-four elected seats (from an initial twenty-eight), however, and reduced the APC and its affiliates to eighteen seats. The twelve Paramount Chiefs in the House also customarily vote with the SLPP.

Although Sierra Leone continues to experience a sizable trade deficit ($28 million in 1961, due largely to unsold diamonds) and needs outside capital and technical assistance for any major development projects, it is considerably better off in terms of economic resources than many larger African states. With diamond smuggling finally under control, the value of diamond exports rose to $44,713,360 in 1961, followed by iron ore ($13,083,938). Indeed, mining now accounts for more than 70 per cent of exports by value, as compared with 30 per cent in 1951. Subsistence agriculture remains the occupation of most of the population.

Somali Republic

Population: 2,000,000 (1963 est.).

Area: 246,000 square miles.

Capital: Mogadiscio (population: 100,000).

Political Status: Independent republic.

Date of Independence: July 1, 1960.

Chief of State: President Aden Abdullah Osman, elected (July, 1961) by Parliament for a 6-year term.

Head of Government: Prime Minister Abdi Rashid Ali Shermarke, appointed (July, 1960) by the President.

Major Political Parties: The Somali Youth League (SYL) was founded during the British occupation of Somalia (World War II), grew in stature during the Italian Trusteeship Administration, and assumed the reins of government with independence in 1960. The Somali National League (SNL) and the Somali United Party (SUP) represent northern constituencies from ex-British Somaliland with 20 and 12 seats, respectively, in the National Assembly to SYL's 83. The Somali National Congress (SNC) was created in 1963 and is composed of former members from all 3 parties.

Legislative Branch: Unicameral. National Assembly of 122 members elected by universal male suffrage for 5-year terms. Next scheduled elections, March, 1964.

Monetary Unit: 1 Somali shilling = US$0.14.

Principal Languages: Somali, Arabic, English, Italian.

External Affiliations: United Nations, Organization of African Unity, European Economic Community (associate).

The Somali Republic enjoys a degree of ethnic, religious, and linguistic homogeneity unique among African states. The Somalis are in Africa, but not entirely of Africa: they apparently originally came from Asia and then gradually absorbed the resident Galla and Bantu of the Horn into their own Somali culture. Islam has also been an important element in creating a Somali national consciousness, for all Somalis claim to trace their descent from the lineage of the Prophet. From this highly developed Somali national consciousness, however, stems the major problem currently disturbing the republic's relations with its neighbors and the West.

When former Italian Somalia and British Somaliland were united in July, 1960, into a single independent republic, the commitment was explicit that the ultimate goal of Somali nationalism must continue to be to bring all other Somalis in the Horn of Africa under the new flag. According to present estimates, those yet to be "ingathered" number over a million—most of them in the Ogaden Province of Ethiopia, the Northern Frontier District of Kenya, and in French Somaliland. Many of these Somalis customarily spend part of the year in the republic, for they are preponderantly (80 per cent) nomadic or seminomadic and their constant search for water and pasture takes them back and forth across the national boundaries of the arid Horn.

Ethiopia has become increasingly sensitive in recent years about the possible political significance of these nomadic movements, and armed clashes between Ethiopian military units and Somali nomads have been frequent since 1961. Somali relations with Kenya, on its southern border, have also been severely strained by the "greater Somalia" issue. In December, 1962, a British fact-finding commission delighted Somali officialdom by concluding that 87 per cent of the population of Kenya's Northern Frontier District was undeniably Somali, and that a majority of this Somali element would prefer to avoid assimilation into an independent Kenya. The Somali Government later severed diplomatic relations with the British Government (March 15, 1963) when it became apparent that the Commission's findings were to be ignored and that the NFD was to remain an integral part of Kenya after independence.

As for the Somali heartland, visible progress has been made since 1960 toward integrating the diverse currencies, pay scales, judicial procedures, administrative concepts, cultural preferences, and uneven skills which the two partners brought with them from Italian and British tutelage. Aside from a brief uprising of British-trained officers in the Northern Region in 1961, the union itself has never been seriously challenged, nor has the predominance of the southern-based Somali Youth League, in decision-making. Various procedures have long been institutionalized to tap grass-roots sentiment on policy issues—e.g., frequent conferences of district and regional commissioners, regular party meetings, sessions of the popularly elected National Assembly—but both initiative and decision-making are centered in the Cabinet. The Somali Youth League holds 83 of 122 seats in the National Assembly, 9 of 12 cabinet posts. Tribal balance is carefully practiced in the distribution of high government offices, but a clear effort has been made to choose modernist, "detribalized" representatives of each of the three main clan-family groups for major appointments. Some Somali intellectuals cite the practice of "tribal balance" as a useful check on the development of one-man authoritarian rule.

Although the Somali Government has been able to increase its revenue beyond its own expectations (from an estimated $15,260,000 in 1961 to an estimated $18,900,000 in 1962), it continues to operate in a chronic deficit position. Bananas (sold at controlled prices to the Italian Banana Monopoly) account for approximately 55 per cent of foreign exchange, but the net gain to the Somali economy is questionable, as 80 per cent of the growers are Italian concessionaires who deposit their lira proceeds in Italy. Other exports—livestock, hides, incense, and agricultural products—total about $500,000 annually.

The pessimistic pre-independence projections on the republic's long-term economic future have been partly softened, however, by a recent American AID survey which concluded that the republic could attain economic "viability"—given sufficient infusions of foreign aid over a prolonged period of time—through optimum exploitation of its scarce water and fisheries resources, agricultural land, and grazing areas. The survey suggests, for example, that an estimated additional 400,000 acres of land could be irrigated from the country's two rivers, and that 2,500,000 more acres of land are basically suitable for dryland farming. Another recent American study noted that there were several possibilities for small industries. U.S. aid, previously concentrated in agriculture, is now helping to develop the Juba River port of Chisimaio, to stimulate cash-crop production along the river, and to improve the harbor facilities in Mogadiscio. Soviet technicians are enlarging the harbor at Berbera, the only port in the Northern Region.

In foreign policy as in domestic policy, Somalis have sought to remain masters of their own fate by effecting a delicate balance among conflicting pressures. The principal sources of economic assistance during the trusteeship period—Italy, the U.A.R., the United Nations, the United Kingdom, and the United States—have been encouraged to continue their help, and the government has succeeded in augmenting this flow with a remarkable amount of additional assistance from the European Common Market, West Germany, the Soviet Bloc, and, during 1963, Communist China.

Concern was expressed in late 1963 and early 1964 that Somali anger and bitterness over the failure of the West to supply the republic with military support commensurate with that accorded to Ethiopia (and to support the principle of self-determination in Somali-inhabited portions of Kenya and Ethiopia) may have caused the Somali leaders to get themselves in deeper with the U.S.S.R. and Communist China than is prescribed under the country's traditional policy of "balance." While precise figures were not available, it was reliably estimated that total Somali indebtedness to the Soviet Union by 1964 could total over $100 million. By mid-1963, Communist China was reported to have extended economic aid totaling more than $23 million.

French Somaliland

Population: 81,000 (1961 est.).

Area: 8,500 square miles.

Capital: Djibouti (population: 41,200).

Political Status: French overseas territory.

Local Head of Government: Governor René Tirant, assisted by an 8-member Council of Government elected from the Territorial Assembly.

Legislative Branch: Unicameral. Territorial Assembly of 32 members elected by universal suffrage. Last election, November 17, 1963.

Monetary Unit: about 225 francs Djibouti = US$1.00.

Principal Languages: French, Dankali, Arabic.

In the 1958 constitutional referendum, French Somaliland's voters opted to join the French Community as an Overseas Territory. Following a postreferendum crisis in the local government, the Territorial Assembly was dissolved and new elections were held. The results of this election confirmed the previously expressed sentiments on the referendum. There has been no serious bid thus far for independence, though there was some pressure in 1963 for further autonomy.

The neighboring Somali Republic is politically committed to the eventual union of all Somali peoples, but the pan-Somali movement is strongly opposed by France. In any case, French Somaliland is not as homogeneous as the other Somali-inhabited states: Only 36,450 of the territory's 81,000 inhabitants are Somalis, with the rest broken down into some 34,020 Danakils, 7,290 Arabs, and 3,240 French. The Danakils predominate in the government.

An arid land, Somaliland has few resources beyond the strategically important French naval base of Djibouti and the Djibouti-Addis Ababa railroad. While France clearly hopes to retain Djibouti under its direct administration as long as possible, subtle changes in French policy since 1957 reflect a realization that the gap between Somaliland and the peoples of neighboring states must be narrowed. Political reforms introduced in recent years have resulted in increased powers over internal affairs for the Territorial Assembly and Council and the first serious efforts at partial Africanization of the administration. Meanwhile, educational opportunities are being expanded and an increasing number of Somaliland students are being sent to French universities in the hope of strengthening cultural bonds for the longer term. The territory is represented in the French National Assembly by a deputy and a senator.

South Africa

Population: 16,122,000 (1961 est.), including 11,007,000 Africans, 3,106,000 Europeans, 1,522,000 Coloreds or mixed, and 487,000 Asians.

Area: 472,685 square miles.

Capitals: Pretoria (population: 423,000); Cape Town (population: 810,000).

Political Status: Independent republic.

Date of Founding: May 31, 1910; became a republic on May 31, 1961.

Chief of State: President Charles Robberts Swart, elected (May, 1961) by an electoral college consisting of members of the Senate and House of Assembly, for a 7-year term.

Head of Government: Prime Minister Dr. Hendrik F. Verwoerd, invested by Parliament (1958).

Legislative Branch: Bicameral. Senate of 54 members, all white (43 elected by electoral colleges, 11 nominated by the government, all for 5-year terms). Last election, October, 1960. House of Assembly of 160 members (156 elected by white adult suffrage, 4 whites elected on a separate roll by Coloreds and Asians in the Cape Province for a maximum term of 5 years). Last election, October, 1961.

Major Political Parties: National Party, led by Prime Minister Verwoerd (105 seats); United Party, led by Sir de Villiers Graaff (49 seats); Progressive Party, led by Dr. Jan Steytler (1 seat); Liberal Party, led by Alan Paton (no seats); African National Congress (banned), led by Albert J. Luthuli; Pan-Africanist Congress (banned), led by Robert Sobukwe and Potlako Leballo.

Principal Languages: Afrikaans, English, Xhosa, Zulu.

Monetary Unit: 1 South African Rand = US$1.40.

External Affiliations: United Nations.

In a new study of South Africa published in November, 1963, Professor Thomas Karis summarizes the internal situation in these terms: "The trend toward the polarization of white and black politics in South Africa since the end of World War II invites oversimplification and analogies to Greek tragedy. Yet South Africa has not ceased to be complex. Within its modern economy

the several racial groups continue to become more interdepend-
ent. Behind the reality of white racial oligarchy and police-state
control of nonwhites and their white allies is also the reality of
social and economic change that is beyond the control of a virtually impregnable political leadership. The wide variety of historical influences actively at work and the continued plurality of
groups makes the possession of political power in South Africa
more vulnerable than appears on the surface. Although a review
of the main developments since 1870 appears to confirm the most
pessimistic predictions of eventual racial violence, there is as yet
no obvious timetable for the future. The period of predictable
stability, however, is fast shortening."* Four "historical water-
sheds" are cited as keys to understanding the contemporary scene
—1870, marking the opening of the diamond mines and the beginning of South Africa's industrial revolution; 1936, the nadir
of South African liberalism, when African voters in Cape Province were removed from the common voting roll; 1948, the coming to power of the first all-Afrikaner government; and 1960,
following the first major clash between African nationalists and
security forces at Sharpeville, the driving underground of those
African leaders who had been committed to multiracialism and
nonviolence.

Since 1948, successive Nationalist governments have worked
systematically toward the objective of creating a closed compart-
mentalized society in which each racial group will have prescribed
living areas, kinds of work, levels of wages, and distinctive educational systems. Since the Africans are, in the folklore of apartheid, only "visitors" from their tribal homelands and (according
to the Promotion of Bantu Self-Government Bill of 1959) "do not
constitute a homogeneous people," they are not to be allowed to
participate in the government of white-governed South Africa.

To justify the denial of voting rights to Africans in "white
South Africa," as well as to segment the 11 million Africans into
discrete, manageable groups, the Afrikaner Government has recently devised the concept of Bantustans. Under the Bantustan

* From the chapter on South Africa in *Five African States: Responses to
Diversity,* edited by Gwendolen M. Carter, published by Cornell University
Press, 1963.

system, the majority of Africans (including most of those born and raised in urban areas) are to be consolidated into seven or eight autonomous tribally based states grouped around a white-governed nucleus; those Africans needed for work in white-controlled areas are to vote in the Bantustan that most nearly reflects their ethnic origin. Even if all the Bantustans evolve as planned, however, it is apparently accepted as inevitable by the government that there will be more Africans and Coloreds than whites in the white-governed portions of the republic.

The areas earmarked as present or prospective Bantustans comprise 13.7 per cent of the republic. All are presently rural in character, dependent on a low level of subsistence agriculture and a considerable amount of imported food, and lacking in known resources. The government announced a modest $160 million five-year development plan for the reserves in January, 1962, to be spent primarily on the construction of thirty-three towns and fencing, improvements in irrigation, and afforestation.

Plans for the first experimental Bantustan, the Xhosa "homeland" in the Transkei, were announced by Prime Minister Verwoerd in January, 1962, and an all-African government was established in November, 1963, after popular election of 46 members of a 109-seat Legislative Assembly. While the Transkei (projected population: 1.4 million) now has many of the institutions of a modern state and can enact legislation on some matters of local concern, the central government retains control over all foreign affairs, communications, internal and external security, currency and banking, immigration, and amendments to the constitution. The President of the republic may refer any legislation the new Assembly may pass back to the Assembly for reconsideration.

Sixty-four seats in the Transkei's 109-seat Legislative Assembly are held by government-appointed chiefs, and the new Chief Minister—Chief Kaiser Mantanzima—was chosen head-of-government by the Assembly despite the fact that candidates supporting his policies won a minority of the elected seats. While Mantanzima has cooperated with the South African Government in establishing this first Bantustan and nominally supports apartheid, observers who knew him as a student at Fort Hare University College predict steadily mounting demands for a lifting of social apartheid, expanded economic aid, adoption of English as the medium of instruction in Transkei schools, more territory, and an accelerated and more precise timetable for the evolution to promised "independence."

There are four significant white parties and two major African nationalist movements in South Africa; the million and a half Coloreds (mixed) and half-million Asians remain politically ineffective and largely unorganized. Within the white community, barriers still exist between the nearly 2 million Dutch-descended Afrikaners and the more than 1 million English-speaking settlers as a result of cultural differences and the bitter heritage of the Anglo-Boer war, but the country's growing isolation and white fear of the insistent pressures of African nationalism have diminished these internal tensions in recent years. The October, 1961, elections gave the Afrikaner-based Nationalist Party a larger parliamentary majority than ever—105 out of 156 seats. The United Party, which favors economic integration and a somewhat more humane form of social segregation, received only 49 seats. The Progressive Party, which advocates a qualified nonracial franchise, made a sizable showing in many constituencies but won only one seat. The "one-man-one-vote" Liberal Party has no elected representation. Since 1961, the Nationalists have made a conscious effort to widen the government's base, as indicated by the appointment of two English-speaking Cabinet officers.

The two banned African political movements—the African National Congress, founded in 1912, and its 1959 offshoot, the Pan-Africanist Congress—both aim at the transformation of South Africa into a nonracial state. The main point of difference between the two movements is that the ANC, while African-led, has generally favored a slower-paced, multiracial popular front attack on apartheid, while the PAC is a militant African party which eschews alliances of expediency with white liberal or leftist groups. Both parties were at their nadir during 1963 because of government repression and arrests of top leadership, but continue to operate at a lower scale of effectiveness as clandestine movements. Originally pledged to nonviolence, each now has one or more guerrilla affiliates engaged in acts of sabotage against the

South African Government. Umkonto We Sizwe ("the Spear of the Nation") and the National Liberation Committee are offshoots of the African National Congress, while Poqo (Xhosa for "pure" or "alone") is said to be an arm of the Pan-Africanist Congress.

To contain African nationalism and discourage the threat of supportive action by the independent African states, South Africa has measurably strengthened its police and military establishment since 1960. Expenditures for national defense rose from $61.6 million in 1960 to $168 million in 1962–63 to $220 million in 1963–64. In addition, a series of laws were enacted in 1962 and 1963 that greatly enlarge the scope of existing apartheid legislation. These extend control over the press; prescribe the death penalty for "sabotage"; authorize detention incommunicado for periods of ninety days, without explanation, and subject to renewal; and authorize extended periods of imprisonment without further trial for persons who have committed offenses under the new security legislation and who have completed their sentences.

At the founding meeting of the Organization of African Unity at Addis Ababa in May, 1963, the independent African states committed themselves to supply "effective assistance of every kind to antiapartheid movements in South Africa to help them carry out their struggle for freedom efficiently."* During 1963, the OAU states concentrated their campaign against the Verwoerd government in the various organs of the United Nations. A trade boycott endorsed by the General Assembly in 1962 has not been successful, however, for some of South Africa's major customers have ignored it and new markets have opened up in the Far East (Communist China, Japan, and Thailand) and Eastern Europe. Moreover, prohibition of South African overflights by most independent African states has caused only minor inconvenience and additional expense. The most significant development was a Security Council resolution calling for the banning of shipments of arms, ammunition, and military vehicles to South Africa, which is to be honored by the U.K. (with reservations), the U.S., and West Germany. An oil embargo is now seen as an early OAU objective, but its effectiveness also remains in question. Even if

* See "The Conference Resolutions," p. 256.

South Africa's traditional suppliers could be persuaded to support a boycott, most of the country's oil needs could (in the short term, at least) conceivably be supplied from nearby Angola.

Internal tension and external pressures have had only a negligible effect thus far on South Africa's economy. The republic, which has forty-five commercially exploitable minerals within its borders, leads the world in the production of gold, diamonds (by value), blue asbestos, and chrome ore, and has impressive reserves of manganese, copper, lead, vanadium, coal, and iron. It has the most advanced banking system, the highest degree of industrialization, and the highest per capita income ($427) on the continent; more than 50 per cent of all capital invested in Africa is invested in the republic. The gross national product for 1962—$8.4 billion —showed an increase of 7 per cent over 1961, the greatest advance in several years; both gold and diamond sales set record highs; production of other minerals (excluding uranium) showed a modest increase; earnings for agricultural production ran at record levels. The balance of payments account showed a surplus of $413 million for 1962, and at the end of May, 1963, gold and foreign exchange reserves stood at $685 million (the highest figure in fifteen years and an increase of approximately $400 million over the 1961 post-Sharpeville low).

Two strikingly different views of the ultimate fate of South Africa have been set forth recently by Colin Legum, writing in the November, 1963, issue of *Africa Today,* and John Mander in the October, 1963, issue of *Encounter.* Mr. Legum, rejecting partition as a feasible solution, anticipates that "South Africa's travail will continue until, one day, fully representative government has been achieved." In his view, "the greatest single hope of all South Africa must be that the final settlement will come while there is still a chance of fitting, if not all of the 3,250,000 Whites, at least the majority of them, into the new South African society." John Mander, on the other hand, reluctantly views partition as inevitable. He sees southern Africa as moving inexorably "towards something like that uncomfortable, but curiously stable equilibrium that exists between Israel and the Arab world." Among many parallels, he notes that the Afrikaners, like the Israelis, "are the only white settlers in Afro-Asia to have succeeded in forging a nation of settler elements" and that both "share the same Bible-bred mythology of persecution, fierce struggle, and God-guided trek to a land set apart for their redemption." Whereas Mr. Legum assumes increasing outside pressure and ultimate intervention, Mr. Mander "cannot see . . . white supremacy being crippled, from within or without, by the efforts of the Addis Ababa powers," and believes also that the African nationalists who look for direct intervention by the great powers or others will be as disappointed as were the Arabs in the Middle East. An important difference between Israel and South Africa, however, is that Israel had the sanction of most of world opinion, whereas South Africa does not.

Southern Rhodesia

Population: 4,013,000 (1963 census, including 224,000 Europeans, 7,700 Asians, and 11,500 Coloreds).

Area: 150,333 square miles.

Capital: Salisbury (population: 301,800, including 84,000 Europeans).

Political Status: Self-governing British colony.

Chief of State: Queen Elizabeth II, represented locally by Governor Sir Humphrey Gibbs.

Head of Government: Prime Minister Winston Field.

Major Political Parties: Rhodesian Front, led by Winston Field; Rhodesia National Party, led by Sir Edgar Whitehead; Peoples Caretaker Council, protoparty led by Joshua Nkomo; Zimbabwe Africa National Union, led by Reverend Ndabaningi Sithole.

Legislative Branch: Unicameral. Legislative Assembly of 65 members, elected under dual voting system in which 50 seats are elected primarily by a higher (i.e., European) roll and 15 seats primarily by a lower (i.e., largely African) roll with the added complexity that each roll is permitted to contribute up to 20 per cent of the total votes cast for the seats on the other roll. Last election, December, 1962.

Monetary Unit: 1 Federal pound = US$2.80.

Principal Languages: English, Shona, Ndebele.

External Affiliations: Federation of Rhodesia and Nyasaland dissolved in December, 1963; future ties uncertain.

European settlement of Southern Rhodesia began when the "Pioneer Column," under the auspices of the British South Africa Company, trekked north from the Cape Colony via Bechuanaland to raise the British flag over Fort Salisbury in 1890. The company operated as the *de facto* government for thirty-three years, parceling out land and making and enforcing its own laws. After the Ndebele Rebellion of the early 1890's was subdued, the country's Africans were governed for years as a conquered people.

Immigrants came in increasing numbers just before and after World War I; by 1923, the white population was sufficiently large and well organized to persuade the British Government to accord Southern Rhodesia the anomalous status of a "self-governing colony." The crucial clause in the 1923 agreement, and the one which occasioned prolonged debate in the House of Commons and the United Nations during 1962 and 1963 on Britain's present responsibilities, is the stipulation that the Crown retains certain reserve powers to intervene in legislation affecting fundamental African rights.

African resentment of settler rule remained unorganized until the late 1950's, when the African National Congress (founded in 1957 under the leadership of Joshua Nkomo) began to challenge, with an increasingly vigorous voice, the monopoly of power by Southern Rhodesia's 200,000 Europeans. The ANC was banned at the time of the Nyasaland emergency of 1959, and each succeeding major African nationalist party has met a similar fate.

In 1961, a predominantly European electorate accepted a new constitution drafted in London that expanded the colony's Legislative Assembly to sixty-five seats, of which fifteen were (for the first time) to be chosen primarily by Africans voting on a lower but still restricted roll. In the first elections held under the new arrangements in December, 1962, African nationalists—by now reorganized into the Zimbabwe African People's Union—revealed unexpected control of the African population by effecting a nearly complete boycott of the polls. The white voters, on their part, decided that incumbent Prime Minister Sir Edgar Whitehead and his United Federal Party (now the Rhodesia National Party) were making too many concessions too fast to African pressures, and gave power instead to the more militant Rhodesian Front, which campaigned on a promise to keep the reins of government firmly in white hands for the foreseeable future. The resulting government—led by fifty-eight-year-old Winston Field, a wealthy tobacco farmer—has tightened security legislation but is also attempting to undercut nationalist support in the rural areas through a program of community development.

Although the African case in Southern Rhodesia was heard and debated for many days in the United Nations during 1963, and was a lively concern of the Committee of Liberation of the Organization of African Unity, the nationalist movement itself reached its lowest point of effectiveness since the 1950's. New government restrictions made it illegal to organize in the reserves, and every meeting or other remotely political activity was hamstrung by an ever increasing mass of security regulations. In mid-1963, moreover, long-existing tensions within the movement culminated in an open split.

Denouncing the "indecisive leadership" of Joshua Nkomo, most of the intellectuals in the upper echelons of the movement broke away to form a new Zimbabwe African National Union under the leadership of the Reverend Ndabaningi Sithole. Nkomo, claiming to have the majority of Africans still behind him, has formed a People's Caretaker Council. The split has penetrated into the labor movement, further dividing unions which were already plagued by confusion from prolonged bickering. Ideological differences do not seem to have figured in the dispute, but there are indications that it has injected an element of tribalism into Southern Rhodesian African nationalism for the first time. The ZANU splinter group appears to have the support of Nyasaland's governing Malawi Congress Party and Northern Rhodesia's predominant United National Independence Party.

Southern Rhodesia's immediate future depends on many imponderables—the possibility of British intervention (in turn partly tied to the forthcoming British general election); the nature and degree of the promised pressure from independent African states through the OAU; the ability of leaders within the country to settle (or at least paper over) their divisions; and the effect of the break-up of the Federation (December, 1963) on the Southern Rhodesian economy.

When the federation was established in 1953, Southern Rhodesian imports stood at $216.6 million while exports (mostly agricultural) were $152.3 million. Federation made it possible to use Northern Rhodesia's favorable trade balance in support of Southern Rhodesian development. In the ensuing decade, the colony rapidly developed its secondary industries until manufacturing now constitutes the largest component in the GNP. Almost 30 per cent of these industrial exports (estimated total value: $320 million) went to Northern Rhodesia and Nyasaland in 1962 under protected tariff arrangements. If these two northern markets should be cut off for political reasons—and other neighboring African states are not likely to be replacements—the dislocation to the Southern Rhodesian economy could become serious. The crucial factor, in the short term at least, is Northern Rhodesia's postfederation attitude toward trade with its southern neighbor.

South West Africa

Population: 572,000 (1962 est., including 73,000 whites).

Area: 318,000 square miles.

Capital: Windhoek (population: 46,958).

Political Status: Administered by South Africa, nominally under a League of Nations mandate.

Chief of State: South African President Charles R. Swart.

Local Head of Government: W. C. du Plessis, Administrator appointed by the Government of South Africa.

Major Political Parties: National Party, led in South West Africa by J. G. H. Vanderwath; United National South West Party, led by J. P. Niehaus; South West Africa People's Organization, led by Sam Nujoma (in exile); South West African National Union, led by Jariretundu Kozonguizi (in exile).

Local Legislative Branch: Unicameral. Legislative Assembly of 18 members elected by white adult franchise. The South African Parliament, which has 10 South West African representatives, all white, has authority over more vital matters.

Monetary Unit: 1 South African Rand = US$1.40.

Principal Languages: Afrikaans, German, Kwanyama.

South Africa occupied the former German colony of South West Africa during World War I, and subsequently undertook to administer the territory under a League of Nations mandate. The Class C mandate allowed South Africa to govern South West "as an integral portion" of its own territory, but required that it promote "to the utmost the material and moral well-being and the social progress of the inhabitants." The United Nations, supported by a 1950 World Court advisory opinion, contends that the supervisory function of the League's Permanent Mandates Commission automatically passed to the U.N., and has pressed South Africa since 1946 to place South West under trusteeship. No decision has yet been rendered on the formal case brought before the World Court by Liberia and Ethiopia in 1960, asking for its binding judgment that South Africa has violated its original mandate.

Meanwhile, the Seventeenth Session of the United Nations unanimously condemned South Africa for refusing to heed the past resolutions, called for the establishment of an effective U.N. presence in South West Africa, and requested the Secretary General to appoint a Technical Assistance Resident Representative for the territory. In May, 1963, the Special Committee on Colonialism (which has assumed the duties of the defunct Special Committee for South West Africa) recommended that the U.N. "presence" should implement an earlier resolution to evacuate South African military from the territory, release political prisoners, abolish apartheid, and prepare for U.N.-supervised elections.

Most of the residents of South West are engaged in some form of pastoral agriculture. For the African population (largely confined to unevenly watered, poorly serviced reserves totaling about one-third of the country), there are few opportunities beyond subsistence farming, small-scale stock-raising, or contract labor in mines or on white farms. Outside the Northern Reserves, areas designated for Africans are small, far apart, and under much closer supervision of white officials than those of the north; in many cases, a single tribe has been broken up into several widely separated reserves in order to facilitate white settlement in selected areas. Movement in and out of all the reserves is restricted and rigorously controlled. With some exceptions, the apartheid laws of the Republic of South Africa are applicable.

The cash economy of South West is almost exclusively confined to the European-owned areas. Although many of the white farmers originally settled this arid, unpromising land with the help of subsidies from South Africa, and remain dependent on various forms of governmental support, recent mineral development has rendered the territory capable of financing a major share of its own capital requirements. Some observers believe that South West's per capita income—already roughly calculated at $164 per year, despite a $17 figure for the northern reserves—may soon be among the highest in Africa. Exports in 1962 totaled roughly $131.6 million, almost double imports ($77 million). Minerals (industrial diamonds, lead, copper, zinc, and other base minerals) account for more than half of current exports, but karakul wool and fish products were also of major significance. Indeed, South West is one of the world's most important producers of karakul. The principal port is Walvis Bay, part of a South African enclave of several hundred square miles.

The National Party, part of the governing party in the republic, entirely monopolizes South West's representation in the South African Parliament and holds sixteen seats in the local legislative body. J. P. Niehaus' UNSWP, which received 40 per cent of the vote in the 1961 Legislative Assembly election but only two seats, advocates more autonomy for the territory, improvement on the most embittering features of apartheid, and the return of "Native Administration" to the South West African Government.

Denied representation at home, the two major African nationalist movements—SWANU, with a claimed membership of some 10,000, and SWAPO, with a claimed 90,000—have contributed a growing number of articulate petitioners to the United Nations. Both parties originally sought U.N. trusteeship status for an interim period, but now press for full independence supported by U.N. technical and administrative assistance. In November, 1963, under pressure from the independent states of the Organization of African Unity, the leaders in exile of SWANU and SWAPO reportedly buried their personal and ideological differences to form a "South West Freedom Fighters' Open United Front" with headquarters in Dar es Salaam, Tanganyika.

In 1963, there were reports that South Africa would shortly introduce a development plan for South West Africa in an attempt to placate world opinion. One of the provisions was said to be the partition of the territory to create a "Bantustan" on the Transkei pattern for at least the 280,000 Africans in the Northern Reserves.

Spanish Guinea

Population: 245,990 (1960 census).

Area: 10,852 square miles.

Capital: Santa Isabel on Fernando Póo (population: 19,869).

Political Status: Two Spanish provinces (Río Muni and Fernando Póo) jointly administered by a Governor-General.

Local Head of Government: Governor-General, Admiral Francisco Nuñez Rodríguez.

Legislative Branch: Six representatives of Spanish Guinea elected to central Cortes in Madrid in 1960; see below for plans for local Legislative Assembly.

Monetary Unit: 60 pesetas = US$1.00.

Principal Languages: Spanish, pidgin English, Fang.

Under a new policy of cautious liberalization announced in 1962 and outlined more specifically in August, 1963, Spain has indicated its intention to grant the two provinces of Spanish Guinea a measure of economic and administrative autonomy and an opportunity to "prepare themselves to be administered and governed by their own sons." This is a major shift from the theme of integration and assimilation introduced in 1958, when Río Muni and Fernando Póo were made integral provinces of the motherland. The new draft reforms, approved by a December 15, 1963, referendum of adult citizens in Spanish Guinea, provide for the establishment of a joint elected Legislative Assembly (Asamblea General) for the two provinces and installation of a Cabinet of eight counselors elected by the Assembly and chaired by a Madrid-appointed President. This cabinet will take over most of the functions of the Governor-General. A High Commissioner will represent Spain locally.

Responding to the Spanish olive branch, several African nationalist leaders re-established their headquarters within Spanish Guinea and campaigned actively in the December referendum. The most important parties as of late 1963 were the Movimiento

Nacional de Liberación de la Guinea Ecuatorial (MNLGE), led by Atanasio Ndong; the Idea Popular de la Guinea Ecuatorial (IPGE), favoring union with Cameroun, led by Dr. Luis Maho and Perea Epota; the Movimiento Nacional de Unión, led by Jaime Nseng; and the Movimiento de Unión Popular de Liberación de la Guinea Ecuatorial, led by Bonifacio Ondo. In the December referendum, 94,655 voters cast their ballots, of whom 54,224 endorsed Spain's offer of autonomy, at least as an intermediate step.

Río Muni is a small rectangular land area of 10,039 square miles bordered by Cameroun, Gabon, and the Gulf of Guinea. A large part of it is dense rain forests. Fernando Póo, largest island in the Gulf (779 square miles) is about 20 miles from the West African mainland. For administrative purposes, Spanish Guinea also includes several less important islands (Annobón, 6.6 square miles; Corisco, 5.8 square miles; Great Elobey, 0.9 square mile; and Little Elobey, 0.07 square mile). Cocoa is the principal commercial crop in Fernando Póo, much of it harvested by 25,000 to 35,000 seasonal Nigerian contract workers. Río Muni exports principally timber products and plantation-grown coffee. The smaller islands have little or no economic activity.

In 1960, Spanish Guinea's exports totaled $33 million. Both the coffee and cocoa output is purchased by Spain at prices well above the world market. Some banana exports since 1957 have elicited anguished protests from rival producers in the Canary Islands.*

* See "Spain Changes Course in Africa," by René Pelissier, *Africa Report*, December, 1963, p. 8.

Spanish Sahara

Population: 23,793 (1960 census).

Area: 105,558 square miles.

Capital: Al Aiún (population 3,000).

Political Status: Province of Spain.

Local Head of Government: Governor-General Pedro Latorre Alcubierre.

Monetary Unit: 60 pesetas = US$1.00.

Principal Languages: Spanish, Arabic, Tachelit.

The Spanish Sahara—more than half the size of Spain itself—is an extremely arid land with a resident population of some 24,000 and an annual rainy season influx of from 30,000 to 80,000 nomads from neighboring countries.

Fishing is the major source of cash income, currently bringing in about $500,000 annually. Spain has not given up hope that oil or mineral riches lie beneath its Saharan sands, and a significant amount of Spanish and other Western capital is being expended in continuing geological exploration and development of Saharan port facilities. The Spanish Mining Service reports that some iron ore deposits have been located at Agracha halfway between Villa Cisneros and Fort Gouraud, Mauritania, but it is of a very low grade. Large deposits of phosphate are found to the south of Al Aiún, the capital and major air center, but problems of transportation may render exploitation impractical. The search for oil has been fruitless thus far.

Spanish Sahara was periodically visited by Spanish explorers from the sixteenth century on. It was claimed as a Spanish colony in 1884, officially allotted to Spain by the Franco-Spanish treaties of 1900, 1904, and 1912, and was actually occupied in 1934. In 1958, the area was established as an integral province of Spain in a move designed to counter renewed Moroccan claims to the territory. When Moroccan irregulars attacked and captured a group of oil prospectors near the northern border in March, 1961, Spain not only protested in strongest diplomatic terms but also concentrated nearly 10,000 troops in the province and reinforced the neighboring Canary Island garrisons. From Mauritania's point of view, Spanish Sahara apparently is a welcome buffer against direct Moroccan attempts to implement its historic claims to Mauritania.

As a province of the motherland, Spanish Sahara is administered by a Governor-General directly responsible to the Director-General of the African Provinces in Madrid. The first elections of provincial representatives (three) to the central Parliament (Cortes) in Madrid were held in May, 1963. An elected Provincial Council and municipal councils were established in 1963.

Sudan

Population: 11,615,000 (1963 est.).

Area: 967,498 square miles.

Capital: Khartoum (population: 75,000).

Political Status: Independent republic.

Date of Independence: January 1, 1956.

Chief of State and Head of Government: General Ibrahim Abboud, President of the Supreme Council of the Armed Forces and the Council of Ministers since November, 1958.

Major Political Parties: All political parties abolished in November, 1958.

Legislative Branch: Unicameral. Central Council, with limited functions, established November, 1963. Its 72 members include 6 representatives chosen by each of 9 popularly elected provincial councils plus 18 members appointed by the central government.

Monetary Unit: 1 Sudanese pound = US$2.80.

Principal Languages: Arabic, English, various African languages in the south.

External Affiliations: United Nations, Arab League, Organization of African Unity.

Africa's largest country is Sudan, which was governed as an Anglo-Egyptian condominium for fifty-six years before it became an independent republic in 1956. The parliamentary institutions developed under British tutelage lasted only two years, however; in November, 1958, the heretofore nonpolitical Sudanese Army intervened "to ward off political chaos."

The small group of military leaders in whom power is centered —there are seven officers in the Supreme Council of the Armed Forces—have been characterized by a recent resident of Khartoum as "austere in their private lives, efficient, accessible . . . and remarkably incorrupt." They have little nostalgia for the untidy years of partisan politics, and appear genuinely convinced that the Sudanese people as a whole could not possibly want to exchange the present governmental and economic stability for a return to free-for-all party life. In the five years it has been in power, the junta has effectively quashed at least three poorly organized countercoups by dissident army factions and has turned a deaf ear to those civilian leaders of the former political parties who have pressed for a return to parliamentary government. It continues to maintain a blanket ban on all political parties, heavy censorship of the once-vigorous Khartoum press, and close supervision of labor unions.

Not until 1963 were the first cautious steps taken to return to the Sudanese citizenry a restricted voice in local and national affairs. In April, voters went to the polls throughout the country to elect 1,580 representatives to sit on 94 municipal councils. These local councils, which also include other members appointed by the central government, in turn elected certain of their numbers to serve on 9 provincial councils. In November, 1963, each provincial council selected 6 representatives from its own ranks to fill the provincial government's quota of 54 of the 72 non-Ministerial seats in a new Central Council. Eighteen other Central Council members are being appointed by the government. The primary function of the Central Council, according to President Abboud, will be to draw up a new constitution for the Sudan.

When the military came to power, the Sudan's economy was in grave crisis. In the wake of the 1956 Suez affair, the Gezira Board set the price of cotton—which normally accounts for more than 60 per cent of Sudanese exports by value—artificially high on the assumption that Egypt's traditional customers would be seeking alternate sources in a seller's market. Instead, the Lancashire textile industry largely ignored the overpriced Sudanese cotton to buy in the United States and Latin America, while French buyers simply continued to purchase from Egypt through the back door. When the military came to power in November, 1958, 20 per cent of the 1957 cotton crop and 45 per cent of the 1958 crop was still unsold. The fiscal year 1957–58 witnessed the largest balance-of-payments deficit in the country's history—more than $67 million as compared with a credit balance of more than $50 million in 1956.

By the fifth anniversary of the revolution, President Abboud could report that Sudan's foreign exchange reserves had risen to

$140,193,200, and that figures available for the end of the first
four months of 1963 indicated that the value of 1963 exports
might exceed imports by a considerable margin. An ambitious
ten-year internal development plan (1961–71) aims at an increase
of 63 per cent in the gross domestic product and 23 per cent in
per capita income by 1971. The plan is based on the assumption
that cotton, gum arabic (Sudan produces 85 per cent of the
world's supply), and a few other cash crops will remain the important sources of revenue in the foreseeable future, but also emphasizes the need to diversify the economy through introduction
of new crops and encouragement of secondary industry. Irrigation
schemes recently completed or now under way are designed to
open several million acres of heretofore unproductive land to
both traditional and experimental crops. Although much of the
financing for the current development plan is scheduled to come
from internal sources, the government anticipates that it will
require about $798 million in external credits to finance current
goals. Pledges of financial support to date have come from the
World Bank, the U.K., the U.S., West Germany, the U.S.S.R.,
Yugoslavia, and U.N. agencies.

The most serious internal problem now facing the Abboud
government is the discontent festering in the Sudan's three southern provinces (est. population: 3.5 million), which are ethnically,
culturally, and linguistically more akin to middle Africa than
to the Sudan's Moslem, Arabized north. Khartoum's efforts
(which antedate the present government) to develop national
unity by introducing a common curriculum and common language of instruction for all Sudanese schools has raised particular
controversy, in part because the new educational policy under-
cuts the heretofore dominant role of Christian missionaries in
southern education.

By 1963, an estimated 80,000 to 100,000 southern Sudanese
had crossed the border to neighboring Uganda, Congo-Leopoldville, the Central African Republic, and Tanganyika, claiming political and religious persecution, and recurrent reports of
strikes, demonstrations, and clashes with northern troops seeped
through tight government censorship. Meanwhile, a southern separatist movement—the Sudan African National Union

(SANU), led by exiled Joseph Oduho and William Deng—took southern grievances to the United Nations. SANU claims a "full mandate from the people of the South" to secure the "right of self-determination" so that they may "keep their African negroid race and culture." The problem of conscience this issue creates for neighboring African states is implicit.

Tanganyika

Population: 9,538,000 (1962 est.).

Area: 362,688 square miles.

Capital: Dar es Salaam (population: 150,000).

Political Status: Independent republic.

Date of Independence: December 9, 1961. Became a republic on December 9, 1962.

Chief of State and Head of Government: President Julius Nyerere, elected (November 1, 1962) by universal adult suffrage. Vice-President, Rashidi Kawawa.

Political Party: Tanganyika African National Union.

Legislative Branch: Unicameral. National Assembly of 71 elected and 10 nominated members (last elected in 1960 under qualified suffrage). Revised 1962 constitution provides for 107 elected members and up to 10 nominated members with adult suffrage for National Assembly elections. Next election must be by October, 1964.

Monetary Unit: 1 East African shilling = US$0.14.

Principal Languages: Swahili, English.

External Affiliations: United Nations, Organization of African Unity, East African Common Services Organization, Commonwealth.

After forty years as a British-administered League of Nations mandate and then a United Nations trust territory, Tanganyika achieved independence on December 9, 1961. Led by an extraordinarily popular and able leader, Julius Nyerere, the nationalist party—the Tanganyika African National Union—had vanquished all opposition in two pre-independence elections. Besides enlightened leadership and a sense of nationhood that largely transcended tribal differences, Tanganyika came to independence with the advantage of a favorable balance of payments and a unique degree of respect abroad. Its overriding problems appeared to be a lack of significant economic resources and a critical need to augment the thin layer of Africans qualified to fill technical and administrative posts.

The TANU party's chief ideologist is Dr. Nyerere, who has spelled out in his writings and speeches a version of African socialism keyed to Tanganyika's specific needs. Thus, TANU doctrine seeks a middle course between the "exaggerated . . . freedom of the individual in the West" and the "other extreme" of Communist society. Dr. Nyerere has frequently argued that it is "natural that young nations which emerge as a result of a nationalist movement having united their people will be governed at first by a nationalist government rather than a party government." The pyramidal party structure of TANU laid out in the 1950's establishes clearly defined lines of communication reaching up from the most remote village to the national executive; the diverse composition of its central institutions (which include labor leaders, tribal elders, university graduates, and even female suffragettes in their membership) reflects a conscientious effort to combine the advantages of the traditional African process of government by consensus and those of a sophisticated modern political party organization. It was not until January, 1963, however, that President Nyerere announced his intention to appoint a commission to study the advisability of enacting legislation that would make Tanganyika a *de jure* as well as *de facto* one-party state.

In March, 1963, author John George probed with rare insight another side of the Tanganyika picture: "Very few of [the British civil servants who have stayed on in Tanganyika] are capable of feeling the creature sympathy for emergent Africans that could make the British a much more constructive force in Tanganyika's present transition. . . . The British misery has other effects, too. A number of Africans (sometimes the ones most aware of their own limitations) have come to regard the continuing official British presence as an unwanted mirror, forever reflecting African faults and inadequacies. Many in TANU believe that the pace of Africanization of the administration must be hastened even at the risk of creating chaos, if for no other reason than to expel these erstwhile colonial bosses now turned critics, informants, and arbiters of moral behavior. . . . The principal political leaders of the country—President Nyerere and most of the Ministers—are aware of the suicidal nature of ejecting the British immediately en masse, and are unlikely to take this drastic step; but pressure from

within the party will continue to hasten the process of Africanization to a precarious degree."* The mutiny of the two battalions
of the Tanganyikan Army against their British officers in January,
1964 (see pp. 225–26), brought these pressures into public view for
the first time and perhaps opened a new chapter in Tanganyika's
political evolution.

Tanganyika's economy is dominated by subsistence agriculture. The most important cash crops are sisal, coffee, cashew nuts,
cotton, and tobacco. Together with diamonds, they supply the major share of the country's revenue. Some iron and coal is known to
exist, but the feasibility of exploitation is not yet certain. Village
regroupment, consumer cooperatives, and direct government
participation in commerce and industry reflect the government's
socialist orientation. Great Britain, the United States, and West
Germany are the main sources of capital for economic development at present, but the roles of the Scandinavian countries, West
Germany, and Japan are expected to expand. Trade and cultural
agreements have been established with several Soviet Bloc countries.

Tanganyika strongly favors the proposed East African Federation; indeed, President Nyerere's commitment to the idea of regional unity was so deeply felt that he tentatively offered in 1960
to postpone Tanganyika's independence until such time as
Kenya and Uganda could also make the transition. Aside from
political considerations, Tanganyika would benefit economically
from the greater flow of foreign investment that a stable federation would make possible. In the absence of federation, Tanganyika will press for the continued administration of certain regional
services—e.g., postal, railway, telecommunications, monetary, and
research—by the existing East African Common Services Organization. Higher education is already "federalized" through the
University of East Africa, which has three constituent university
colleges in Kenya, Uganda, and Tanganyika.

On the national level, Tanganyika's development plans give priority to improvements and diversification of agriculture, establishment of small industries (especially food processing), and
rapid development of education.

* See "How Stable Is Tanganyika?," *Africa Report,* March, 1963, p. 5.

Togo

Population: 1,642,000 (1962 est.).

Area: 21,850 square miles.

Capital: Lomé (population: 80,000).

Political Status: Independent republic.

Date of Independence: April 27, 1960.

Chief of State and Head of Government: President Nicolas Grunitzky, elected (May 5, 1963) by universal suffrage for a five-year term.

Major Political Parties: Union Démocratique des Populations Togolaises (UDPT); Parti de l'Unité Togolaise (PUT); Mouvement de la Jeunesse Togolaise, whose slogan (Justice, Union, Vigilance, Education, Nationalisme, Tenacité Optimisme) forms the initials JUVENTO; Mouvement Populaire Togolais (MPT).

Legislative Branch: Unicameral. National Assembly of 56 members, elected from a single agreed "List of National Unity and Reconciliation" (consisting of 14 candidates from each of 4 major Togolese parties) for 5-year terms. Last election, May, 1963.

Monetary Unit: 247 CFA francs = US$1.00.

Principal Languages: French, Ewe, Kabre, Hausa.

External Affiliations: United Nations, Organization of African Unity, Union Africaine et Malgache, European Economic Community (associate), franc zone.

Togo, the smallest independent state in Africa, aside from Rwanda and Burundi, is the eastern portion of the former German colony of Togoland. From 1919 until it became independent in April, 1960, the territory was administered by France, first as a League of Nations mandate and later as a United Nations trust territory. (The western half of Togo, administered by the U.K. after World War I, subsequently became an integral part of Ghana. Thus, President Nkrumah's argument for the unification of the two countries is based on ethnic and historical links, as well as on a more generalized objection to the "balkanization" of Africa into political units of Togo's dimensions.)

The military junta that assassinated President Sylvanus Olympio and seized power in January, 1963, cited four basic reasons for the revolt: (1) the government's inattention to "daily increasing unemployment"; (2) the pervasive atmosphere of authoritarian paternalism; (3) the "sterile isolationism" of Togo's external policy; and (4) President Sylvanus Olympio's "profound contempt for the military." Although much has been made of the irony that West Africa's first military *coup d'état* should occur in the nation with the smallest army in the area (250 men), this is not entirely correct. The insurrection was not organized by members of Togo's armed forces but rather by disgruntled Togolese veterans of the French Army who had returned home in recent years to find that there were neither vacancies waiting for them in the new national army of Togo nor any jobs offering status commensurate with their experience. The austere fiscal policies adopted by President Olympio in support of his overriding goal of economic independence precluded the luxury of a prestigious standing army.

The all-party provisional government established by the military junta, subsequently given legal status in a nationwide election and constitutional referendum held in May, 1963, has rejected economic independence as a feasible goal for a country with the limited resources of Togo. Accordingly, new "links of friendship" were forged with France in July, 1963, including (1) a diplomatic convention specifying that the French Ambassador will be dean of the diplomatic corps in Togo and that the two countries will confer on foreign policy; (2) a defense agreement; (3) a technical assistance agreement; (4) an establishment convention; and (5) a judiciary convention.

Although Togo's economic prospects are clearly limited, its largely agricultural economy is sufficiently diversified to protect the country from fluctuating prices on world markets. Since only one-fourth of the land surface is in productive use at any one time, there is room for considerable expansion of agricultural output. Phosphate is the principal nonagricultural resource, and Togo's deposits—which only came into production in 1961—are said to contain more than 50 million tons, much of it high grade. The phosphate project, which aims at annual production of

600,000 tons, is owned 20 per cent by the Government of Togo and 80 per cent by six French concerns.

The economic development plans of the Olympio regime for the Oti and Mono valleys and for increased production and diversification of agriculture through the Jeunesse Pionnière Agricole and various rural community programs are being continued, and a pending project for the construction of a deep-water port at Lomé, with West German financial and technical assistance, has been approved. Olympio's plans for a separate Togolese central bank and currency, however, seem to have been dropped.

Tunisia

Population: 4,300,000 (1962 est.).

Area: 63,078 square miles.

Capital: Tunis (population: 700,000).

Political Status: Independent republic.

Date of Independence: March 20, 1956.

Chief of State and Head of Government: President Habib Bourguiba, elected by universal adult suffrage (1959) for a 5-year term.

Political Party: Neo-Destour.

Legislative Branch: Unicameral. National Assembly of 90 members elected by universal adult suffrage for 5-year terms. Last election, November, 1959.

Monetary Unit: 1 dinar = US$2.16.

Principal Languages: Arabic, French.

External Affiliations: United Nations, Arab League, Organization of African Unity, participates in franc-zone arrangements.

Although Tunisia is the smallest and poorest of the North African states, it is a country rich in human resources. Unlike those states of Africa that were for so many years insulated from the rest of the world by physical or climatic barriers, Tunisia's position as a crossroads between Europe and the Middle East, inviting climate, coastal plains, and natural harbors opened it for centuries to wave after wave of Mediterranean influences. Thus it entered the age of modern nationalism with three vital advantages—a sophisticated political elite, a high degree of social and geographical homogeneity, and a population receptive to change.

By 1956, when Tunisia became an independent state, President Habib Bourguiba had already developed a pioneering mass party that functioned in every village and had created both the symbols and reality of national unity. Under Neo-Destour leadership, Tunisia is markedly free from corruption, and the gap between the country's upper and lower economic strata is not as wide as in other parts of North Africa.

Until the Bizerte crisis of August, 1961—when French troops killed 1,037 Tunisians engaged in an abortive attempt to force the pace of France's evacuation of the military base retained "temporarily" after independence—Bourguiba maintained an almost mystical reputation for infallibility. His obvious miscalculation of the French response to a direct Tunisian military move against Bizerte seriously damaged this image, and also cast doubt on the political wisdom of the unequivocal Western orientation of his foreign policy.

In December, 1962, at the end of a year in which the Neo-Destour machine showed increasing signs of sluggishness, a plot to assassinate the President was uncovered. Involved were a motley assortment of disgruntled army officers, a few party militants, former *résistants,* and some ex-Youssefists (followers of Salah Ben Youssef, exiled former secretary-general of the Neo-Destour) brought together by various grievances, including frustration over the government's ineffectiveness in solving the Bizerte crisis, discontent because of denial of promotion in the Party, and resentment on the part of former *résistants* that they had not been given sufficient rewards for their heroic fight against the French.

In 1963, President Bourguiba reasserted his political skills. The Neo-Destour structure was overhauled, France was persuaded to evacuate Bizerte, and greater participation in party decisions was promised to critics of government policy, especially intellectuals and students. By year's end, the regime appeared to have restored much of its earlier rapport with its constituency.

Although Tunisia's political problems appear to be surmountable with internal resources, its economic needs clearly require continuing outside assistance. The uncertainty of rainfall causes crop yields to vary from year to year—a problem that touches all of Tunisian life since agriculture employs much of the population and supplies some two-fifths of the national income. Mining (especially for phosphates) accounts for 30 per cent of the value of exports, but only about 5 per cent of national income. With population increasing at about 3 per cent yearly, the present national output is insufficient to prevent unemployment (now estimated at 350,000) from continuing to increase. However, the current development plan (1962–71)—nearly half of which will be financed by foreign assistance, reinforced by an efficient system of taxation—could start Tunisia on the way toward economic self-sufficiency.

Uganda

Population: 6,845,000 (1961 est.).

Area: 94,000 square miles.

Capital: Kampala (population: 47,000). Some government offices remain in the former administrative center of Entebbe, 28 miles away.

Political Status: Independent sovereign state. Although Uganda ceased to be a dominion in October, 1963, with the election of its first President (see below) to replace Governor-General Sir Walter Coutts, it did not become a republic out of deference to the "substantial monarchial element" in the country.

Date of Independence: October 9, 1962.

Chief of State: President, Sir Edward Mutesa II, the Kabaka of Buganda, elected by the National Assembly for a term of 5 years. First election, October, 1963.

Head of Government: Prime Minister Milton Obote, leader of the governing coalition since May, 1962.

Major Political Parties: The Uganda People's Congress, led by Prime Minister Obote; its coalition partner in the central government, the Buganda-based Kabaka Yekka movement; the opposition Democratic Party, led by Benedicto Kiwanuka and Basil Bataringaya.

Legislative Branch: Unicameral. National Assembly of 82 elected members and 9 "specially elected" members chosen by the Assembly voting as an electoral college. Of the 82 elected members, the 21 from the Kingdom of Buganda may be directly or indirectly elected at the option of the Buganda Parliament. In 1962, they were indirectly elected. Last election, April, 1962.

Principal Languages: English, Luganda, Runyoro, Runyankore, Ateso, Lwo, Acholi.

Monetary Unit: 1 East African shilling = US$0.14.

External Affiliations: United Nations, Organization of African Unity, Commonwealth, East African Common Services Organization.

First penetrated by Europeans in 1862, Uganda is a land of great natural beauty, fertile soil, and pleasant climate. With a stable and self-sufficient agricultural economy, a small but well-educated African elite (Makerere University College was established in

1921), no white-settler problem to complicate political change, and a paternalistic colonial government sympathetic to Africanization, Uganda was a logical candidate to become one of Africa's first independent states. Instead, the very absence of issues capable of arousing national consciousness slowed the development of national political parties, and gave full rein to personality, religious, ethnic, and regional jealousies.

The most serious barrier to national unity during the 1950's was the distrust between the new nationalist parties and the hereditary governing groups of Uganda's four traditional kingdoms. Tension between traditional centers of power and modernist parties is a familiar phenomenon in Africa, but in Uganda the prospects of establishing a cohesive central government seemed especially slim because the most powerful of the kingdoms, Buganda, occupies more than a quarter of the country (25,390 square miles), contains a majority of the educated elite, and accounts for nearly 60 per cent of the total revenue of Uganda. It was not until the June, 1962, constitutional conference in London that Buganda warily dropped the threat of secession and tentatively acknowledged its stake in the central government then being shaped.

It is generally agreed that the progress which Uganda made toward nationhood between 1961 and 1964 was due largely to the tactical skill of Prime Minister Obote and the tacit cooperation of younger Baganda politicians whose ideological sympathies lie with Mr. Obote's party even if they dare not risk an open break with the Buganda establishment. In pursuing one overriding goal —to bring modern politics and tribal tradition peacefully to terms—Obote has quietly and methodically worked his way from one ledge to another, frequently compromising on matters affecting the semblance (but not the substance) of power, and studiously avoiding any direct challenge to Buganda's Kabaka or the other traditional rulers.

The current phase of Uganda political development began in September, 1961, when Obote effected an unlikely alliance between his radical Uganda People's Congress and Buganda's newly formed Kabaka Yekka movement. This union (described by the opposition party as "an unholy alliance of horsetraders") accomplished three interrelated objectives: It committed Buganda to drop its boycott of the central government; provided access to the parliamentary majority needed to establish a government under UPC leadership; and assured British approval of an early independence date.

Although the UPC-KY alliance has often been strained in the months since independence, it has outlasted all predictions of its longevity. Operating on the assumption that time and logic are on the side of the modernizing forces of Uganda, and that every Muganda actively engaged in a constructive role on the larger national scene is unwittingly chipping away at Buganda parochialism, Obote has not attempted to hurry the pace. Respectful of the sensitivities of the tribal kingdoms, the government readily agreed that the "anti-monarchial" term "republic" should be avoided when Uganda replaced the Governor-General (representing Queen Elizabeth II) with an elected President in October, 1962, and that the ceremonial position of head of state should be assigned by law to one of the fifteen hereditary rulers of Uganda. Moreover, the Prime Minister gave his full support to the election of the Kabaka of Buganda as the first President—despite the bitter opposition of many UPC rank and file. Obote's marriage in November, 1963, to a beautiful Baganda secretary, symbolizing the partnership of the north with Buganda, added yet another thread to the web of national unity he hopes to construct.

Meanwhile, the UPC's parliamentary position has steadily improved. Although the tentative proposal of nineteen progressive Kabaka Yekka deputies that the two coalition parties merge into a single "national movement" during 1963 was promptly dismissed by the Buganda establishment, the UPC has nonetheless picked up several seats through individual shifts in party loyalties. In the April, 1962, elections, the UPC received thirty-seven elected seats and six "specially elected" seats, for a total of forty-three out of ninety-one; the Democratic Party secured twenty-four elected seats; and the Kabaka Yekka had twenty-one elected and three "specially elected." By December, 1963, forty-eight of the ninety-one deputies were committed to UPC; Kabaka Yekka's parliamentary strength had dropped (through seven Baganda defections, including two Ministers) to seventeen, and the Democratic Party's to twenty. While this means that the UPC could now technically govern without Kabaka Yekka's support, Mr. Obote apparently feels that it is safer politically to keep the creaky alliance functioning and avoid a premature polarization between the progressives and neotraditionalists in Buganda. In an unexpectedly forthright campaign speech at Lira on January 7, 1964, however, Obote made it clear that his ultimate objective for Uganda is a one-party socialist state.

Over the past sixty years, ever since the railway from the ocean reached Lake Victoria just after the turn of the century, Uganda's economic growth has been steady if unspectacular. It remains primarily an agricultural country, but nobody goes hungry and more than $120 million worth of coffee, cotton, tobacco, sugar, copper, and a few other products are exported annually. Coffee and cotton, which account for 80 per cent of exports by value, are almost entirely grown on small African peasant farms or (in Buganda) on larger-scale African-owned plantations. Although industry is far less developed than in Kenya, the Owen Falls hydroelectric scheme, inaugurated in 1954, has permitted the development of a growing range of secondary industries—notably in plywood, steel, textiles, soap, and building supplies.

The 1962–67 development plan includes 160 separate projects, with the main emphasis on increasing agricultural production per acre and improvements in the quality and diversity of agricultural and animal products; transportation, education, tourism, health, and information services also are receiving attention. If the plan's goals are reached—and this is not certain, since the government is still some $42,000,000 short of the estimated capital requirement of $200,760,000—cotton production will be increased from an average of 370,000 bales per year to 500,000. An all-out attack against the tsetse fly is also under way, with the objective of stocking some 2,000 square miles of idle grassland with cattle; meanwhile, efforts are being made to improve the quality of the indigenous long-horned Ankole cattle by crossbreeding with other varieties.

The development program follows closely the recommendations presented by a World Bank mission in 1960. In economic policy, as in politics, the government has deferred to local sensibilities during the first fourteen months of independence by confining the role of government largely to "guiding, advising, and helping."

Although Uganda participates in the East African Common Services Organization and is committed, in principle, to the idea of an East African Federation, it has more reservations about the union than Tanganyika and Kenya. Cut off from the coast and with a smaller population than either of the other two territories, Uganda is apprehensive that it might become the slighted junior partner. The traditional kingdoms are especially wary of the scheme because of their fear that they would soon lose their separate identity in a federation led by such advocates of highly centralized government as Jomo Kenyatta's KANU and Julius Nyerere's TANU.

United Arab Republic

Population: 27,000,000 (1963 est.).

Area: 363,000 square miles.

Capital: Cairo (population: 3,000,000).

Political Status: Independent republic.

Date of Independence: February 28, 1922.

Chief of State: President Gamal Abdul Nasser, who led the Free Officers' *coup d'état* in 1952 and succeeded General Mohammad Naguib to the presidency in 1954.

Head of Government: Premier Ali Sabri, chairman of an Executive Council of Ministers established by President Nasser in September, 1962.

Major Political Party: Arab Socialist Union, conceived in 1962 to replace the unsuccessful National Union.

Legislative Branch: The bicameral Egyptian Parliament was abolished in 1952. The unicameral National Assembly called for in the 1956 constitution was formed in 1957 but gave way to a combined U.A.R. National Assembly when Egypt and Syria merged in 1958; this body was, in turn, dissolved when Syria withdrew from the union in September, 1961. In May, 1962, President Nasser convened a broadly based National Congress of Popular Powers (comprised of 1,500 elected and 250 appointed members) to approve a Draft Charter outlining a new constitution envisaged by the government. This constitution provides for a central legislative body, elected in March, 1964.

Monetary Unit: 1 Egyptian pound = US$2.85.

Principal Languages: Arabic, English.

External Affiliations: United Nations, Arab League, Organization of African Unity.

Shortly after Gamal Abdul Nasser became President of Egypt, he described the objectives of the revolution in these terms: "This is a middle-class revolution against capitalism and against communism. For two thousand years Egypt has been ruled by an alliance of capitalists and landlords. Under parliamentary democracy, parties acted merely as their agents, with the politicians taking their rake-off. Of our 22,000,000 Egyptians, about 2,000,000 are free, and 20,000,000 live in fear and poverty. We have got to liberate 20,000,000 from fear and raise their standard of living, despite the gigantic rate of population increase. Politics for me means only one thing—solving the social problem. Somehow we have got to create a political party which people join, not for what they get out of it, but for what they put in. That's a completely new idea here, and that's why I have to exclude all the old politicians and prevent the capitalists and landlords from muscling in. The new party must be composed of people . . . with a sense of public service."*

Although President Nasser has thus far failed in his various efforts to achieve meaningful union with selected partners in the Middle East and Africa—notably with Syria, with Iraq, with Yemen, in the Maghreb, and within Africa's shortlived "Casablanca Bloc"—he has gone far in this first decade toward his overriding domestic goal of transforming Egyptian society. Moreover, aside from the brief power struggle of 1954—when Nasser replaced Naguib as President—there has been a high degree of continuity within the governing junta. Most of the men in policy-making positions today were among the small group of officers who overthrew the monarchy in the early hours of July 23, 1952. They have added some gray hairs, acquired new skills, and become more precise in defining their ideology; but their personal lives and their aims for Egypt have remained remarkably unchanged.

In the decade just ended, the party politicians of King Farouk's era have long since been dispatched into exile, retirement, or prison. Land reforms, designed to end the political and economic predominance of the wealthy landlords, have been institutionalized through the organization of cooperatives, reduction of rents for tenant farmers, establishment of a ceiling of 100 acres on land-holdings, and the provision of a variety of peasant social services. Similarly, Egypt has moved beyond the nationalization of foreign corporations to take over ownership of all but the smaller locally owned economic enterprises and, through new taxation, has imposed an effective ceiling on all incomes above $28,000. Birth control is being officially encouraged as a long-term measure to combat the appallingly unfavorable land-population ratio.

---

* See *New Statesman*, January 22, 1955.

The current development plan seeks to double Egypt's national income between 1960 and 1970. The annual rate of growth of the GNP has been running at about 4.5 per cent in recent years (though not yet at the intended 7.2 per cent). The value of industrial output (doubled between 1952 and 1962) has for the first time overtaken the value of cotton production. The Suez Canal, now running more traffic more efficiently than under the previous private ownership, earns more than $143 million gross revenues annually (as compared with $15 million for Egypt in 1956). Government expenditures for development of productive sectors in agriculture, industry, and transportation have risen twelvefold since 1950, for education fivefold, for health fourfold.

The drag on further development remains heavy, however. Egypt's gains have been achieved at the cost of high (if nearly equally balanced) indebtedness to the Soviet Bloc and the West of altogether about $530 million in utilized credits, and extensive domestic borrowing amounting to $2 billion. Military expenditures stand at about $280 million annually or 7 per cent of GNP (more than any European NATO country). Birth control cannot be made retroactive, and Egypt must cope with the fact that its population has tripled since the turn of the century, despite no appreciable decline in the death rate.

Unless union with underpopulated or oil-rich neighbors can somehow be effected, Egypt's future will depend on its ability to continue to borrow outside capital, to sell its industrial products, and to find means of watering and thus utilizing its largely uninhabited desert. Above all, the future will depend on the Egyptian leaders' ability to organize the masses politically and socially for a very long and very hard pull. The major domestic failure of the regime thus far has been its inability to build a structured mass political movement to bridge the gap between rulers and ruled.

Upper Volta

Population: 4,400,000 (1963 est.).

Area: 105,900 square miles.

Capital: Ouagadougou (population: 63,000).

Political Status: Independent republic.

Date of Independence: August 5, 1960.

Chief of State and Head of Government: President Maurice Yameogo, invested (April, 1959) as Prime Minister by National Assembly; unanimously elected (December, 1959) President by National Assembly. The 1960 constitution calls for Presidential elections by universal adult suffrage for a 5-year term. However, elections were postponed and the mandate of the existing government extended.

Political Party: Union Démocratique Voltaique.

Legislative Branch: Unicameral. National Assembly of 50 seats, all members of the governing party, elected by universal adult suffrage for 5-year terms. Last election, April 20, 1959.

Monetary Unit: 247 CFA francs = US$1.00.

Principal Languages: French, More, Bambara; also Peulh, Gourounsi, Gourmantche.

External Affiliations: United Nations, Organization of African Unity, Union Africaine et Malgache, Conseil de l'Entente, European Economic Community (associate), franc zone.

What is now Ouagadougou, Upper Volta, was the seat of the powerful Mossi Empire from the eleventh to the seventeenth century. The establishment of Upper Volta as a distinct entity within French West Africa in 1947 and its subsequent emergence as an independent state in 1960 was largely in response to the demands of the dominant Mossi population (1.7 million, or almost half of the present Voltaic total) for a political base.

The independence movement was consolidated in the Union Démocratique Voltaique, a branch of the regional Rassemblement Démocratique Africaine. It was led by Ouezzin Coulibaly, whose sudden death in 1958 left a political vacuum that was later to be filled by Maurice Yameogo. Mr. Yameogo, a former government clerk—who is a Mossi but not of the Mossi aristocracy—

became first President of the republic in 1959. In consolidating his power since independence, President Yameogo has used Mossi history to kindle a new sense of Voltaic nationhood. For example, he has implemented a 1947 decision (ignored for more than a decade) to transfer the seat of government from Bobo-Dioulasso, key city on the principal trade route between Ivory Coast and Mali, to Ouagadougou, center of the Mossi Empire. At the same time, however, President Yameogo undertook to render the traditional Mossi leader Moro Naba politically impotent by gradually reducing his powers to those of a ceremonial chief. The last open threat to the regime from its right flank was eliminated in 1960 when the French failed to support an abortive attempt by the traditional ruler to seize power by force.

Other elements of discontent exist in the country—the resentful citizenry of dying Bobo-Dioulasso; the non-Mossi in the southwestern section of the country who charge that the government practices tribal discrimination; educated young Voltaics who resent the lack of economic progress and their country's close ties with the more conservative French-speaking countries of Africa; and disgruntled, underemployed veterans of the French Army. But whether any of these elements will coalesce sufficiently to challenge the government directly is yet to be seen. It is noteworthy that eight Ministers were dismissed or imprisoned between 1961 and 1963 in an effort to tighten security.

Ninety per cent of the Voltaic population is employed in subsistence farming or herding; however, less than 7 per cent of the land area is cultivated. Many traditionally migrate to Ivory Coast or Ghana to work as farm laborers, and Voltaics formerly enlisted in large numbers in the French Army. The country's main cash income is from French aid (estimated at about $10 million annually, plus the services of more than 300 technicians), veterans' pensions, military expenditures, and the migratory wages. Recorded exports include small quantities of peanuts, meat, and cotton. A Fifteen Year Development Plan launched in 1963, to be financed largely by the EEC and France, seeks to double agricultural output by 1978, improve transport, establish some small industries, and continue the search for minerals.

Although Upper Volta has been a member of the Conseil de

l'Entente (with Ivory Coast, Dahomey, and Niger) since 1959, and was a founding member of the Union Africaine et Malgache, President Yameogo's foreign policy has also had a puckish quality. In 1960, Upper Volta came close to joining the Mali Federation; in 1961, Yameogo publicly flirted with the idea of closer economic ties with Ghana, apparently with the idea that Upper Volta might be able to use its strategic geographical position to become the essential connecting link within both the Entente and the Ghana-Guinea-Mali Union; even within the UAM, President Yameogo has sometimes clearly chafed at his role. Relations with the wealthier Ivory Coast, crucial economically, are complicated by personality differences at the leadership level; psychological legacies of the period (1923–47) when Upper Volta was split up among the Ivory Coast, Niger, and Mali; and a chronic dispute over customs regulations along the common frontier.

Zanzibar

Population: 299,111 (1958 est.; Zanzibar, 165,253; Pemba, 133,858).

Capital: Zanzibar town (population: 57,923).

Area: 1,020 square miles. Zanzibar, 640 square miles; Pemba, 380 square miles.

Political Status: Independent constitutional monarchy.

Date of Independence: December 10, 1963.

Chief of State and Head of Government: President Abeid Karume, installed by *coup d'état,* January 12, 1964.

Major Political Parties: The majority Afro-Shirazi Party, led by Abeid Karume; the Ummah Party, led by Abdul Rahman Mohammad Babu. The Zanzibar Nationalist Party (ZNP), led by Sheikh Ali Muhsin, and the Zanzibar and Pemba People's Party (ZPPP), led by former Prime Minister Sheikh Mohammed Shamte Hamadi, have been banned.

Legislative Branch: Prior to the *coup d'état* of January 12, 1964, the legislative branch consisted of a unicameral National Assembly of 31 members, including 3 ex officio, 5 appointed by the Sultan, and 23 elected by universal adult suffrage for 3-year terms. Last election, July, 1963. Plans for a new legislature have not been announced.

Principal Languages: English, Arabic, Swahili, Gujurati.

Monetary Unit: 1 East African shilling = US$0.14.

External Affiliations: United Nations, Organization of African Unity, Commonwealth.

At the end of the seventeenth century, the inhabitants of Zanzibar —a fifty-mile-long island off the coast of Tanganyika—drove out the Portuguese with the assistance of the Arabs of Oman, and an Arab governor was subsequently sent to govern; in 1822, the ruler of Oman transferred his capital to Zanzibar. In the nineteenth century, Zanzibar's golden age, the island prospered on its clove plantations and the slave trade, and the port of Zanzibar was the most important in East Africa. Government and most of the wealth were in the hands of the governing Arab sultan and the Arab minority, while Asians served as middlemen and Africans provided the labor. In 1890, the island (together with neighboring Pemba) became a British protectorate, though the Sultan remained the nominal ruler.

The end of the slave trade and a dwindling demand for cloves (which comprise 80 per cent of Zanzibar's exports) have brought economic decline in this century. The price of cloves has dropped from \$112 per hundred pounds to roughly \$12.60 over the past 6 years, and the 2 most important customers, India and Indonesia, have cut their purchases back sharply. In 1962–63, the government was only able to balance its accounts with the help of a \$1,265,600 grant-in-aid from the U.K.

Zanzibar's political instability, which culminated in the *coup d'état* of January, 1964, is a product of its racial diversity and economic structure. The island nation (including Pemba) is divided into four major ethnic categories—about 17 per cent Arabs (who, prior to the events of early 1964, held most of the arable land, largely staffed the upper ranks of the civil service, and dominated the political life of the island); some 60 per cent Shirazis, an intermixture of indigenous Africans and the Persians who immigrated to Zanzibar in large numbers in the seventh century; 20 per cent who are descendants of slaves from the mainland or more recent African immigrants; and some 20,000 Asians, who long controlled virtually all of the retail trade. Most of the population is Moslem.

At independence on December 10, 1963, Zanzibar was governed by a coalition government consisting of the Arab-led Zanzibar People's Party (twelve seats) and a conservative Shirazi movement, the Zanzibar and Pemba People's Party (six seats). The opposition party—which gained over half of the total popular vote in 1963 elections, but only thirteen seats—was the Afro-Shirazi Party, supported by the mainland African immigrants and the remaining section of the Shirazis. Since the ASP had the recorded electoral support of 54 per cent of the islanders, as well as close ties with African leadership groups in mainland Tanganyika and Kenya, it was evident that the traditional Arab-dominated power structure of the island could not survive indefinitely.

The particular character of the bloody January 12, 1964, *coup d'état* was a surprise to most observers, however. The resulting government combined four diverse and potentially competitive elements: (1) President Abeid Karume, leader of the majority Afro-Shirazi Party, a veteran African nationalist whose only external loyalty would appear to be to Tanganyika's President Julius Nyerere; (2) Vice-President Abdullah Kassim Hanga, leader of the left wing of the ASP, who married an American-born Russian wife while attending Patrice Lumumba University on a scholarship; (3) Foreign and Defense Minister Abd al-Rahman Mohammad Babu, a half-Arab journalist and leader of the small Marxist Ummah Party, whose financial support in recent years appears to have come from Peking; and (4) the mystical "Field Marshal" John Okello, who trained and led the estimated 600 armed insurgents who carried out the *coup*.

The new government's request that British civil servants employed on Zanzibar remain at their posts, its early SOS for Tanganyikan police to help restore order, the expressed intention to remain in the Commonwealth, and the anxious concern about diplomatic recognition from West as well as East suggested that it might be premature to categorize Zanzibar as "Africa's Cuba." The ultimate character of the new government would appear to depend on which of the principal leaders emerges as its real power center.

CHART I. THE UNIVERSITIES OF AFRICA, 1964

States	Universities	Year founded	Number of students (1963 figures)
Algeria	University of Algiers	1879	2,500 (est.)
Basutoland	University of Basutoland, Bechuanaland and Swaziland (formerly University College of Pius XII, est. 1945)	1964	177
Burundi	University of Usumbura (formerly the University of Ruanda-Urundi, est. 1960)	1963	85
Cameroun	Université Federale du Cameroun, Yaoundé	1962	518
Congo-Leopoldville	Lovanium University, Leopoldville	1954	1,200
	Université Officielle du Congo	1956	250
	Université Libre du Congo (formerly Université de l'Etat, Elisabethville)	1963	30
Ethiopia	Haile Selassie I University, Addis Ababa (incorporating University College of Arts and Sciences, est. 1950)	1961	1,093
Ghana	University of Ghana, Legon (formerly University College of Ghana, est. 1948)	1961	1,300
	Kwame Nkrumah University of Science and Technology, Kumasi (formerly Kumasi College of Technology, est. 1951)	1961	1,300
Ivory Coast	University College of Cape Coast	1961	150
	University of Abidjan	1963	1,035
Kenya	University of East Africa (incorporating the Center of Higher Education, est. 1959) (Kenya Component: The Royal College, est. 1956, Nairobi)	1963	478
Liberia	University of Liberia, Monrovia	1951	350 (est.)
	Cuttington College, Suacoco (originally founded 1888 but closed from 1929 to 1948)	1961	150
Libya	The Libyan University	1955	1,500
Malagasy Republic	University of Madagascar, Tananarive (incorporating the Institute of Higher Studies, est. 1955)	1961	1,731
Morocco	University of Rabat	1957	n.a.
	Qarawayin University, Fez	859	n.a.

States	Universities	Year founded	Number of students (1963 figures)
Nigeria	University College of Ibadan	1948	1,779 (1962)
	University of Nigeria, Nsukka (incorporating Enugu branch of the Nigerian College of Arts, Science and Technology)	1960	1,200 (1962)
	Ahmadu Bello University, Zaria (incorporating Zaria branch of the Nigerian College of Arts, Science and Technology)	1962	425 (1962)
	University of Ife (incorporating Ibadan branch of the Nigerian College of Arts, Science and Technology)	1961	244 (1962)
	University of Lagos	1962	130 (1962)
Rwanda	University of Butare	1963	50
Senegal	University of Dakar	1957	2,006
Sierra Leone	University College of Sierra Leone, Freetown (formerly Fourah Bay College, est. 1827)	1960	435
South Africa	University of Cape Town [a]	1918	5,010 European (1962) 475 non-European[b]
	University of Natal,[a] Durban and Pietermaritzburg (including non-white medical school in Durban—founded 1951)	1909	3,164 European (1962) 750 non-European[b]
	University for Christian Higher Education,[a] Potchefstroom (est. as college 1869)	1951	1,901 (1962)
	The University of the Orange Free State[a] (est. as college 1855)	1950	2,125 (1962)
	Rhodes University,[a] Grahamstown (est. as college 1904)	1951	1,062 European (1962) 106 non-European[b]
	University of Stellenbosch[a]	1916	4,818 (1962)
	University of Pretoria[a] (est. as college 1908)	1930	9,368
	University of the Witwatersrand,[a] Johannesburg	1922	5,662 European (1962) 222 non-European[b]
	University of South Africa (correspondence courses serving all races)	1873	9,920 European 2,175 non-European 1,117 post-graduates of all races

Country	Institution	Date	Enrollment
	University College of Zululand	1959	131 non-European
	University College of Fort Hare	1923	196 non-European
	University College of the North, Turfloop	1959	228 non-European
	University College of the Western Province	1959	321 Colored
	University College for Indians, Durban	n.a.	670
Southern Rhodesia	University College of Rhodesia and Nyasaland, Salisbury	1955	480 (inc. 141 Africans)
Sudan	University of Khartoum (formerly Gordon Memorial College, est. 1902)	1956	2,200
Tanganyika	University of East Africa (Tanganyika Component: University College of Dar es Salaam, est. 1961)	1963	84
Tunisia	University of Tunis (incorporating the Institute of Higher Studies, est. 1945, and Zitouma University)	1960	3,298
Uganda	University of East Africa (Uganda Component: Makerere University College, Kampala, est. 1950)	1963	749
United Arab Republic	University of al-Azhar	970	7,500
	Cairo University	1908	42,000
	American University of Cairo	1919	900
	Alexandria University	1942	25,000
	Ain Shams University	1950	31,000
	University of Assiut	1957	4,200

n.a.: Not available.

[a] Restricted to Europeans by law since 1959.

[b] Non-European students enrolled in courses prior to 1959 and allowed to complete studies.

PART TWO

The Armies of Africa

Explanatory Notes for
"The Armies of Africa"

Size of Armed Forces refers to the estimated strength of standing armies and other clearly military forces, normally under the Ministry of Defense.

Police and Other Security Forces differ from "armed forces" in that they are concerned primarily with the maintenance of law and order. Usually they are under the Ministry of Interior rather than the Ministry of Defense and are normally untrained for military tactics. But some (as the police strike force in Libya) are paramilitary in organization and function, thus complicating the task of distinguishing policemen from soldiers.

Most of the budgetary figures cited under the heading *Approximate Annual Defense Budget* are informed but rough estimates of defense operating budgets only and should not be regarded as a record of actual expenditures. Precise details on the extent of foreign subsidies and grants to African armies are closely held and, even when made available, are often incomplete and therefore misleading. All figures have been converted into dollar equivalents.

Sources of External Military Assistance are considered here to include past and current external sources of supply, whether gifts or purchases, and training, whether provided in Africa or elsewhere. The list is doubtless incomplete and does not necessarily reflect ongoing assistance programs.

The figures cited under the heading *Contribution to U.N. Congo Force* represent the peak monthly contribution to U.N. military force in the Congo between August, 1960, and May, 1963.

1. The Armies of Africa

compiled by GEORGE WEEKS

ALGERIA*

Size of Armed Forces: 48,000.

Police and Other Security Forces: 10,000.

Approximate Annual Defense Budget: $66 million (1963).

Sources of External Military Assistance: France, Soviet Union, United Arab Republic, Czechoslovakia, Cuba.

Defense Agreements With: Arab League Unified Military Command (est. 1964).

Contribution to U.N. Congo Force: None.

During the seven years of the Algerian war, the FLN became one of the world's most effective and battle-hardened guerrilla armies.* Now making the difficult transition to an orthodox military force, the Algerian Army seeks to preserve something of its "popular revolution character" by taking an active role in postwar reconstruction of the country and by participating in the training of rebel forces for Angola and other still-dependent African territories. After the March, 1962, cease fire, Algeria was divided into military regions, each with its independent army command.

In 1958, France had 400,000 troops in Algeria; by the terms of the Evian Agreement of March, 1962, as revised in a joint communiqué in May, 1962, French forces in the country had been reduced to 80,000 in 1963, and are scheduled to be completely evacuated in 1964. The revised agreement further permits France to use its nuclear and missile-test sites in the Sahara until 1967, to retain use of the naval air base at Mers-el Kebir for fifteen years on a lease renewable by mutual agreement, and to continue to use Algerian air communications facilities subject to

* See "When the FLN Takes Over," *Africa Report*, April, 1962, p. 5, for a vivid description of its tactics and organization.

certain conditions (e.g., the facilities at the Colomb Bechar, Reggane, and In-Amguel airfields were to remain in French hands for five years from the date of agreement, after which they are to be transformed into civilian airfields according France technical facilities as well as landing rights). At the Bône and Boufarik airfields, France will have technical facilities as well as landing, refueling, and repairing rights for a five-year period. The agreement stipulated that the installation "will under no circumstances be used for aggressive purposes."

Much of the present Algerian military equipment was diverted from withdrawing French troops. The Soviet Union and U.A.R. subsequently provided both training assistance and modern equipment, including tanks, aircraft, and heavy guns. The Algerian Air Force was said in October, 1963, to include six MIG fighters. Communist Chinese military delegations visited Algeria during 1963 and an Algerian military delegation visited a tank school and other Peking installations in October, 1963. During the border war with Morocco in October-November, 1963, some shipments of military supplies reportedly arrived from the U.S.S.R., Czechoslovakia, the U.A.R., and Cuba.

BASUTOLAND

Size of Armed Forces: None.
Police and Other Security Forces: 550.
Source of External Military Assistance: United Kingdom.

As a British High Commission Territory, Basutoland has no armed forces of its own and relies on British forces to be flown in when needed to supplement the territory's police forces.

BECHUANALAND

Size of Armed Forces: None.
Police and Other Security Forces: 500.
Source of External Military Assistance: United Kingdom.

As a British protectorate and High Commission Territory, Bechuanaland relies on British forces for security when needed. The police force numbered 500 in 1960, including 60 European officers.

BURUNDI

Size of Armed Forces: 800.
Police and Other Security Forces: 8,500.
Approximate Annual Defense Budget: $1.2 million (1962).
Source of External Military Assistance: Belgium.
Defense Agreements With: None.
Contribution to U.N. Congo Force: None.

Belgium maintained a highly mobile 1,400-man paracommando unit in the U.N. Trust Territory of Ruanda-Urundi before the twin kingdoms became independent and went their separate political ways in July, 1962. In addition, pre-independence Burundi had an indigenous force of about 800 men under 50 Belgian officers and NCO's. Prime Minister André Muhirwa, exercising an option granted by the United Nations, decided against retaining the Belgian paracommandos, but some 43 Belgians remained as advisers to the indigenous force. They were exercising some command functions during 1963 while Burundi continued to build its own officer corps. Legislation enacted during 1963 would limit the armed forces to 1,300 men.

CAMEROUN

Size of Armed Forces: 2,700.
Police and Other Security Forces: 5,900.
Approximate Annual Defense Budget: $15.6 million (1963).
Sources of External Military Assistance: France, United States.
Defense Agreements With: France, Union Africaine et Malgache.
Contribution to U.N. Congo Force: None.

When Cameroun became independent in January, 1960, it had no army of its own to deal with the five-year-old uprising still festering in the southwestern part of the country. Invoking the wide-ranging defense agreement signed with France three days before independence, President (then Prime Minister) Ahmadou Ahidio urgently requested the assistance of French troops in mounting an all-out campaign against the terrorists. During the height of the crisis, up to 1,000 French troops and 200 officers were serving in Cameroun.* The defense agreement authorizes the French Army to maintain a base at Douala.

By 1963, only a few pockets of terrorist resistance remained, and the task of maintaining internal security had been transferred to the 2,700-man Cameroun Army. This new force—trained and supplied by France and still largely officered by Frenchmen—has been created at a cost to France of about $7,000,000 annually since 1961 under a bilateral military-assistance agreement. An air arm was formed around a nucleus of three single-engined Broussards, a DC-3, and a helicopter, all received from France. Non-French military assistance included $321,000 in vehicles and a C-47 from the United States in 1962–63. Cameroun has been a member of the mutual defense organization of the Union Africaine et Malgache since 1961. It has attended meetings of the Equatorial Defense Council, but as of late 1963 was not a member. Other security forces in early 1963 included the Camerounian Guard (expanded from 740 to 2,000 men since 1960), a 3,000-man gendarmerie, and 900 municipal police.

CENTRAL AFRICAN REPUBLIC

> *Size of Armed Forces:* 500.
>
> *Police and Other Security Forces:* 1,450.
>
> *Approximate Annual Defense Budget:* $2,105,000 (1963).
>
> *Sources of External Military Assistance:* France, Israel.
>
> *Defense Agreements With:* Union Africaine et Malgache, Equatorial Defense Council (France, Gabon, Central African Republic, Congo-Brazzaville, Chad).
>
> *Contribution to U.N. Congo Force:* None.

The Central African Republic (formerly known as Ubangi-Shari) had no armed forces of its own before independence in August, 1960, because the defense of Equatorial Africa was then a collective responsibility of the French Community. Thousands of Ubangi soldiers fought in the ranks of the Free French Forces in World War II, however, and several wear the Cross of the Liberation, the highest decoration instituted by General de Gaulle. The 500-man C.A.R. Army, created with French technical assist-

---

* See "Cameroun Faces Troubled Future," *Africa Report*, January, 1960, p. 2.

ance since 1960, included in 1962 four infantry companies with a headquarters unit. In addition to those French officers seconded to the C.A.R. Army for training purposes under the 1960 military technical-assistance agreement, France maintains a small standby force in the country in accordance with the terms of a multilateral agreement with the Equatorial Defense Council and/ or other unpublished agreements dealing with the availability of French forces in certain emergencies. Other security forces include 450 gendarmes and a 670-man Republican Guard, and 330 police. It should be noted that the 1963 budget estimate of $2,105,000 for the defense establishment includes, atypically, the gendarmerie; it does not include French support for the C.A.R. Army.

Israeli army officers are in charge of a project to train the country's youth in modern farming. The United States provided $200,000 in vehicles and other equipment in 1962 under an internal-security assistance program.

There were unconfirmed reports of a short-lived army revolt in one military installation in Bangui in September, 1963. Discontent over pay and lack of amenities was cited as the cause.

CHAD

Size of Armed Forces: 400.

Police and Other Security Forces: 1,950.

Approximate Annual Defense Budget: $1.5 million (1962).

Source of External Military Assistance: France.

Defense Agreements With: Equatorial Defense Council, Union Africaine et Malgache.

Contribution to U.N. Congo Force: None.

Chad had no armed forces of its own before independence in 1960. It had long been an area of high recruitment for the French armed forces, however, and was the first of the French African territories to rally in support of Free France in 1940, subsequently serving as a supply base for the Allied theaters of operations in East Africa and the Mediterranean. Chadian troops fought well in the campaigns in Fezzan, Tripolitania, and Tunisia.

The present 400-man army, built around a nucleus of these veterans, inherited French equipment and facilities and retains a number of French officers in both command and advisory positions. Chad is bound to France militarily by a 1960 bilateral military technical-assistance agreement (similar to that signed between France and all of its former African colonies except Guinea and Mali) and a multilateral defense agreement between France and the Equatorial Defense Council. In addition, France was authorized at independence to maintain its existing military base at Fort Lamy for a period which has not been specified publicly; part of the force of up to 1,000 French commandos stationed there was flown to Brazzaville in August, 1963, during the demonstrations that preceded the resignation of President Fulbert Youlou.* Chad adhered to the mutual defense pact of the Union Africaine et Malgache in September, 1961.

CONGO-BRAZZAVILLE

> *Size of Armed Forces:* 700.
>
> *Police and Other Security Forces:* 500.
>
> *Approximate Annual Defense Budget:* $3.7 million (1962).
>
> *Source of External Military Assistance:* France.
>
> *Defense Agreements With:* Union Africaine et Malgache, Equatorial Defense Council.
>
> *Contribution to U.N. Congo Force:* None.

Congo-Brazzaville (formerly Moyen Congo) had no armed forces of its own before becoming an independent republic in 1960, since its defense needs were previously a collective responsibility of the French Community. Brazzaville had long been a center of French military operations and influence in Equatorial Africa, however, and Radio Brazzaville played a vital role in the Allied war effort during World War II.

The army numbered about 700 men in mid-1963; it is French trained and includes a considerable number of French officers and NCO's. As in most states of former French Africa, it includes an understrength infantry battalion, a communications company, a transportation company, a patrol boat, and an air arm comprised of three single-engine planes, one DC-3, and a helicopter. Part of the officer corps joined forces with labor leaders in Au-

---

* See "Austerity in Brazzaville," *Africa Report,* October, 1963, p. 22.

gust, 1963, to force the resignation of President Fulbert Youlou; however, the new Provisional Government established at that time did not include any army officers in ministerial positions.*

Congo-Brazzaville signed a bilateral military technical-assistance agreement with France at independence, and is also bound to France militarily by a multilateral defense agreement signed in 1960 between France and the four African states of the Equatorial Defense Council. France maintains about 500 standby troops in the country (at Pointe-Noire) in addition to those French officers and NCO's actually serving in the Congo Army. During the August, 1963, demonstrations leading to the downfall of the Youlou government, additional French troops were airlifted to Brazzaville from the Central African Republic and Senegal under the terms of a special series of agreements, the details of which are not available, but which is known to permit certain African states to appeal to France to "intervene directly" in the case of a threat to peace and public order. In the Brazzaville instance, French forces set a precedent of carefully avoiding taking sides in the internal dispute. Congo-Brazzaville adhered to the defense pact of the Union Africaine et Malgache in September, 1961.

CONGO-LEOPOLDVILLE

Size of Armed Forces: 30,000.

Police and Other Security Forces: 15,000.

Approximate Annual Defense Budget: $10 million (1963).

Sources of External Military Assistance: Belgium, United Nations, United States, Israel (Anticipated: Nigeria, Italy).

Defense Agreements With: None.

Contribution to U.N. Congo Force: 791.

When the Congo became independent in June, 1960, the Belgian-trained Force Publique (est. strength: 25,000) was regarded as one of the best-disciplined armies in Africa. In the first weeks of independence, this linchpin of Congolese stability gave way as troops mutinied against the entirely Belgian officer corps in protest at the soldiers' unchanged lot in the "new Congo." Three years later, as the UN peace-keeping operation enters its final phase,

* See "Austerity in Brazzaville," *Africa Report,* October, 1963, p. 22.

the reconstituted and expanded Armée Nationale Congolaise is once more seen as the key to Congolese stability.*

By mid-1963, more than 400 Congolese officers and senior NCO's had been trained in Belgium or elsewhere, and another 200 were in school. In September, 1963, Joseph Mobutu, ANC Chief of Staff, was among 219 Congolese completing paratroop training in Israel. The reconstituted army includes only those individuals in the Katanga gendarmerie who applied for transfer when the provincial force was disbanded in 1963—about 3,600 out of a force variously estimated at 12,000 to 20,000. Some 6,000 rebellious troops from Kasai have been asked to lay down their arms.

Under a plan proposed in March, 1963, by Prime Minister Cyrille Adoula, six nations were to be invited through the U.N. to participate in the final preparation of the ANC for its new role —Belgium (infantry), Italy (air force), Norway (navy), Israel (paratroops), Canada (communications and transport), and the United States (supply and administration). This multilateral scheme foundered because of Afro-Asian objections to the primarily European character of the training package, and indications are that the Adoula government will confine itself to bilateral military technical-assistance agreements. Under the first of these, a sizable Belgian training mission began to arrive in Leopoldville in June, 1963, for assignment to the infantry. The full extent of Belgian military aid under the new agreement is not known but was expected to be less than the $59 million Belgium spent on the Force Publique in 1959. The cost of Italy's initial contribution was expected to be about $5 million.

United Nations military costs in the Congo between July, 1960, and June, 1962, amounted to $240 million, almost half of which was paid by the United States. The budgeted figure for U.S. bilateral military aid to the Congo in 1962–63 was $3,378,000. (Twelve African nations were among 35 contributing troops to the U.N. force, which had a peak strength of about 20,000.)

The police of the Congo are under the jurisdiction of the provincial administrations. Nigeria was assisting in police training in 1963.

* See "The Congo Begins To Stir," by M. Crawford Young, *Africa Report,* October, 1963, p. 9.

DAHOMEY

> *Size of Armed Forces:* 1,000.
> *Police and Other Security Forces:* 1,700.
> *Approximate Annual Defense Budget:* $1.1 million (1963).
> *Sources of External Military Assistance:* France, United States, Israel.
> *Defense Agreements With:* France, Union Africaine et Malgache.
> *Contribution to U.N. Congo Force:* None.

In October, 1963, Dahomean army and labor leaders joined forces in a bloodless *coup d'etat.* President Hubert Maga was succeeded temporarily as chief of state by Colonel Christophe Soglo, commander of Dahomey's armed forces, pending the drafting of a new constitution. The modest force which Colonel Soglo commands was created, with extensive French help, following independence in August, 1960. The specific character of Franco-Dahomean cooperation in the military field is set forth in a 1960 military technical-assistance agreement and a bilateral defense agreement. Token military assistance has been provided by the United States (eight jeeps, three motor launches, and eight trucks in 1962, plus some aid for the police); and by Israel (four jeeps, exchange visits, etc.).

In April, 1963, President Hubert Maga announced a new system of compulsory military service for Dahomeans of both sexes. He emphasized that the principal objective of conscription was not to prepare for war, but rather to make national unity a reality by giving each citizen an opportunity to carry out certain social, economic, and civic responsibilities. Young men were to serve for eighteen months and women for twelve.

Besides the army, other security forces include 350 police, about 1,000 gendarmes (with an air arm), and other units.

ETHIOPIA

> *Size of Armed Forces:* 25,000 to 35,000.
> *Police and Other Security Forces:* 30,000.
> *Approximate Annual Defense Budget:* $17.9 million (1963).
> *Sources of External Military Assistance:* United States, Sweden, Norway, India, Israel, United Kingdom (1947–51).
> *Defense Agreements With:* Kenya.
> *Contribution to U.N. Congo Force:* 3,133.

Ethiopia in 1963 had armed forces variously estimated at from 25,000 to 35,000 (depending on how many tribal irregulars were serving with regulars) and a 30,000-man police force.* Modernization of Ethiopian military forces, now well under way, is a product of extensive external aid and advice since World War II, and sizable internal spending. The Army was trained during 1947–51 by British officers. More recently, United States aid— amounting to a cumulative total of $73,799,000, or about half the U.S. military-aid program in all Africa through June, 1963— had been a major factor in the modernization and support of four Army commands, including the 6,000-man Imperial Guard, and in the creation of the Air Force and Navy. In addition, there have been Swedish advisers for the Air Force, which is headquartered at Debre Zeit and has a training school at Bishoftu; Norwegian instructors for the Naval School at Massawa; Indian instructors for the Imperial Guard and Harar Military Academy; and Israeli instructors in various branches of the military establishment. A mutual-defense agreement with neighboring Kenya was ratified in December, 1963.

The Ethiopian Army today includes 23 infantry and 4 artillery battalions, an armored squadron, an airborne rifle company, and the 9 infantry battalions of the Imperial Guard. The Air Force includes a squadron of F-86 jet fighters, 5 T-33 jet trainers, and a transport squadron with DC-3's and C-47's (all U.S.-made), as well as 18 piston-engined Swedish Saab-91 training craft and 2 squadrons of Saab-17 light bombers. The latter are currently being replaced with more modern craft. The Navy includes 5 95-foot U.S. coastal patrol boats, 2 Yugoslav motor torpedo boats, and an 18-year-old reconverted U.S. seaplane tender outfitted as a patrol-boat tender, training vessel, and flagship for Emperor Haile Selassie. At least 400 sailors have trained aboard the training ship, which has participated in joint U.S.-U.K.-French maneuvers. The royal yacht Brioni, a gift of Yugoslavia, was returned to that country in 1959.

The United States maintains about 1,300 military personnel

---

* For an analysis of the past and potential political role of the armed forces, see "Ethiopia: Reshaping an Autocracy," by Alphonse A. Castagno, *Africa Report,* October, 1963, p. 3.

at the leased Kagnew communications station at Asmara, as well as a military advisory group for the Ethiopian forces. The agreement on Kagnew, signed in May, 1953, runs for 25 years.

Ethiopia sent its fabled Kagnew Battalion to Korea; 3,133 Ethiopian troops and half an air squadron participated in the United Nations military operations in the Congo.

GABON

> *Size of Armed Forces:* 600.
> *Police and Other Security Forces:* 900.
> *Approximate Annual Defense Budget:* $2.5 million (1963).
> *Source of External Military Assistance:* France.
> *Defense Agreements With:* Union Africaine et Malgache, Equatorial Defense Council, France.
> *Contribution to U.N. Congo Force:* None.

Gabon had no armed forces of its own before independence in 1960, since its defense was a responsibility of the French Community. Under the terms of a military technical-assistance agreement signed at independence, France has helped the new republic create and train its present modest national army around a nucleus of French army veterans, supplying training cadres as well as equipment. There were about twenty African officers in late 1963, but some thirteen command positions are held by French officers. Air and naval support, provided by France, includes a helicopter, a DC-3, at least three single-engine Broussards, and a harbor patrol boat. Army and naval cadets are training in France. The 1963 defense appropriation was $1 million higher than in 1962.

Under the terms of a multilateral defense agreement between France and the four African states of the Equatorial Defense Council, mutual collaboration on various defense problems is assured. Gabon also has a bilateral defense agreement with France. About thirty-five French officers are stationed in Gabon, and additional French troops in Chad and Congo-Brazzaville are available in case of emergency. Gabon adhered to the defense agreement of the Union Africaine et Malgache in 1961.

Other security forces include 700 gendarmerie and 200 police.

GAMBIA

Size of Armed Forces: None.
Police and Other Security Forces: 560.
Approximate Annual Defense Budget: None.
Source of External Military Assistance: United Kingdom.

Beginning in the early 1900's, the Gambia Company (later the Gambia Regiment) was part of Britain's Royal West African Frontier Force (RWAFF). British West African forces fought in East Africa in World War I and in Ethiopia and Burma in World War II. As a British colony, Gambia has had no armed forces of its own. A 150-man Field Force within the 560-man Gambia Police Force carries out certain defense, security, and ceremonial duties of the now-disbanded Gambia Regiment, however, and will presumably be the nucleus for an army when Gambia becomes independent, probably in 1964.

GHANA

Size of Armed Forces: 8,000.
Police and Other Security Forces: 9,000.
Approximate Annual Defense Budget: $35.3 million (1963).
Sources of External Military Assistance: United Kingdom, Soviet Union, Yugoslavia, Canada, Pakistan, India, Israel, United States, Australia, New Zealand.
Defense Agreements With: None.
Contribution to U.N. Congo Force: 2,624.

Accra served as the command headquarters for Britain's Royal West African Frontier Force until it was disbanded in 1956, and the RWAFF's Gold Coast Regiment—which was to become the Ghana Army at independence in 1957—participated in the 1914 campaigns in the German Cameroons and Togoland and in Britain's African operations of World War II.

Although only 10 per cent of the Ghana Army officer corps was Africanized at independence, the 8,000-man army is now commanded entirely by Ghanaian officers, though expatriates of diverse origins are still used in training roles. The first major step to Africanize the officer corps and balance British military influence with that of other nations came in September, 1961, with the dismissal of the Army's British Commander as well as 200 other British officers and NCO's. Although British influence is still strong in the Army—40 Ghanaian cadets had trained at Sandhurst by mid-1962, and much of the equipment is still of British origin—Ghana has made considerable progress toward its goal of diversifying sources of military assistance. Besides British advisory and training programs, Ghana has accepted (1) an offer of Soviet training for 100 cadets as well as Soviet arms estimated by Western sources to be worth more than $1 million; (2) Yugoslav assistance in constructing a naval base; (3) a Canadian training mission plus several aircraft (purchased); (4) limited training assistance from Pakistan, India, Israel, and the United States; and (5) some arms (purchased) from Australia and New Zealand. Minister of Defense Kofi Baako announced in September, 1963, the establishment of two new elements within the armed forces: (1) a farm company "to instill in the soldiers the love for working on the land," and (2) the women's auxiliary corps which "will offer employment to a great number of girls in a disciplined environment."

In 1962, the Ghana Navy had 2 inshore minesweepers acquired from the Royal Navy in 1959, 2 Glasgow-built seaward defense boats, and was having 2 corvettes built by a British firm. The Air Force, formed in 1959, reportedly had 26 single-engined Beavers and Otters from Britain and Canada by 1962, plus 8 twin-engined Caribou transport aircraft, 12 Chipmunk trainers, 1 Heron V1B transport, 6 turbine-engined Whirlwind helicopters, and 5 Indian-built Hindustan HT-2 trainers. Further Ghanaian orders with de Havilland (Canada) amounted to about $7.5 million. Ghana bought 8 Ilyushin-18 transport planes from the Soviet Union at more than $1.5 million each on credit in 1961, but returned 4, along with a cargo plane, and retained 4 for Ghana Airways. A number of Air Force planes are used for patrol, air ambulance, government travel, and survey work. There are air bases at Takoradi and Tamale.

A major reorganization of the police force was ordered in January, 1964, following the abortive attempt of a constable to assassinate President Kwame Nkrumah. As a first step, Commissioner E. R. T. Madjitey and nine other senior police officers were dismissed from their posts and/or detained. The 9,000-man force has heretofore been trained in the British tradition of nonpolitical public service. Some observers in Ghana predicted that the purge would shortly extend to the Army.

GUINEA

> *Size of Armed Forces:* 4,800.
> *Police and Other Security Forces:* 3,300.
> *Approximate Annual Defense Budget:* $5.8 million (1962).
> *Sources of External Military Assistance:* Soviet Union, West Germany, France.
> *Defense Agreements With:* None.
> *Contribution to U.N. Congo Force:* 749.

Of the approximately 22,000 Guinean soldiers in the French army when Guinea voted to sever ties with France in 1958, some 10,000 serving abroad elected to remain in the French Army and roughly 12,000 were quickly demobilized. Piqued by Guinea's "no" vote on membership in the French Community, Paris cut all political, economic, and military ties. French military installations in Guinea were dismantled of all movable equipment almost overnight and all military technicians were withdrawn from the country. Guinea was left with thousands of unemployed veterans but no organized military force except a gendarmerie lacking necessary equipment.

Faced with a two-edged problem—to create a new national army quickly from scratch, and also to ensure that the thousands of returning veterans did not become a disruptive political force—President Sékou Touré chose the most reliable of the veterans for the nucleus of the army and quickly organized the others under the umbrella of the Parti Démocratique de Guinée to play specific roles in the task of national reconstruction. Within three months of independence, the French-trained gendarmerie and selected veterans had been combined in a functioning army of 2,000 officers and men.* Compulsory military service was subsequently established as part of the government's over-all effort to instill a sense of common nationality among Guineans of different

* See "The Role of the Army in Guinea," *Africa Report,* January, 1963, p. 3.

ethnic and cultural backgrounds. Only a small percentage of those in the army in 1963 (now approaching a figure of 5,000 officers and men) ever served in the French Army. Those pre-1958 veterans who remain have been carefully screened for loyalty to the Guinean revolution, and political indoctrination is a significant aspect of the training program for all new recruits.

With the withdrawal of French military technical assistance, Guinea had to look for other sources of help. The Soviet Bloc stepped in to fill the vacuum, providing training personnel and what has been estimated as "more than $1 million" in arms and equipment between 1958 and 1962. By 1963, Guinea had begun to broaden its sources of economic and military assistance; among other developments was West Germany's announcement of an agreement to train and outfit three engineer companies and expand road and communications networks.

The Army's 1962 operating budget of $5,850,000 included some funds for agricultural, forest, and road work. For six months in 1960, the U.N. Congo operation was a testing ground for 749 Guinean troops.

IVORY COAST

> *Size of Armed Forces:* 4,000.
> *Police and Other Security Forces:* 2,280.
> *Approximate Annual Defense Budget:* $8.7 million (1962).
> *Sources of External Military Assistance:* France, Israel, United States.
> *Defense Agreements With:* Union Africaine et Malgache, Regional defense agreement with Niger and France.
> *Contribution to U.N. Congo Force:* None.

Although many Ivoiriens fought in the French Army in both World Wars (as many as 20,000 in World War I, according to French sources), the Ivory Coast itself had no military force before independence in August, 1960. The territory was within the Third Brigade Area of French West Africa, and its defense was a responsibility of the French Community. Under terms of a regional defense agreement signed at independence with Niger and France, French forces remained in the country to assure against external attack until an indigenous force adequate to the task could be developed. Under the terms of a bilateral military technical-assistance agreement signed at the same time, France has taken a major role in training and equipping a new national army that was nearing 5,000 in mid-1963. On September 28, 1963, however, President Félix Houphouet-Boigny revealed plans to reduce and reorganize the army into a small professional force with the function of defending the country's frontiers. This announcement followed closely on the reported discovery of a second major plot to overthrow the government, which was said to involve military as well as civilian elements.* A militia, composed of loyal *militants* from the governing Parti Démocratique de la Côte d'Ivoire, was to be created for the express purpose of ensuring an orderly transfer of power within the party in case of the President's death.

In an address to the National Assembly in 1962, President Houphouet-Boigny emphasized that French military presence in the country was in response to Ivoirien initiative: "It is important to remember that France no longer has any strategic interests in Abidjan; the French troops are stationed here at our request; there can be no doubts that France will be greatly relieved when she is asked to withdraw her troops." As for the new national force, Houphouet promised that "never shall an Ivory Coast soldier engage in an offensive action against an African state, and never shall our territory be used as an offensive base against an African country."

Israeli officers in 1963 were organizing an army school for civic action near Bouaké and advising the Ivory Coast Army on the operation of six farms. In July, 1963, the government announced that Israeli officers would organize an Ivoirien women's army unit. The U.S. in 1961 gave $292,000 in vehicles, communications, field and laboratory equipment, and training aids for the police, and $144,000 for similar equipment in 1962; jeeps were included in a $218,000 U.S. military shipment in 1962. The 1962 defense operating budget of $8.7 million did not include the cost of maintaining the 1,500 gendarmes and 780 police.

* See "New Plot Reported in Ivory Coast," *Africa Report,* October, 1963, p. 21.

Ivory Coast adhered to the mutual defense pact of the Union Africaine et Malgache in 1961.

KENYA

> *Size of Armed Forces:* 2,500.
> *Police and Other Security Forces:* 11,500.
> *Approximate Annual Defense Budget:* Not available.
> *Source of External Military Assistance:* United Kingdom.
> *Defense Agreements With:* Ethiopia.
> *Contribution to U.N. Congo Force:* None.

Kenya's standing force consisted in 1963 of three well-trained battalions of the King's African Rifles (KAR), which became the Kenya Rifles upon independence in December, 1963. This force, originally raised in the late 1800's to control Arab slave traders and to protect the interests of the Imperial East Africa Company, gives independent Kenya the strongest military force among East African territories now contemplating federation. (See Uganda and Tanganyika.)

The Kenya Army has light mortars, scout cars, and troop carriers but lacks tanks and artillery. Africanization of the officer corps at independence was more advanced than in Uganda or Tanganyika at a comparable political stage, though 150 British officers and men were serving with the Kenya Army at the end of 1963, and British officers still held top command positions as of January, 1964. Kenya's 11,500-man police force was in 1963 the largest and best equipped in East Africa; it includes a light-plane wing and is trained for riot control.

Under the terms of the December, 1963, independence agreement, the U.K. agreed to phase out, over a 12-month period, the 4-battalion, 5,000-man strategic reserve of British troops stationed in Kenya, as well as support units and two RAF transport squadrons. It was anticipated that the strategic reserve would gradually be transferred to Aden or used to fill gaps in the British Army of the Rhine. Some British officers were scheduled to remain to help with expansion of the Kenya Rifles and establishment of a small air force.

This timetable was at least temporarily disrupted in January, 1964, when Prime Minister Jomo Kenyatta called for emergency British assistance to break up a strike at the headquarters of the 11th Battalion of the Kenya Rifles near Nakuru in protest against inadequate pay and the continued presence of expatriate officers. The mutiny in Kenya had been anticipated by the government after similar uprisings in neighboring Tanganyika and Uganda earlier in the same week appeared to have resulted in major concessions from hard-pressed ministerial negotiators. In Kenya, unlike Uganda and Tanganyika, Prime Minister Kenyatta made the punishment and disciplining of the mutineers strictly an Army matter.

Despite some evidence of outside machinations by troublemakers in the wave of East African army mutinies, the facts as known in January, 1964, seemed to indicate that the chain reaction that began in Tanganyika shortly after the Zanzibar revolution and then swept through Uganda and Kenya was set in motion by the existence of common grievances among all the lower ranks of the former King's African Rifles of East Africa.

Some 700 additional British troops arrived in Kenya from Aden or the U.K. during the emergency, though some were to replace units sent to Uganda or Tanganyika.

LIBERIA

> *Size of Armed Forces:* 3,580.
>
> *Police and Other Security Forces:* 700.
>
> *Approximate Annual Defense Budget:* $2.4 million (1963).
>
> *Source of External Military Assistance:* United States.
>
> *Defense Agreements With:* United States.
>
> *Contribution to U.N. Congo Force:* 462.

The Liberian Army—known as the National Guard—has been largely trained and equipped by the United States. Under the terms of an agreement signed between the two countries in 1959, the U.S. is pledged to consult with the Liberian Government on appropriate defense measures "in the event of aggression or threat of aggression against Liberia"; a second article reaffirms that the United States will "continue to furnish the Government of Liberia such assistance as may be mutually agreed upon . . . in order to assist Liberia . . . in the effective promotion of its economic development and in the preservation of its national independence and integrity."* Cumulative U.S. technical military assistance totaled $4,645,000 through June, 1963; in addition, Roberts Air Field was built with American assistance. A fifteen-man U.S. Military Assistance Advisory Group has served in Liberia since 1959, and several Liberians are trained each year in military installations in the United States.

Although the National Guard Commander, Colonel David Thompson, was arrested in February, 1963, on a charge of having tried to instigate a plot against the government (he was reported to have said that "if only 250 Togolese soldiers could overthrow their government, a Liberian Army of 5,000 could seize power easily"), the army in general appears to have been absolved of involvement.

The loosely organized national militia (about 20,000) maintains order in the interior. There is also a 700-man police force (which has had some American training) and an 80-man coast guard equipped with at least two U.S. Coast Guard cutters and two patrol boats.

LIBYA

Size of Armed Forces: 5,000.

Police and Other Security Forces: 11,000.

Approximate Annual Defense Budget: $14 million (1962–63).

Sources of External Military Assistance: United States, United Kingdom, Italy, Turkey, West Germany.

Defense Agreements With: United Kingdom, Arab League Unified Military Command (est. 1964).

Contribution to U.N. Congo Force: None.

Created in 1952 around a core of veteran Cyrenaica tribesmen who had served with British forces in World War II, the Libyan Army has been improved and expanded in recent years with major assistance from the United States and Britain, and supplementary aid from Italy, Turkey, and West Germany. All Libyan males

* See *Africa Report,* September, 1959, p. 6.

are now subject to three years of compulsory military service. Plans were announced in 1963 to expand the army to 7,000.

Under the terms of a mutual-defense agreement signed on July 29, 1953, Britain maintains a Royal Air Force base in Libya, as well as an army-training facility for 1,000 or more troops and support personnel. The 1953 agreement gave the U.K. "exclusive and uninterrupted use for military purposes" of specified areas and facilities.

Wheelus Air Force Base, near Tripoli, was built by and for the United States under the terms of a 1954 agreement. Base rights continue until 1971. Wheelus, primarily a tactical training center, has also been a staging base for U.S. logistical support of United Nations operations in the Congo and a relay point for U.S. emergency food shipments to various countries of Africa. U.S. servicemen at Wheelus number about 4,000. The U.S. Military Assistance Advisory Group (MAAG) to the Libyan Army included five officers and six enlisted men in 1962. The cumulative total of U.S. military assistance to Libya was $7,168,000 as of July, 1963.

Libya's fledgling air force, started in 1959 with acquisition of two Egyptian-built Gomhouria fighters, was augmented in August, 1963, by a U.S. gift of two T-33 jet trainers and the assignment of a U.S. air-training mission. West Germany announced in June, 1963, that it was training fifteen pilots and ground personnel. Other pilots have trained in Turkey and Italy. The RLAF uses Wheelus Air Base facilities. The facilities cost $76 million to build and now represent an investment of more than $100 million.

The 10,000-man police force has had some U.S. training assistance. At least 47 members have had special police work in the States.

MALAGASY REPUBLIC

    Size of Armed Forces: 2,600.

    Police and Other Security Forces: 5,900.

    Approximate Annual Defense Budget: $9 million (1963).

    Sources of External Military Assistance: France, West Germany.

Defense Agreements With: France, Union Africaine et Malgache.

Contribution to U.N. Congo Force: None.

Before independence in June, 1960, Madagascar had no armed forces of its own. With cadets trained in France or at the local Ecole Nationale Militaire de Fianarantsoa (established in October, 1961), and troops instructed locally by French and Malagasy officers, the new republic has now developed a 2,600-man army and an air wing consisting of a DC-3, a Bell helicopter, and 5 Broussards. The Malagasy forces assumed control of the historic French installations at Fort Dauphin (on the southeast shore) in February, 1963, but about 8,000 French ground, air, and naval forces remained on the island. Most of the remaining French military personnel are at the strategic Indian Ocean naval base of Diégo Suarez on the northern tip of Madagascar. The terms of Franco-Malagasy defense cooperation are set forth in a full bilateral defense agreement, as well as a military technical-assistance agreement.

Military assistance is said to account for some 40 per cent of French aid to the Malagasy Republic, which totaled about $90 million over-all in 1963. West Germany announced in June, 1963, that it was providing the Malagasy Republic with 5 coastal boats and that 55 Malagasy seamen were being trained in Germany. West German aid was believed to total $1,640,000 in 1963, including 30 German jeeps. Some minor United States aid (about $193,000) has been provided in the form of equipment for the gendarmerie (4,000 men recruited only from the career army), and the police (1,900 men).

The Malagasy Republic adhered to the Union Africaine et Malgache defense pact in September, 1961.

MALI

Size of Armed Forces: 3,100.

Police and Other Security Forces: 1,250.

Approximate Annual Defense Budget: $8.7 million (1962).

Sources of External Military Assistance: France, Soviet Union, United States.

Defense Agreements With: None.

Contribution to U.N. Congo Force: 577.

Consistent with the Mali Government's over-all policy of ensuring freedom of action by obtaining maximum diversification of sources of external aid, the postindependence Mali Army has gradually reduced French training and material assistance, meanwhile seeking alternative help from the Soviet Bloc (perhaps as much as $3 million worth of arms and equipment) and the United States (equipment for several units of the Malian armed forces, and training of a paratroop unit for use in the inaccessible hinterland, totaling $2.27 million between 1961 and 1963).

The last French base (at Kati, near Bamako) was evacuated in late 1961. Mali—formerly French Soudan—was a major area of recruitment for the French Army for more than a century, and most of the officers and NCO's of the present Mali Army, gendarmerie, and other security forces are veterans of service in World War II, Viet-Nam, and/or even Algeria. The Commander, General Abdoulaye Soumare, served with French forces throughout World War II and in Viet-Nam and rose to the rank of Colonel in the French Army before Malian independence.

In October, 1963, 420 officers, NCO's, and other ranks from Mali's army, gendarmerie, police, and other security forces met in Bamako for the first national Seminar on Defense and Security. Discussion focused on the "history and vocation of the colonial army," the role of the "national revolutionary army," and the "political role of Mali army officers." A final resolution stressed the need for unity of political and military command, and reaffirmed that the Mali Army should be a "force for constraint in internal affairs and for defense in external affairs."

MAURITANIA

> *Size of Armed Forces:* 500.
> *Police and Other Security Forces:* 400.
> *Approximate Annual Defense Budget:* $4 million (1963).
> *Source of External Military Assistance:* France.
> *Defense Agreements With:* France, Union Africaine et Malgache.
> *Contribution to U.N. Congo Force:* None.

Before Mauritania acceded to independence in November, 1960, its defense was a responsibility of the French Community, and the only military service open to Mauritanians was in the French Army. Part of Mauritania was within the command of the First Brigade of French West Africa headquartered at St. Louis (Senegal), and a smaller segment was under the jurisdiction of the Third Brigade, headquartered at Bamako. Atar, Mauritania, was (and is) the site of one of the major French air bases in West Africa.

Although a Mauritanian Army and a small Air Force have been developed since independence with French budgetary assistance and training cadres, an unspecified number of French troops have also remained in the country under the terms of a full bilateral defense agreement signed at independence to help the new republic cope with Moroccan irredentism on the north and (until the 1963 border settlement) possible Malian border incursions on the south and west. The French troops, stationed principally at Port Etienne, are under the jurisdiction of the Dakar-based French Overseas Command Zone I.

Projected Ministry of Defense expenditures of $4 million for the 1963 fiscal year represented 21.5 per cent of the country's operating budget, an increase from 1962; this includes projected expenditures for the National Guard and certain other security forces that were under the Ministry of the Interior in 1962. Legislation enacted on June 14, 1962, established compulsory two-year military service. Meanwhile, French forces in the country, as well as the military assistance received from France under the terms of a 1961 military technical-assistance agreement, were being reduced as the regional security situation improved.

Mauritania adhered to the UAM defense pact in September, 1961.

MOROCCO

> *Size of Armed Forces:* 34,848.
>
> *Police and Other Security Forces:* 24,300.
>
> *Approximate Annual Defense Budget:* $93 million (1963).
>
> *Sources of External Military Assistance:* France, Spain, Soviet Union, United States.
>
> *Defense Agreements With:* Arab League Unified Military Command (est. 1964).
>
> *Contribution to U.N. Congo Force:* 3,259.

The main body of the Moroccan Army, one of the five strongest military forces on the continent, was recruited (from Berber tribes) and trained by France before independence; the army now also includes about 4,000 guerrilla fighters of the Moroccan Army of Liberation, veterans of the Spanish Army (including a full general), and veterans of French Army service in World War II and Indochina. It includes infantry, cavalry, motorized, parachute, and engineer units, many of which participate in civic-action projects. About 100 French officers have been retained to assist with training—in the field and at Morocco's Dar el-Beida military academy. Some of the more than 900 Moroccan officers (including the commander of the Moroccan detachment in the Congo) have been trained at St. Cyr in France. A *lycée militaire* was established at Kenitra in 1962. Spain at one point was providing officer-training for 100 Moroccans a year.

Most of the original equipment was an independence gift from France, which has continued since 1956 to provide some technical assistance. In recent years, however, Morocco has also received substantial military assistance from the United States and the Soviet Union. Soviet assistance reportedly includes artillery and heavy equipment as well as communications material on a 12-year credit. The 1963 Moroccan operating defense budget of $93 million exceeded the outlay of $82 million in 1962 and $75 million in 1961, but the defense share (20.2 per cent) of total expenditures was about the same as in the 2 previous years.

The 1,930-man air force, formed in 1956, is equipped with 12 Soviet MIG-17's and 2 MIG-15's, all purchased; an unspecified number of U.S. C-119 transports; a flight of M.S. Criquet observation monoplanes, and a communications flight of Heron, Broussard, and Twin-Bonanza light transports. The 400-man navy was started with a corvette, a patrol vessel, and a seaward patrol craft, all acquired from France. Construction was reported under way in 1962 on at least 12 ships. Other security forces include 1,800 gendarmes, 14,000 national police, and an auxiliary of 8,500. Some U.S. training has been provided for the police.

The historic French bases at Fez, Agadir, Marrakech, Meknes, and Khouribga were evacuated in 1961 under the terms of a September, 1960, agreement. The United States, which landed about

1 million soldiers at Moroccan ports in World War II, later established a complex of bases in the country under the terms of a 1950–51 agreement with France at a cost of more than $500 million. They were the Strategic Air Command bases of Nousseur, Benguerir, Sidi Slimane, and Ben Slimane, and the $70 million Port Lyautey Naval Station at Kenitra. Former President Dwight D. Eisenhower and the late King Mohamed V agreed in 1959 that all the bases would be evacuated by the end of 1963, and President Kennedy reaffirmed the 1959 agreement in March, 1963, when he discussed with King Hassan alternative forms of assistance the U.S. might be able to provide in converting the bases to Moroccan use, including the possibilities of a new international airport at Nousseur near Casablanca, hospitals, and various kinds of civilian-training centers. By August, 1963, SAC bombers had been withdrawn and U.S. personnel reduction from the peak of 15,000 was being accelerated.

On January 1, 1964, the Moroccan Royal Armed Forces took over Strategic Air Command bases at Nousseur, twenty-five miles from Casablanca; Benguerir, forty-two miles north of Marrakech; and Sidi Slimane.

NIGER

Size of Armed Forces: 1,200.

Police and Other Security Forces: 1,500.

Approximate Annual Defense Budget: $3.4 million (1963).

Sources of External Military Assistance: France, United States.

Defense Agreements With: Union Africaine et Malgache; regional defense agreement with Ivory Coast and France.

Contribution to U.N. Congo Force: None.

Niger's Army was formed in August, 1961—a year after independence—from three former companies of the French Army. The highest rank among the ten African officers in the force in 1962 was a lieutenant colonel, but the pace of Africanization of the officer corps was increased in 1963. French Army personnel serve in both training and command positions under a military technical-assistance agreement reached at independence. In addition, an estimated 1,000 French troops are based in the country under terms of a regional-defense agreement with Niger and Ivory Coast. In 1961, the United States supplied $225,000 worth of vehicles and communications equipment to the Ministry of Interior to "augment the internal security capacity of the Sûreté, Gendarmerie and Garde Républicaine." Assistance from the U.S. in 1962–63 consisted of $114,000 worth of civic-action equipment and some police-training. In an address to the nation on December 18, 1963, President Hamani Diori described the national army as "an offspring of the nation and entirely at the service of the nation," and expressed confidence that it would "never follow the ambitious agitators who would like to lead it into adventure."

NIGERIA

> *Size of Armed Forces:* 8,000.
>
> *Police and Other Security Forces:* 23,000 (federal plus regional).
>
> *Approximate Annual Defense Budget:* $28 million (1963).
>
> *Sources of External Military Assistance:* United Kingdom, West Germany, United States, Canada, India, Pakistan, Ethiopia.
>
> *Defense Agreements With:* None.
>
> *Contribution to U.N. Congo Force:* 1,898.

Nigeria's 8,000-man army, now being rapidly strengthened and expanded with assistance from several external sources, is a derivative of the old Royal West African Frontier Force. Only about 25 per cent of the officer corps was Nigerian at independence in 1960, but at least 60 Nigerian officer candidates had trained at Sandhurst by mid-1962 as part of an accelerated program of Africanization. Nigeria is also one of the first African states to participate in an ROTC-type training program in the United States aimed at helping developing nations produce professional military officers. More than 20 Nigerian cadets are to train in Canada, and officer-training assistance has also been provided in India, Pakistan, and Ethiopia; some are likely to go to Israel in 1964. British as well as Indian officers are serving on the staff of the military academy at Kaduna.

West Germany is helping to build a Nigerian Air Force for troop transport and frontier patrol, initially supplying two Dornier-27 trainers and seven instructors for employment in Nigeria and training ninety Nigerians in Germany. Other help is expected from Commonwealth countries. In announcing the creation of the Air Force and establishment of an arms factory in April, 1962, Defense Minister Alhaji Muhammadu Ribadu emphasized that Nigeria was at peace with "everybody" and without territorial ambitions, but noted that "it would be foolish to make no preparations and rely on good will alone." M. T. Mbu, Federal Minister of State for the Navy, said in November, 1962, that Nigeria's ten-ship fleet would be increased to twenty by 1970. As of 1962, the Navy had one frigate, three seaward defense boats, and smaller vessels to aid in prevention of smuggling.

Although Nigeria and Britain canceled a "widely misunderstood" mutual defense agreement in 1962, close military cooperation continues and Britain remains the major source of military equipment and other forms of assistance. U.S. military aid to Nigeria in 1963 totaled $325,000, all for training.

PORTUGUESE AFRICA

ANGOLA—*Size of Armed Forces:* Portuguese forces, 45,000; Rebels (trained), 7,500 est.
Police and Other Security Forces: 5,000.

MOZAMBIQUE—*Size of Armed Forces:* Portuguese forces, 20,000.
Police and Other Security Forces: Not available.

PORTUGUESE GUINEA—*Size of Armed Forces:* Portuguese forces, 6,000; Rebels (trained), 1,000 est.
Police and Other Security Forces: Not available.

A high percentage of Portugal's Army has been tied down in Africa since the revolt in Angola began in 1961, followed by rebellion in Portuguese Guinea in 1962. In September, 1963, there were between 45,000 and 50,000 metropolitan troops in Angola, about 20,000 in Mozambique, and about 6,000 in Portuguese Guinea. The Portuguese defense budget in 1962 was $200 million. In 1963, there was a special unspecified appropriation to cover the "extraordinary expenses" of military forces abroad.

Although all able-bodied "assimilated" Africans have military-service obligations and some recruits are customarily taken from among "nonassimilated" Africans, the percentage of Africans in the Portuguese military establishments in all three African territories has been sharply reduced in recent years as increasing numbers of reinforcements come from the metropole. The police forces, used to maintain local order, are in large part African with Portuguese officers.

The rebel guerrilla force opposing Portuguese rule in Angola has been variously estimated at 5,000 to 25,000 men. The effective core of the rebel force—i.e., those trained in North Africa or across the border near Thysville in the Congo and equipped with small arms—appeared to be about 7,500 in late 1963. Algeria is a primary source of arms and training assistance, with the Organization of African Unity providing financial help. Rebel forces in Portuguese Guinea have received training and material assistance from Algeria, Ghana, Morocco, Guinea, and Senegal, but claim that most of their arms are captured from Portuguese installations.*

RHODESIAS and NYASALAND

Federal Armed Forces Prior to Dissolution of the Federation of Rhodesia and Nyasaland in December, 1963: 7,000, not including 1,100-man Air Force. (*Post-December, 1963:* Southern Rhodesia, 3,400; Northern Rhodesia, 2,900; Nyasaland, 1,500, not including distributed units of federal Air Force.)

Police and Other Security Forces: Federal, 7,000. (*Post-December, 1963:* Southern Rhodesia, 5,000; Northern Rhodesia, 7,000; Nyasaland, 3,000.)

Approximate Annual Federal Defense Budget: $23.7 million (1963).

Source of External Military Assistance: United Kingdom.

Defense Agreements With: None.

Contribution to U.N. Congo Force: None.

Before the Federation of Rhodesia and Nyasaland was dissolved in December, 1963, the 7,000-man federal regular army included: (1) four white-officered African battalions—one in Nyasaland (dating back to 1896), one in Northern Rhodesia (which evolved out of the constabulary of the British South Africa Company), and two of more recent origin in Southern Rhodesia; (2) an all-white battalion; and (3) certain specialist units (including a paratroop and an armored reconnaissance squadron). Africanization of the

* See "The Angola Rebellion," by John Marcum, *Africa Report*, February, 1964, p. 3; and, by I. William Zartman, "Portuguese Guinea: Africa's Quiet War," *Africa Report*, February, 1964, p. 8.

officer corps of the African battalions was only getting under way in 1963 via scholarships or upgrading warrant officers and NCO's. Besides the regular army, there was a 7,000-man Royal Rhodesia Regiment, a part-time but well-trained territorial force of European reservists, and an emergency call-up register of 46,000 unorganized whites. European youths underwent compulsory military training, and then were assigned for three years to local army units for regular drill.

The Royal Rhodesian Air Force had about 90 planes and 1,100 men, of which 900 were European and the rest African ground personnel. The force included at least 18 Canberra bombers, 14 Vampire fighter-bombers, 12 supersonic Hawker Hunter Fighters; a reconnaissance squadron of Provosts; and a transport support squadron with Canadair North Star, Dakota, and Pembroke aircraft, and Alouette helicopters. In addition to their role in internal security and defense, the air units contributed to Commonwealth operations in the Middle East or Mediterranean as needed. Troops from Central Africa fought in World War II, and one battalion from Nyasaland participated in the Malayan emergency, beginning in 1948. British military aircraft used Federation bases on training flights.

Sir Malcolm Barrow, Deputy Prime Minister of the Federation, told the Federal Parliament on October 21, 1963, that the armed forces would be transferred to the individual territories according to their dispositions as of that date, except that "A" Squadron of Selous Scouts would be disbanded and "C" Squadron of the Rhodesian Special Air Services Regiment (comprised of 150 parachute commandos) would be transferred from Northern Rhodesia to Southern Rhodesia.

Southern Rhodesia's regular army will comprise about 3,400 officers and other ranks, under command of Major General J. Anderson. Besides the squadron noted above, the force will include one European and one African battalion—the Rhodesian Light Infantry and the Rhodesian African Rifles—and support units. The Territorial Force training system will continue, with trainees completing an initial eighteen-week basic course before being assigned to active or reserve battalions, depending on whether they live in urban or rural areas. The bulk of the Royal Rhodesian Air Force (RRAF), traditionally manned largely by Southern Rhodesians, was also assigned to the southern territory, under command of Air Vice-Marshal A. M. Bentley; headquarters will remain in Salisbury, with air stations in New Sarum and Thornhill. However, the force was to be reduced by one Canberra light bomber squadron, a number of Vampire aircraft, and some heavy transport craft; their disposal was to be a matter of consultation with the U.K. Ghana charged at the United Nations in September, 1963, that transfer of the RRAF to Southern Rhodesia would constitute a threat to international peace.

Northern Rhodesia will have a regular army of two infantry battalions—the 1st Northern Rhodesian Rifles and the 2nd King's African Rifles—and an armored car squadron. This ground force will be supported by an air wing of transport and reconnaissance craft, to be built around a nucleus of four Dakota and two Pembroke aircraft transferred from the RRAF. The Lusaka and Ndola squadrons of the RRAF volunteer reserve will become auxiliary squadrons for Northern Rhodesia. An additional infantry battalion will be added some time after July, 1964, to bring the regular army strength to 182 officers and 2,750 men. The military forces of the territory are to be known collectively as the Northern Rhodesia Defense Force, commanded by Brigadier C. M. Grigg, a seconded British Army officer who previously commanded the Southern Rhodesia Southern District.

Nyasaland is expected to build its army around one African battalion transferred from the Federal Army. It earlier had laid claim to both the 1st and 2nd King's African Rifles, the main bodies of which were recruited in Nyasaland.

Other security forces include 7,000 police in Northern Rhodesia, 3,000 in Nyasaland, and 5,000 (one-third white) in the British South Africa Police (BSAP) of Southern Rhodesia, which also has 12,000 in reserve. All three forces have been responsible to their territorial governments rather than the federal government. The BSAP has some armored cars and light infantry weapons.

RWANDA

> *Size of Armed Forces:* 900.
> *Police and Other Security Forces:* 650.
> *Approximate Annual Defense Budget:* $1.3 million (1962).

Source of External Military Assistance: Belgium.
Defense Agreements With: Union Africaine et Malgache.
Contributions to U.N. Congo Force: None.

Although the Government of Rwanda decided not to retain the optional 1,400-man Belgian paracommando force when the territory became independent in July, 1962, 28 Belgian military advisers are helping train and command a 900-man national army.

The 1962 defense budget of 1.3 million was 9 per cent of the operating budget.

SENEGAL

Size of Armed Forces: 2,500.
Police and Other Security Forces: 4,000.
Approximate Annual Defense Budget: $9 million (1963).
Sources of External Military Assistance: France, United States.
Defense Agreements With: France, Union Africaine et Malgache.
Contribution to U.N. Congo Force: None.

Dakar was for many years the headquarters for the French West African Defense Zone, and Senegalese troops fought for France in every war from the Napoleonic period through World War II. Thus, while Senegal had no national army at independence in 1960, it had the trained manpower for a military force and one of the best-developed military establishments in French-speaking Africa. Under terms of a military technical assistance agreement signed at independence, France subsequently trained and equipped the country's present 2,500-man army, including 350 Senegalese officers and NCO's. Equipment provided includes aircraft, vehicles, coastal patrol vessels, and a converted subchaser. Under the terms of a full bilateral defense agreement signed at independence, the headquarters for France's Overseas Command Zone I are located in Dakar, and 5,000 French military personnel (including a 1,000-man strategic reserve task force and air and naval forces) are based here. Another source of external assistance is a $3 million United States military-aid program for the training and equipping of an engineer battalion for civic action.

The revised 1962–63 defense budget of $9 million covered both personnel and material. The austerity budget proposed by President Senghor for 1963–64 would cut back in many areas but increase spending for defense. Loyalty of paratroopers to President Léopold Senghor was a decisive factor in the outcome of the December, 1962, political crisis.* Other security forces include 1,000 gendarmes, 1,500 municipal police and detectives, and 1,500 rural police.

SIERRA LEONE

Size of Armed Forces: 1,850.

Police and Other Security Forces: 2,000.

Approximate Annual Defense Budget: $2.2 million (1962).

Sources of External Military Assistance: United Kingdom, Nigeria.

Defense Agreements With: None.

Contribution to U.N. Congo Force: 122.

With independence in April, 1961, the Sierra Leone battalion of the former Royal West African Frontier Force became the nucleus of the country's new army. The present force of 1,850 includes personnel operating small craft in coastal defense, and 122 troops assigned to the U.N. Congo Force for 14 months in 1962–63.

Only 10 out of 50 officers were Africans by 1962 (the highest a major); however, both the U.K. and Nigeria were assisting with an accelerated program of officer-training. The first commander of Sierra Leone's armed forces was a Brigadier seconded from the British Army.

Other security forces upon independence numbered 2,000, including 600 in a special constabulary. Each chiefdom has a small police force.

SOMALI REPUBLIC

Size of Armed Forces: 4,600 (but expanding).

Police and Other Security Forces: 4,800.

Approximate Annual Defense Budget: $3.9 million (1963).

Sources of External Military Assistance: Italy, Soviet Union, United Arab Republic, United Kingdom.

Defense Agreements With: None.

Contribution to U.N. Congo Force: None.

* See "What Happened in Dakar," *Africa Report,* January, 1963, p. 6.

The Somali Army—which includes some personnel from the historic Police Camel Corps of British Somaliland—was engaged in an accelerated expansion and modernization program in 1963. In late 1963, the government rejected a tripartite offer of more than $10 million in military assistance from the U.S., West Germany, and Italy because of "quantitative and qualitative inadequacies and above all because of political conditions which accompanied it." Under the tripartite plan, which was to have run from 1964 to 1968, Germany would have carried the major operational responsibility. Instead, the Somali Government decided to accept a substantially larger Soviet military aid offer—unofficially reported at about $30 million.

Prior to the build-up now in progress, most of the Somali Army equipment had come from Italy, the U.K., or the U.A.R. Included were British and Italian armored cars, tanks, artillery, light planes, and Dakota transports. The estimated 1963 defense budget was 15.2 per cent of total operating and development expenditures. U.S. assistance for the 4,800-man police force (one of Africa's best) is expected to total $1,566,000 by 1964; this aid program has included training in the U.S., construction of a police school, and provision of radio communications equipment, 2 patrol boats for antismuggling operations, aircraft, and vehicles.

In 1961, a northern (i.e., former British Somaliland) officer trained at Sandhurst led an unsuccessful attempt to seize the northern administrative center of Hargeisa.

SOUTH AFRICA

Size of Armed Forces: 25,000.

Police and Other Security Forces: 28,325.

Approximate Annual Defense Budget: $219.8 million (1963–64).

Sources of External Military Assistance: United Kingdom, United States, Canada, France, Switzerland, West Germany.

Defense Agreements With: None.

Contribution to U.N. Congo Force: None.

The South African Army, as of early 1963, included a well-equipped and trained permanent force of 12,000 men and 10,000 trained reserves. Volunteer "skiet-commando" units, in the tradition of the old Boer fighters, were being organized. The growing air arm was equipped with complex tactical weapons (air-to-air missiles, etc.) for external defense as well as aircraft designed for internal security purposes.

In October, 1963, the government announced the establishment of a National Institute for Rocket Research which reportedly seeks to develop a locally made radar guided ground-to-air missile. The 3,000-man navy was equipped with 2 destroyers, 3 frigates, 2 ocean minesweepers, 10 coastal minesweepers, 10 seaward defense boats, and about 20 other craft by 1963. Most of the vessels were purchased from the U.K. The proposed defense budget for 1963–64 was $219,800,000, an increase of $53,200,000 from the previous year. Increased military spending has been justified by Defense Minister J. J. Fouche on the grounds that military action against South Africa is being "openly advocated and secretly planned" by other African states (March 12, 1962), and that "we must prepare ourselves to be of value to the West when the call comes" (March 18, 1963).

Although South Africa has an expanding munitions industry of its own, the major source of heavy arms and aircraft purchases has been the U.K. On August 2, 1963, U.S. Delegate to the United Nations Adlai Stevenson announced that the United States (subject to future review "in the light of requirements for assuring international peace and security") would terminate all sales of military material to South Africa by the end of 1963, except for existing commitments to supply certain items for external defense. Canada, source of aircraft, communication, and other equipment, made a similar announcement in October, and Switzerland (antiaircraft guns) in December, after completing delivery on an earlier contract. West Germany earlier halted sale of vehicles and other equipment. On August 7, 1963, the U.N. Security Council adopted a resolution which "solemnly calls upon all states to cease forthwith the sale and shipment of arms, ammunition of all types, and military vehicles to South Africa" in protest against the republic's apartheid policies. The vote was 9–0 with the U.K. and France abstaining. France on October 31 explained that it would prevent sale of arms that might be used for "oppression." The U.K. position, as of late 1963, was that it would not sell arms which could be used for enforcement of apartheid, but that it would continue to license sales of equipment for external defense.

In December, 1963, the Security Council unanimously approved a resolution appealing to all nations to obey its August call for an arms embargo and to extend the embargo to cover "equipment and material" for making and maintaining arms and ammunition.

On March 18, 1963, Defense Minister J. J. Fouche reminded "our friends in the Western world" of the "valuable strategic and scientific support" South Africa provides. This support includes the Simonstown naval facilities, which are available to the U.K. in peace and to the U.K. and its allies in wartime, as well as tracking sites for the U.S. space program and an important station for the U.S. Atlantic Missile Range network.

SPANISH AFRICA

> Size of Armed Forces: 20,000.
> Police and Other Security Forces: Not available.

Spain's armed forces in Africa are conservatively estimated to number at least 20,000, in addition to about 7,000 in the Canary Islands. An estimated 6,000 in crack cadres (including infantry, cavalry, artillery, mechanized units, marines, engineers, and other support units) are currently in the Spanish Sahara; about 700 troops are reported to be at Ifni, the tiny Spanish enclave on the Atlantic coast of Morocco; and garrisons are stationed at Ceuta and Melilla on the Moroccan coast. Precise figures for troops stationed on Fernando Póo and in Río Muni (i.e., Spanish Guinea) are not available.

SUDAN

> Size of Armed Forces: 11,000.
> Police and Other Security Forces: 10,000.
> Approximate Annual Defense Budget: $21.5 million (1963).
> Sources of External Military Assistance: United Kingdom, West Germany, Soviet Union, Yugoslavia, United Arab Republic.
> Defense Agreements With: Arab League Unified Military Command (est. 1964).
> Contribution to U.N. Congo Force: 487.

The Sudan emerged as an independent state with a well-trained and hard-disciplined army of 8,000 (commanded entirely by Sudanese officers since 1956), whose impressive military tradition and *esprit de corps* have continued to be a source of public pride. In November, 1958, the army staged a successful *coup d'état* under the leadership of General Ibrahim Abboud. Since then, executive and legislative authority has been centered in a seven-officer Supreme Council of the Armed Forces chaired by General Abboud.

By 1963, the army had grown to 11,000 men, supported by an estimated yearly budget (1963) of $21.5 million. The officer corps —well paid by Sudanese wage scales—is selected from secondary school graduates by competitive examination; the officers are then trained for two years at the Military College at Omdurman. Although the establishment of a Staff College in the Sudan has been proposed, most senior staff members still receive their advanced training in the United Kingdom. The overwhelming majority of the officers are from the Moslem north. After the 1955 mutiny of southern troops against their northern officers, the tribal pattern of organizing troops was discontinued, and all companies now integrate both northern and southern troops from a broad variety of tribal backgrounds.

The modernization of the military has been undertaken with help from several external sources: the U.K. (scout and armored cars, arms and equipment, aircraft, and training); the U.S.S.R. (six armored cars, a number of troop carriers); Yugoslavia (naval and air training, and patrol boats); and West Germany (vehicles, radios, and training). The Air Force had a minimum of four jet Provost trainers, some piston Provost and Egyptian-built Gomhouria trainers, and two Pembroke light transports in 1963.

SWAZILAND

> *Size of Armed Forces:* None.
> *Police and Other Security Forces:* 370.
> *Source of External Military Assistance:* United Kingdom.

When local police were unable to cope with labor disorders in this British High Commission Territory in June, 1963, a battalion of the U.K. 1st Gordon Highlanders from Kenya and thirty-five police from Bechuanaland were airlifted to Swaziland.

TANGANYIKA

> *Size of Armed Forces:* 2,000.
>
> *Police and Other Security Forces:* 5,000.
>
> *Approximate Annual Defense Budget:* $1.75 million (1963–64).
>
> *Sources of External Military Assistance:* United Kingdom, Israel.
>
> *Defense Agreements With:* None.
>
> *Contribution to U.N. Congo Force:* None.

Asked about his government's military plans and needs, Tanganyika's President Julius Nyerere said during a 1961 press conference in Washington: "We'd rather spend our money on bread." The modest army inherited at independence in 1961 was comprised of two battalions of Tanganyika Rifles (formerly the 6th and 26th King's African Rifles), neither of which had much heavy equipment. Most of the recruits for these two units were once drawn from elsewhere in East Africa, but the force now has a local character.

Tanganyika's proximity to Mozambique, the key role of Dar es Salaam as an operational base for political exiles from other southern African territories, and diminishing prospects for an early East African Federation prompted new concern about the adequacy of Tanganyika's military establishment during 1963. Foreign and Defense Minister Oscar Kambona announced in the National Assembly in June, 1963, that the government was considering the establishment of an air force and an aviation school, as well as some expansion in the size of the army.

By early 1964, there was also increasing political pressure for more rapid Africanization of the officer corps and diversification of sources of military technical assistance. (The first African officers in the Tanganyikan Army were not commissioned until 1961, and all officers above the rank of Captain remained British in mid-1963, though some Tanganyikan officers were receiving special training in Israel.) When the Army's two battalions mutinied in late January, 1964, ousting approximately thirty British officers, President Nyerere hesitated for two days, then called for emergency military assistance from the U.K. to disarm the mutineers and restore government control of strategic installations. Some 500 British Royal Marine commandos were brought by ship and then helicopters from Aden for the task; leading the initial assault was Brigadier Patrick Sholto Douglas, whom the insurgents had deposed as their commanding officer three days earlier. The mutiny in Tanganyika was followed in swift succession by similar, but less widespread, outbreaks in neighboring Uganda and Kenya.

In a radio address to the nation on January 25, President Nyerere announced that those "who drank the poison of mutiny will be severely punished"; he also indicated that the Tanganyika Rifles would be disbanded and a new army organized. Toward this end, he called on members of the Youth Wing of the governing party to register as recruits. On January 27, he dispatched a message to all African heads-of-state, requesting that the Foreign and Defense Ministers of member states of the Organization of African Unity convene as soon as possible in Dar es Salaam to confer on the "critical" situation in East Africa. (See also Uganda and Kenya.)

TOGO

Size of Armed Forces: 250 (but expanding).

Police and Other Security Forces: 280.

Approximate Annual Defense Budget: Not available.

Source of External Military Assistance: France.

Defense Agreements With: France, Union Africaine et Malgache.

Contribution to U.N. Congo Force: None.

The military junta that assassinated President Sylvanus Olympio and seized power in Togo in January, 1963, was tacitly supported by the officer corps of the Togo Army, but its actual leaders were unemployed veterans of the French Army. One of four grievances cited in their manifesto—Olympio's "profound contempt for the military"—reflected the veterans' bitter rejection of the late President's dictum that a country as small and poor as Togo could not afford the luxury of a standing army large enough to absorb some 300 returning veterans. (In 1962, the defense budget was only $500,000.)

Although the civilian government established by the military Insurrectionary Committee was subsequently given legal status through national elections, the military remains a powerful force behind the scenes. All three of the former French Army sergeants who led the *coup d'état* are now in command positions in the expanding National Togolese Army.*

Reversing the policy of militant independence pursued by the predecessor regime, Togo signed a full bilateral defense agreement with France in July, 1963, as well as a new military technical-assistance agreement. The new government also adhered, in 1963, to the Union Africaine et Malgache and the UAM's defense pact. Israeli Army experts have been assisting with the establishment of agricultural projects for Togolese youth.

TUNISIA

> *Size of Armed Forces:* 20,000.
>
> *Police and Other Security Forces:* 4,600.
>
> *Approximate Annual Defense Budget:* $11.4 million (1962).
>
> *Sources of External Military Assistance:* France, United States, Sweden, United Kingdom.
>
> *Defense Agreements With:* None.
>
> *Contribution to U.N. Congo Force:* 3,165.

Created shortly before independence in 1956, the Tunisian Army has grown from 5,000 to 20,000. Key officers were chosen by the governing Neo-Destour Party from among politically reliable elements of the resistance movement, but the bulk of the force was drawn from the French Army, including veterans of World War II and Indochina. France provided most of the initial equipment and training. Under the terms of the 1956 agreement, France was to retain occupancy of the naval base at Bizerte "temporarily"—a vague stipulation that resulted in a major military clash (1,037 Tunisians killed) between French and Tunisian forces in August, 1961, when Tunisia attempted to expel French troops by force. The base was finally evacuated in October, 1963, except for a dozen French advisers. With the deterioration in Franco-Tunisian relations over Bizerte, Tunisia sought to diversify its sources of

* See "Filling the Togo Vacuum," *Africa Report,* February, 1963, p. 7; and "Recent Developments in Togo," *Africa Report,* June, 1963, p. 25.

military aid, looking particularly to the United States as an additional source. A number of Tunisian officers and officer candidates were undergoing special training in the United States in 1963, and the U.S. has also supplied a considerable amount of arms and ammunition.

The nucleus of a Tunisian Air Force—fifteen Saab-91D Safir primary trainers, plus an air training mission—was provided by Sweden in 1960–61. France furnished two helicopters. The navy consisted in 1962 of a corvette and a seaward patrol craft provided by France in 1959.

Tunisia's 3,165-man U.N. detachment withdrew from the Congo during the Bizerte crisis but returned at half-strength later.

Other security forces include 4,600 gendarmes and police; about 100 police have had U.S. training.

UGANDA

> *Size of Armed Forces:* 2,000.
>
> *Police and Other Security Forces:* 5,500.
>
> *Approximate Annual Defense Budget:* $1.5 million (1962–63).
>
> *Sources of External Military Assistance:* United Kingdom, Israel.
>
> *Defense Agreements With:* None.
>
> *Contribution to U.N. Congo Force:* None.

The nucleus of the present Uganda Army was the British-trained 4th King's African Rifles (renamed the Uganda Rifles in October, 1962), which saw action alongside other Commonwealth forces in World War II. Until 1963, the army consisted of a single battalion, and the expenditure for defense in 1962–63 was $1.5 million, or 1.6 per cent of the total recurrent budget for that year. Confronted with a heavy influx of refugees from Rwanda and Southern Sudan, border cattle raids, and disorder among Ruwenzori hillsmen, the government decided in 1963 to add another battalion to the army; indications were that defense expenditures for 1963–64 would total about 5 per cent of the recurrent budget and 7 per cent of the development budget.

In January, 1964, Prime Minister Milton Obote requested an emergency airlift of some 450 British troops stationed in Kenya to assist the government in maintaining law and order in a "confused situation" following a demand by troops stationed at Camp Jinja on Lake Victoria for an increase in pay from 105 shillings ($14.70) to 300 shillings ($42) per month. Reports were mixed as to whether the troops had also demanded the ouster of some 22 British officers and 16 NCO's serving with the Uganda Rifles. Prime Minister Obote blamed the unrest on "misbehavior by a newly recruited company," and said that the loyalty of the army as a whole was not in question. (Africanization of the officer corps began only recently: The first Ugandan did not enter Sandhurst until 1960. Some officer candidates were being trained in Israel in 1963.)

The government of Prime Minister Obote has shown considerable interest in the plans for military cooperation with neighboring Kenya and Tanganyika. John Babiha, national chairman of the governing Uganda People's Congress, said on June 7, 1963: "We need in East Africa one strong land force, one air force, and to build a strong navy in the Indian Ocean along the African coast. . . . Unity is strength." Military coordination is not a function of the East African Common Services Organization, created in 1960.

Despite some evidence of outside machinations by troublemakers in the wave of East African army mutinies, the facts as known in January, 1964, seemed to indicate that the chain reaction that began in Tanganyika shortly after the Zanzibar revolution and then swept through Uganda and Kenya, was set in motion by the existence of common grievances among all the lower ranks of the former King's African Rifles of East Africa.

UNITED ARAB REPUBLIC

Size of Armed Forces: 120,000.

Police and Other Security Forces: 150,000.

Approximate Annual Defense Budget: $212 million (1963).

Sources of External Military Assistance: Soviet Union, United States, United Kingdom.

Defense Agreements With: Arab League Unified Military Command (est. 1964); Arab Collective Security Pact (est. 1950).

Contribution to U.N. Congo Force: 519.

The invasion of Egypt by Israel, France, and Britain in 1956 reinforced President Gamal Abdul Nasser's determination to rebuild his country's defenses. Today, the U.A.R. has one of the largest and best-equipped military forces in Africa and the Middle East. All citizens are subject to military conscription for three years.

Although the Egyptian Army that seized political power from King Farouk in 1952 was entirely British-trained and British-equipped, most of the equipment now used by U.A.R. forces has come from Soviet sources. (The U.A.R. is one of six primary recipients [Syria, Indonesia, Iraq, Cuba, and Afghanistan] of Soviet military credits.) In addition, the U.A.R. has employed a number of West German and other European scientists with the objective of eventually producing jets, submarines, missiles, and other military items locally; a few prototype ground-to-ground missiles had been assembled locally by 1963. Some defensive items, including mine-detectors and antiaircraft control systems, have been purchased from the United States.

As of mid-1963, the U.A.R. Army was said to include 7 infantry brigades and armored units with an estimated 30 Mark III Centurions, 50 Joseph Stalin III's, 250 T-34's, and 40 light French tanks and 350 Soviet-made armored troop carriers. Two infantry divisions and an armored division were reportedly being added to the armed forces in 1963. Air strength was estimated at 3 squadrons of Il-28 and TU-16 Badger jet bombers and reconnaissance craft; 4 transport squadrons of Il-14's and C-47's; 12 squadrons each with 12 MIG-17 and MIG-15 fighter-bombers and some supersonic MIG-21's and MIG-19's; other Soviet and Czech craft; and Egyptian-built Gomhouria trainers. The navy had an estimated 6,200 men, 6 Soviet destroyers, 2 British destroyers, 9 Soviet submarines, 4 British frigates, 6 Soviet ocean mine-sweepers, 2 corvettes, 20 motor torpedo boats, 20 landing craft, and other vessels. About 20,000 U.A.R. troops participated in the revolt against the Royalist regime in Yemen in September, 1962.

Other security forces include a 50,000-man National Guard, as well as more than 100,000 civil policemen, about a dozen of whom have trained in the U.S.

The Chief of Staff of the U.A.R. Army, Lieutenant General Ali Amer, was named head of the Arab Unified Military Command formed in January, 1964, in Cairo by the 13 Arab League members. Egypt was also among the seven signatories (Iraq, Syria, Jordan, Yemen, Lebanon, Saudi Arabia) of the Arab Collective Security Pact of April 13, 1950.

UPPER VOLTA

Size of Armed Forces: 1,000.

Police and Other Security Forces: 1,335.

Approximate Annual Defense Budget: $2.8 million (1963).

Sources of External Military Assistance: France, United States, Israel.

Defense Agreements With: Union Africaine et Malgache.

Contribution to U.N. Congo Force: None.

What is now Upper Volta was a prime source of African manpower for the French Army from the Napoleonic Wars through World War II. There are 200,000 veterans—astounding for a nation of 4 million. Most, if not all, cadres of the Voltaic Army were under African command in late 1963. This military tradition may be one reason that Ouagadougou was selected in 1961 as the seat of the Union Africaine et Malgache Defense Council, which promotes cooperation among the fourteen member states of the UAM in the training of troops, standardization of equipment, and collective security.

Under the terms of a military technical-assistance agreement signed at independence in 1960, France agreed to train and equip a national army for the new republic. In the 1957–61 period, France provided $17.6 million, including costs of maintenance of the French Army, and $25.4 million for administration of veterans' affairs and military pensions. There are no French Army bases in Upper Volta, however, and Upper Volta apparently did not sign a full bilateral defense agreement with France.

In addition to the Army, other security forces in early 1963 included 880 republican guards, 170 municipal guards, and 285 police. Israel has assigned police experts to Upper Volta. The United States has provided limited police training and $114,000 in military equipment for civic action.

ZANZIBAR

Size of Armed Forces: None (as of January, 1964).
Police and Other Security Forces: 800.
Source of External Military Assistance: United Kingdom.
Defense Agreements With: None.
Contribution to U.N. Congo Force: None.

A garrison of the King's African Rifles, sent from Kenya to rein-force Zanzibar's 800-man police force during the June, 1961, election violence and its aftermath, was withdrawn in March, 1963. British troops also helped maintain order during July, 1963, elections. Zanzibar had no armed forces at the time of inde-pendence in December, 1963, and turned down the offer of a defense agreement with Britain.

Before dawn on January 12, 1964, some 600 armed insurgents of diverse political allegiances broke into the police arsenal and government armory, stealing hundreds of automatic rifles and submachine guns. The islands' 800 police offered minimal resist-ance. Within 6 hours, the rebels had captured all strategic build-ings and installations on the island and overthrown the elected government of Prime Minister Mohammed Shamte Hamadi. A request from the ousted Zanzibar Government for the interven-tion of British troops was turned down. Early reports indicated that the rebels included a few Africans trained in Cuba, perhaps including self-styled Field Marshal John Okello. The Okello faction was only one of several involved in the *coup d'état,* how-ever, and the ultimate character of the new Zanzibar army now being created—and the government itself—remained uncertain at this writing. At the urgent request of the new Provisional Govern-ment, about 150 police from Tanganyika arrived to restore order after the January disorders.

2. The Role of French Military Assistance in Africa*

All the former French African colonies except Guinea and Mali have signed technical-assistance agreements with France, and most have also signed defense agreements. The defense agreements are of two sorts, regional and bilateral. Two regional agreements have been signed—between France and the Central African Republic, Congo-Brazzaville, Chad, and Gabon, and between France and Ivory Coast and Niger. France has signed full bilateral defense agreements with Senegal, Gabon, Mauritania, Cameroun (signed in November, 1960, the text remains secret), Togo, and the Malagasy Republic. In both the regional and bilateral defense agreements the provisions are much the same: collaboration on defense problems, mutual provision of military facilities, aid, and assistance.

Collaboration on defense problems involves under each agreement a political and military permanent organization known as Committee of Defense (in bilateral agreements) and Regional Council of Defense (in the multilateral agreements). The permanent secretariats of these organizations usually comprise the French officer commanding forces stationed in the African territory and the higher ranking local African officers. The task of each Committee or Council is to study common problems and prepare plans relating to mutual defense.

One of the key clauses in each of the agreements is that which allows African governments to appeal to French armed forces to assume the "maintenance of the organization of their own armies," even in cases where this involves the defense of the integrity of the African state. In response to such an appeal, France may "intervene directly" in the African state. The agreements

* Reprinted, with permission, from *West Africa* (London), August 24, 1963.

further provide for establishment of French bases and military installations which, after consultation with the Council or Committee of Defense, are found necessary to enable France to fulfill her obligations under the agreements. Most of the agreements include, in the interests of common defense, an article under which the parties agree to follow a common policy with regard to defense materials such as those used in the creation of atomic energy.

Military technical-assistance agreements, less extensive than the defense agreements, have been signed between France and Senegal, Chad, the Malagasy Republic, Central Africa, Congo-Brazzaville, Gabon, Cameroun, Ivory Coast, Dahomey, Niger, Upper Volta, Togo, and Mauritania. These agreements fix the amount of aid which France gives for the organization, equipment, and training of African national armies and police forces. A Bureau of Military Aid organizes this aid in each state.

France also has special agreements with most of its African ex-colonies to deal with the participation of French armed forces in the maintenance of public order. These agreements, which are signed for a limited period with an option to renew, have not been published. It was presumably under such a clause that French troops first intervened in Brazzaville in August, 1963; that French troops were moved toward the Ghana-Togo border in December, 1962; and that French troops were asked to intervene in the quarrel that resulted in the breakdown of the Mali Federation in August, 1960. Although these particular agreements remain secret, they appear to provide for the indigenous government to call upon French troops to intervene in case of a threat to peace and public order. The call may be refused, and must anyway be approved by a decision of the French cabinet.

France's forces in Africa have dwindled considerably in the last two years, partly as a result of African independence and partly because of France's own defense policy which has been reoriented to include nuclear strategy. Nearly 20,000 Africans serving with French forces in Africa have returned to take service in African national armies; 283,000 men left Africa (including Algeria) between January 1, 1962, and January 1, 1963, while a further reduction of 82,000 is envisaged by the end of 1963. French forces stationed in black Africa numbered about 20,000 in August, 1963.

French military installations have also been cut. Strategic bases are at Mers-el-Kebir in Algeria, in Dakar, and in the Malagasy Republic. Other major bases are at Fort Lamy (Chad), Pointe-Noire (Congo-Brazzaville), Douala (Cameroun), and Port Etienne (Mauritania). French policy has in fact been to withdraw from Africa; and to build up, within France, a force capable of intervening at short notice abroad.

Military agreements in French-speaking Africa take two forms: those concluded bilaterally or multilaterally with France and those concluded between African states themselves. Although the Casablanca Group in fact made provision for common defense, and went so far as to set up a permanent organization with headquarters in the U.A.R., since the Addis meeting the defense pact between the UAM states is the chief formal agreement which remains.

The defense pact of the UAM (UAMD) was signed in September, 1961. Its preamble defines its spirit as an attempt to organize strictly defensive action in conformity with the principles of the United Nations Charter and to maintain peace and security in UAM member states. If one state is threatened the others agree to go to its defense. The pact does not have a common army nor a common command and no member state appears to want this; nor does it invalidate the separate or regional defense agreements which all members have with France.

CHART 2. U.S. MILITARY GRANT AID TO AFRICA, IN DOLLARS

Country	Fiscal year 1962	Cumulative, 1950–63
Algeria	—	—
Cameroun	284,000	321,000
Central African Republic	—	—
Chad	—	—
Congo-Brazzaville	—	—
Congo-Leopoldville	—	3,378,000
Dahomey	104,000	122,000
Ethiopia	11,734,000	73,799,000
Gabon	—	—
Ghana	—	207,000
Guinea	—	—
Ivory Coast	120,000	218,000
Kenya	—	—
Liberia	1,803,000	4,635,000
Libya	721,000	7,168,000
Malagasy Republic	—	—
Mali	243,000	2,272,000
Morocco	n.a.[a]	n.a.[a]
Niger	104,000	114,000
Nigeria	—	329,000
Rhodesia-Nyasaland	—	—
Senegal	2,476,000	2,901,000
Sierra Leone	—	—
Somali Republic	—	—
Sudan	—	—
Tanganyika	—	—
Togo	—	—
Tunisia	n.a.[a]	n.a.[a]
Uganda	—	—
Upper Volta	108,000	114,000
Zanzibar	—	—
Africa area[a]	16,759,000	42,660,000
Total	*34,365,000*	*138,238,000*

[a] "Africa area" aid includes expenditures for regional programs and the undisclosed totals for Tunisia and Morocco.

NOTE: Africa's share of over-all U.S. military aid abroad is very modest. The amount earmarked for Africa during fiscal year 1964—$24,511,000—represented only 2 per cent of projected over-all U.S. military assistance for that year. As in previous years, Ethiopia, site of a key U.S. communications station, receives almost half of the African total. Other sizable percentages go to Libya and Morocco. The remainder is divided among the other African countries, with $9.5 million going to tropical Africa.

SOURCE: Derived from a report on Proposed Mutual Development Assistance Programs for 1964, presented to the U.S. Congress on April 29, 1963, by David E. Bell, Administrator of the Agency for International Development.

PART THREE

The Organization of African Unity

CHART 3. THE SEARCH FOR AFRICAN UNITY: SOME MILESTONES SINCE 1945

All-African / Sub-Groupings	1945	1953	1958	1959	1960	1961	1962	1963
Pan-African Congress	The Fifth Pan-African Congress, Manchester, Oct. 13–21 (organized by W. E. B. DuBois)	The Sixth Pan-African Congress, Kumasi (Gold Coast) Dec. 4–6						
Conference of Independent African States			at Accra, April 15–22, attended by eight states		at Addis Ababa June 15–24, attended by 13 states			Founding Conference of the Organization of African Unity held at Addis Ababa, May 22–26
All-African Peoples' Conference			at Accra, Dec. 5–13		at Tunis, Jan. 25–31	at Cairo, March 23–31		
Pan-African Freedom Movement for East, Central, and Southern Africa (PAFMECSA)			at Mwanza (Tanganyika), Sept. 16–18	at Moshi (Tanganyika), September	at Mbale (Uganda), Oct. 25–27		at Addis Ababa, Feb. 1–9 — at Leopoldville, Dec. 28–31	Formal dissolution pending; most of its functions taken over by the Committee of Liberation of the OAU

Organization							
Union Africaine et Malgache (UAM) (Heads-of-State)	at Abidjan, Oct. 24–26	at Brazzaville, Dec. 15–19	at Yaoundé, March 26–28	at Tananarive, Sept. 7–12	at Bangui, March 25–27	at Libreville, Sept. 12–14	at Ouagadougou March 10–14; at Cotonou July 27–30
Casablanca Group (Heads-of-State)	at Casablanca, Jan. 4–7	at Cairo, June 15–18	Absorbed into the Organization of African Unity				
Ghana-Guinea-Mali Union of African States (UAS) (Heads-of-State)	at Accra, April 27–29	Dissolution announced by Guinea President Sékou Touré June 2, 1963					
Inter-African and Malagasy States Organization (IAMO) (Heads-of-State)	at Monrovia, May 8–12	at Lagos, Jan. 25–30	Absorbed into the Organization of African Unity				

SOURCE: Compiled by John Marcum.

1. The Achievements of the Addis Ababa Conference

As Seen by 18 Observers or Participants in Africa, Europe, Asia, and the United States

DAR ES SALAAM

Let us say this to those enemies—to those enemies of Africa who will want to belittle the significance of this conference by saying that it did not achieve very much. I think we ought to send this challenge: if, when the nations of the world reassemble at the United Nations, they approach the problems of the world in the same spirit of good will and cooperation as the nations of Africa assembled here have approached their African problems, then the human race, like the African people, shall have taken an immense step toward universal brotherhood.

> —*Tanganyika's President Julius Nyerere, concluding his speech to the Addis Conference, May 25, 1963.*

PARIS

The Addis Ababa Conference did not abolish frontiers between languages because the delegates were given earphones for simultaneous translation, nor between Arabic and Bantu cultural groups because President Nasser received a warm ovation, nor between the revolutionaries and the moderates because the Casablanca and Monrovia groups were the founders of the common organization created by the charter. But each of these barriers was shaken and was revealed to be more artificial than had been thought. As Mr. Senghor said, one must still speak of Africas; but the fragments are no longer so widely scattered. . . .

In any case, it has become apparent that Africa has ceased to want to go it alone, to be simply "against." In coming together in this way, it has delivered itself of its *fièvre obsidionale,* of its negative obsessions, of its haunting fear of . . . being once again the victim of aggression and domination. In getting rid of the complexes deriving from division and weakness, it ceases to harangue its case and begins to engage instead in a dialogue and a positive effort.

—*Jean Lacouture, writing in* Le Monde, *June 3, 1963.*

LAGOS

. . . Although some feel that disarmament can never be achieved, still others feel that it is most important that the Powers continue to talk about it; because the more they talk about it, the less danger there will be of an open clash. I am glad that they have seen fit to invite some of the African countries to participate in their disarmament talks. . . . If there is a war now, there would be nothing—everything would go. . . . The mere fact that Africa has been declared a nuclear-free zone will not make Africa free in the event of a world war. If there is a war, we in Africa will be directly involved. . . . Some people have suggested that we should organize ourselves into a defense bloc . . . that we should embark on an arms race in Africa. All of us know very well that we are at present incapable of joining in such a race. . . . We should not be talking about an arms race. All we should talk about, sir, is how to stop it.

—*From an address by Nigerian Prime Minister Tafawa Balewa, May 28, 1963.*

DAKAR

The Addis Ababa Conference was a success because it was the first time independent African heads of state met to institute international bodies. Clashes between Arabs and Africans and between French- and English-speaking Africans were expected, but there was confrontation and we came to agreement. There was no disagreement between reformists and revolutionists; we transcended such disagreement. We consolidated what united us and excluded what divided us. This is a step forward toward African unity. . . .

My idea of African unity is similar to General de Gaulle's

about Europe. Africa should be made up of countries because we are too different from one another, as much in race as in culture and language. . . . At no time did we renounce cooperation with Europe and Asia or with France. We did not envisage the disappearance of the Union Africaine et Malgache, which is a regional grouping.

—Senegal's President Léopold Senghor, in a press conference in Paris, May 30, 1963.

ACCRA

The new all-African charter is a product of compromise, with the advocates of radical African nationalism setting the pace. In addition to the points that are common ground between the various African blocs, it pushes forward to embrace many points contained in the 1958 Accra conference decisions and in the subsequent decisions of the Casablanca group and the All-African People's Conference.

These points, which are a total departure from the Monrovia point of view, should be carefully enumerated. They are: (1) the principle of nonalignment with any power bloc—article 3, section 7; (2) coordination of policies in the fields of culture, economy, defence, foreign affairs, and diplomacy—article 2, section 2; (3) determination to fight neo-colonialism in all its forms —preamble 6; (4) active and armed support for the struggle of dependent African territories against colonialism and apartheid —article 2, section 1-d; (5) the end of foreign military bases in Africa and the withdrawal of African states from military pacts with foreign powers; (6) settlement of disputes between African states by direct talks or mediation—article 3, section 4; (7) the setting up of a permanent machinery made up of an assembly of heads of state and government, a council of foreign ministers, a secretariat, and specialized commissions dealing with economy, culture, health, research, and defence—articles 7 and 20.

Thus analyzed, the Addis Ababa summit was a positive victory for the forces of radical African nationalism. It is a significant advance for the African revolution. It is, however, not a total victory, for the great goal of an African union government still belongs to the future. But there can be no gainsaying the fact that the Addis Ababa summit has laid a firm foundation for a future takeoff into the realms of a single government for a "united states of Africa."

—From a broadcast over Radio Ghana, May 28, 1963.

BAMAKO

The people of Mali and the Union Soudanaise are firmly united in their desire for achievement of African unity. Thus in January 1961 the US–RDA delegated us to represent the party in Casablanca, where the Casablanca Charter was created. A few months later we formed the Union of African States with Ghana and Guinea. There is no need to dwell on and discuss these two organizations, but we should recognize their contribution to the increased awareness of Africans, because within a few months the Union Africaine et Malgache (UAM) was created and later the so-called Lagos group.

Africa was thus divided into a revolutionary Africa—the Casablanca charter group—and a moderate Africa—the Lagos charter group. Little by little, Africa was crystallizing into two blocs. . . . Certain newspapers treated the Casablanca group states as being adherents to the socialism camp, while the states of the Lagos charter appeared as brothers of the Western camp. . . .

The discreet attempts of the officials of Mali to achieve our objective—the meeting of the two blocs in order to constitute a single group and consequently to liquidate the two groups— were crowned with success in the meeting . . . of the African heads of state in Addis Ababa. . . .

There was considerable discussion at Addis Ababa of the abolition of the various groups formed in Africa. The conference discussed the idea of regrouping the African states on an economic basis. This is because we have all realized that individually our countries cannot fulfill the conditions of a truly modern economy and of a truly modern development policy. . . . You already know that the press has often suggested a regrouping of Mauritania, Senegal, Guinea, and Mali. Among other suggestions made was that of regrouping Ivory Coast, Upper Volta, Mali, Niger, and Dahomey.

—From President Modibo Keita's report
to the people of Mali, June 1, 1963.

LONDON

The lesson is a simple one. There is no longer any hesitation on the part of any African State in denouncing the South African and Southern Rhodesian regimes, and Portuguese rule. A leader as conservative as the Emperor Haile Selassie, as closely linked with the West as President Tubman, as insular as the King of Libya, is here no less emphatic than President Nkrumah or Dr. Nyerere. Even those French-speaking leaders who formerly seemed indifferent to such matters now feel as strongly on them as anybody else. It is no longer possible to divide Africa theoretically into "moderate" and "militant" States—as the extinction of the Monrovia and Casablanca Groups shows. On affairs which are the special concern of the British Government all Africa is united —and often against British policies.

> —*From the weekly,* West Africa, *May 25, 1963.*

What has emerged from Addis Ababa falls far short of Ghana's concept of a Union Government of Africa. In the modesty of the achievement, however, lies its potential strength. It quickly became clear that, in the words of Sir Abubakar Tafawa Balewa, the Prime Minister of Nigeria, "only a very small minority" wanted political unity. A decision in these circumstances to surrender substantial powers to a central authority would have been merely an empty gesture.

Was the conference, therefore, a defeat for President Nkrumah of Ghana? In the sense that the Addis Ababa charter is much nearer to that of the Lagos or Monrovia group of African powers than to the Casablanca group, it could certainly be depicted in that light. However, Dr. Nkrumah showed a realization from the beginning that if he insisted on all his points he would end in isolation and he accordingly came in a spirit of compromise. He proclaimed that unity was essential but indicated that he would be satisfied with a declaration of the principle of unity.

> —*An assessment of Conference results,*
> the Times, *May 27, 1963.*

Even though the language of violence is . . . used against Portugal, what in fact is being built up is a deterrent, since the hope still is that the United States and Britain will pull the rug from under Dr. Salazar. . . . Most notably at Addis, there was carrot as well as stick for the West. The resolutions did not in any way let up on anti-colonialism—one of them, especially directed at the United States, "informs the allies of colonial powers that they must choose between their friendship for the African peoples and their support of Powers that oppress African peoples." Yet one only has to contrast their language and tone with that of the resolutions carried at the Moshi Conference of the Afro-Asian Solidarity Movement last February to notice the great gulf that, for the time being, separates the independent African states from the international Communist line.

—Keith Kyle for Forum Service, *June 15, 1963.*

ADDIS ABABA

Our independence cannot be complete as long as a single African country is dependent. Rhodesia, Angola, South Africa, Mozambique, and other African countries are shouting for our full assistance in their struggle for independence. Their demand should never be ignored. Would it not be a betrayal and a mouthing of empty words if we simply watch the blood streaming like water without joining our brothers in action? We must say: Struggle hard; never be disheartened; all of Africa is with you. We must act as their advocates. Not only that, we must also remember that if we just said this, causing them to shed their blood without sacrificing ours with them, it would be shameful and regrettable. . . .

Steps toward African common defence are essential, and we should cooperate. It must be our duty to defend Africa against outside invasion. If Africa is to be able to resist outside aggression, the existence of some sort of defence organization is essential. It is our duty to preserve our independence by defending it against both the West and the East. . . .

—From Emperor Haile Selassie's address
to the Conference, May 23, 1963.

UNITED NATIONS

The African members of the United Nations served notice during the first week of June that they were about to take their fight

against Portugal's colonial rule and South Africa's race-segrega-
tion policies into the Security Council. . . . At first glance it seems
strange that they are turning to the Security Council, where their
voting strength is much less than in the Assembly and they have
no chance of getting the seven votes required for any kind of
sanctions resolution.

One reason for the selection of the Council is the fact that the
African members do not want to delay a public hearing of their
charges until September, when the Assembly will open its 18th
session.

The timing of the appeals to the Security Council has been influenced by the fact that, under the Council's system of rotating
the presidency according to alphabetical order, Africans will
be in the chair—Ghana is president for June and Morocco for
July. The president has considerable influence over Council pro-
ceedings.

But the basic aim, as indicated last week by Alex Quaison-
Sackey of Ghana, is to put pressure on the United States and
Britain to side with the African members. . . . The United States
and British representatives in the Council will be more in the spot-
light—and more on the spot—than they would be in the Assembly
with its membership of 111.

—*Thomas J. Hamilton, writing in the*
New York Times, *June 9, 1963.*

LEOPOLDVILLE

Situated at the heart of Africa, with 10 inter-African frontiers, the
Congo has never lost sight of the duties which are imposed on it
by its location. Neither can the Congo forget that it is the pivot
between the English-speaking countries and those of French expression.

Moreover, the line of demarcation between free Africa and the
Africa still under colonial domination passes today along its frontiers. This historical fact adds to our responsibilities. We have always been conscious of their importance. Despite the difficult
hours we have traversed, we never have failed in our duty. We
always have answered "present" at all the African *rendezvous,* and

this without exception. Our anxiety to preserve the possibilities of African unity even have led us to deprive ourselves of advantages which adhesion to a specific bloc might have brought us. . . .

We intend to take an active part in this confrontation, and to bring to it a contribution in proportion with the importance and the reality of the Congo of 1963 which—I would like to stress—is not the Congo of 1960.

—From Congo Prime Minister Cyrille Adoula's
comments at the Addis Conference, May 20, 1963.

ALGIERS

Ben Bella's impact on the African scene should not be overlooked. At one closed session, the Algerian leader turned on one of his colleagues who wished to keep his role in supplying and moving arms to rebel forces secret. Ben Bella had been arguing that everybody should openly state their collaboration with the liberation movements and he said with great emotion: "I have not come here because of any special interest in African charters. My primary aim is to help liberate those parts of Africa not yet liberated. If this conference doesn't share my concern I will refuse to be a signatory to any charter." He won his point. There is no reason to suppose that his influence will grow less in the days ahead.

—Colin Legum, writing in the Observer,
London, June 2, 1963.

CAIRO

The mere convocation of this conference manifests the presence of a free, joint African will. We did not come here by accident or without effort. We have come by different ways and only after great efforts which were finally able to attain realization because they sprang from an overpowering, irresistible desire for unity from which others could not bar us.

This is accentuated by the fact that all the groupings or organizations which were set up in the past to handle phases of African action have realized that the time has come when they must unreservedly join hands so that their entente may engender the free, joint will of Africa. It is also demonstrated by the fact that the traditional picture of Africa—an Africa dissected by colonialism into northern, southern, western, or eastern Africa, or into French-speaking and English-speaking Africa—has been replaced by the true picture of Africa—an Africa that speaks the common language of a common fate, although the ways of expression may differ. . . .

This does not mean that Africa should be turned into an international bloc. . . . Let there be an African league, or an all-African charter, or periodical meetings of African heads of state or representatives, or anything. One thing the U.A.R. does not want: To go out from here with just enthusiastic words or formal, ineffective façades and formations. That way we would be fooling no one but ourselves. Let us begin coordinating African cooperation toward an African common market; let us draw up projects for scientific and cultural cooperation; and let us set a deadline for the liquidation of colonialism. . . .

Dear friends, the UAR came here with an open heart and an open mind. It is ready to carry out to the furthest extent its historical responsibilities toward the African continent. We have come here without any selfish intention of discussing the problem which we consider to be our gravest problem—the problem of Israel, which the Casablanca powers have rightly realized was one of the tools of imperialist infiltration into Africa and one of its bases of aggression. We will not propose this problem for discussion in this conference, in the belief that the progress of free African action will, by experience, reveal the truth day by day and lay bare any false images of it before the African conscience.

—*From U.A.R. President Gamal Abdul Nasser's address to the Conference, May 24, 1963.*

TEL AVIV

Whether or not the "white" Arab countries of North Africa should form an integral part of a united Africa is one of the questions uppermost in the minds of several of the African statesmen attending the conference. There are those who say that, while Egypt is part of the African continent from the strictly geographical point of view, she has, in fact, no real affinity with the Africans south of the Sahara; neither cultural affinity, nor common political heritage, nor any possible share in the concept of negritude propounded by President Senghor of Senegal. Those advocating this viewpoint claim that the Sahara Desert is a much more effective boundary to "black"Africa than the shores of the Mediterranean, and that the Arabs of North Africa rightfully form part of the Mediterranean basin and not of Africa.

There can be no doubt that this thesis contains a great deal of truth. But, from a political point of view, the proposition is false. Egypt is an integral part of Africa, and Nasser was right when he wrote in his *Philosophy of the Revolution:* "Can we ignore that there is a continent of Africa in which fate has placed us and which is destined today to witness a terrible struggle over its future? This struggle will affect us, whether we want it or not." For Egypt, above all, is the Nile—and the Nile has the whole of Africa behind it. . . .

In future, therefore, we can expect an increased Egyptian presence in Africa—and the Addis Ababa Conference will make these increased activities all the easier. For the lowering of the barriers between the Casablanca and Monrovia groups means that Egypt will now have access to countries which were hitherto barred to her. . . .

In view of this tremendous importance of Africa for Egypt, Israel's success in gaining such firm African friends and in preventing Egypt's bid to bar her from the continent is all the greater. If, as we presume, Egypt fails to push through an anti-Israel resolution at Addis Ababa, it will be a deserved victory for the Israelis —and clear proof that their travail has not been in vain.

> —*From an editorial in the* Jewish Observer and
> Middle East Review, *May 24, 1963.*

MOGADISCIO

We Somalis know what problems are facing us. We know of the bitterness we feel at the splitting of our land and its present situation. We wanted to speak about this at the conference, although other states did not like this and regarded it as something likely to harm the atmosphere and spirit of the conference. However, we spoke up and had the courage to do so.

I think that because of what we said there—perhaps our words were the cause—the charter recommended the establishment of a committee to deal with disputes among states. It will be one of many committees which will be set up. We have prayed to God that He may help and stand by those who signed this charter so that they may succeed. . . .

The man who is the Emperor of Ethiopia [and I] talked together and had two meetings. We met once before my speech, and we had another meeting to discuss matters after my speech, only two evenings ago. We talked for quite a while, and he told me: "Tell the Somali nation that we shall agree to settle whatever matters exist between us. We shall negotiate. However, our relationships should be normal so that we may be able to talk in a friendly atmosphere." Therefore, as you can see, we will negotiate.

—From President Aden Abdullah Osman's speech
on his return to Mogadiscio, May 28, 1963.

MOSCOW

It is true that the colonial circles and their agents worked hard to obstruct the conference. Before it started, the Western press and news agencies stubbornly forecast inevitable failure of the summit meeting. . . . During the conference the colonialist press literally applauded any remark directed, in one way or another, against the creation of an effective instrument of all-African unity, any call for "no hurry" in working out practical recommendations, and any attempt to sow the seeds of discord among the African countries. . . . But it is results that matter, and results of the conference show with ample clarity that proper foundations have been laid in Addis Ababa for the unity of emerging Africa. The heads of the independent African nations have worked out documents of major importance.

—From a broadcast over Radio Moscow, May 27, 1963.

PEKING

A burning anti-imperialist, anti-colonialist atmosphere dominated the conference throughout. Whoever took a firm stand against im-

perialism and colonialism in his speech was warmly received. That was why Algerian Premier Ben Bella received the warmest applause when he said that his government would resolutely support the national liberation movement with volunteers and arms.
. . .

During the conference, correspondents were very much impressed by the profound friendship between the Chinese and African peoples. Premier Chou En-lai's message of greetings drew enthusiastic applause. Many African delegations took the initiative to contact and chat with [Chinese] correspondents. Some delegations from countries which still do not have diplomatic relations with China expressed the hope that the Chinese correspondents would visit their countries.

—From an article in the People's Daily, *June 3, 1963.*

WASHINGTON, D.C.

In creating the Organization of African Unity, Africa's leaders have demonstrated a political maturity of the highest order. It is an answer most convincing to those who tend to regard the nations of Africa as less politically mature, less possessed of the experience necessary to effective international cooperation than the more sophisticated developed countries who too seek political, economic, and social progress through one form of unity or another.

Those who gathered at Addis Ababa were able to set aside the dramatic rhetoric which creates headlines, but often little else, to reject the use of the conference as a platform from which to advance special interests in favor of addressing themselves to the needs and interests of all of the peoples of Africa. They have declined to place emphasis on oratory as an instrument to influence other peoples of the world and instead demonstrated an understanding of the problems of others.

They have pledged their allegiance to certain basic principles but publicly acknowledged their own failure always to live up to these principles. They have rededicated themselves to helping in the achievement of independence for all who would be independent, but have recognized that independence is no end in itself; that without economic and social development there can be no lasting political independence and that this independence will only be achieved through joint action and mutual cooperation of a kind that accepts a self-responsibility for its achievement.

All of this is reflected in the charter signed at Addis Ababa. . . . It is an example of truly independent action, formulated independently of the influence of this nation—or any non-African nation—and subscribed to without promise of aid or assistance except that which the signees have pledged toward their common cause. It reflects Africa's determination to rally its own resources behind its own efforts.

—Congressman Barratt O'Hara of Illinois, Chairman of the
Subcommittee on Africa of the Foreign Affairs Committee,
recorded in the U.S. House of Representatives,
May 29, 1963.

2. The Conference Resolutions

(Final Version, Dated May 25, 1963)

I. DECOLONIZATION

The Summit Conference of Independent African States meeting in Addis Ababa, Ethiopia, from May 22 to May 25, 1963; *having considered* all aspects of the questions of decolonization; *unanimously convinced* of the imperious and urgent necessity of coordinating and intensifying their efforts to accelerate the unconditional attainment of national independence by all African territories still under foreign domination; *reaffirming* that it is the duty of all African independent states to support dependent people in Africa in their struggle for freedom and independence; *noting* with deep concern that most of the remaining dependent territories in Africa are dominated by foreign settlers; *convinced* that the colonial powers by their forcible imposition of the settlers to control the governments and administration of those territories are thus establishing colonial bases in the heart of Africa; *have agreed* unanimously to concert and coordinate their efforts and action in this field, and to this end have decided on the following measures:

(1) *Declares* that the forcible imposition by the colonial powers of the settlers to control the governments and administration of the dependent territories is a flagrant violation of the inalienable rights of the legitimate inhabitants of the territories concerned;

(2) *Invites* the colonial powers to take the necessary measures for the immediate application of the declaration on the granting of independence to colonial countries and peoples by insisting on the fact that their determination to maintain colonies or semi-colonies in Africa constitutes a menace to the peace of the continent;

(3) *Invites* further the colonial powers, particularly the United Kingdom with regard to Southern Rhodesia, not to transfer the powers and attributes of sovereignty to foreign minority governments imposed on African peoples by the use of force and under cover of racial legislation. A transfer of this kind would amount to a violation of the provisions of United Nations resolution 1514 on independence;

(4) *Reaffirms* its support of African nationalists of Southern Rhodesia and solemnly declares that if power in Southern Rhodesia were to be usurped by a racial white minority government, the states members of the Conference would lend their effective moral and practical support to any legitimate measures which the African nationalist leaders may devise for the purpose of recovering such power and restoring it to the African majority. The Conference undertakes henceforth to concert the efforts of its members to take such measures as the situation demands against any state according to such recognition;

(5) *Reaffirms* that the territory of South West Africa is an African territory under international mandate and that any attempt by the Republic of South Africa to annex it would be regarded as an act of aggression; *Reaffirms* also its determination to render all necessary support to the second phase of the South West Africa case before the International Court of Justice; *Reaffirms*, further, the inalienable right of the people of South West Africa to self-determination and independence;

(6) *Intervenes* expressly with the great powers so that they cease without exception to lend directly or indirectly any support or assistance to all those colonialist governments which might use such assistance to suppress African national liberation movements, particularly the Portuguese Government, which is conducting a real war of genocide in Africa. *Informs* the allies of colonial powers that they must choose between their friendship for the African peoples and their support of powers that oppress African peoples;

(7) *Sends* a delegation of Ministers of Foreign Affairs to speak on behalf of all African states at the meeting of the Security Council which will be called to examine the report of the United

Nations Committee of 26 on the situation in African territories under Portuguese domination;

(8) *Demands* the breaking off of diplomatic and consular relations between all African states and the Governments of Portugal and South Africa so long as they persist in their present attitude towards decolonization;

(9) *Asks for an effective boycott* of the foreign trade of Portugal and South Africa by (a) prohibiting the import of goods from those two countries; (b) closing African ports and airports to their ships and planes; (c) forbidding the planes of those two countries to overfly the territories of all African states;

(10) *Earnestly invites* all national liberation movements to coordinate their efforts by establishing common action fronts wherever necessary so as to strengthen the effectiveness of their struggle and the rational use of the concerted assistance given them;

(11) *Establishes* a coordinating committee consisting of Ethiopia, Algeria, Uganda, U.A.R., Tanganyika, Congo-Leopoldville, Guinea, Senegal, and Nigeria, with headquarters in Dar es Salaam, responsible for harmonizing the assistance from African states and for managing the special fund to be set up for that purpose;

(12) *Establishes* a special fund to be contributed by member states with the deadline (July 15) to supply the necessary practical and financial aid to the various African national liberation movements;

(13) *Appoints* the day of May 25, 1963, as African Liberation Day and organizes popular demonstrations on that day to disseminate the recommendations of the Heads of State Conference and to collect sums, over and above the national contributions, for the special fund;

(14) *Receives,* on the territories of independent African states, nationalists from liberation movements in order to give them training in all sectors, and afford young people all the assistance they need for their education and vocational training;

(15) *Promotes,* in each state, the establishment of a body of volunteers in various fields, with a view to providing the various

African national liberation movements with the assistance they need in the various sectors;

(16) *Fixes* a deadline for the accession of all African territories to independence.

II.   APARTHEID AND RACIAL DISCRIMINATION

The Summit Conference of Independent African States, *having considered* all aspects of the questions of apartheid and racial discrimination; *unanimously convinced* of the imperious and urgent necessity of coordinating and intensifying their efforts to put an end to the South African Government's criminal policy of apartheid and wipe out racial discrimination in all its forms; *have agreed* unanimously to concert and coordinate their efforts and action in this field, and to this end have decided on the following measures:

(1) Creation of a fund for concerted financial assistance to the anti-apartheid movement in South Africa.

(2) Effective assistance of every kind to anti-apartheid movements in South Africa to help them carry out their struggle for freedom efficiently.

(3) The immediate release of Mr. Mandela, Sobukwe, and all other political prisoners in South Africa.

(4) Granting of scholarships, educational facilities, and possibilities of employment in African government service to refugees from South Africa.

(5) Supporting the recommendations presented to the Security Council and the General Assembly by the Special Committee of the United Nations on the apartheid policies of the South African Government.

(6) Dispatch of a delegation of Foreign Ministers to inform the Security Council of the explosive situation existing in South Africa.

(7) Coordination of concrete measures of sanction against the Government of South Africa.

(8) Appeal to all states, and more particularly to those which have traditional relations and cooperate with the Government of South Africa, strictly to apply U.N. resolution 1761 of November 6, 1962, concerning apartheid.

(9) Appeal to all governments who still have diplomatic, consular, and economic relations with the Government of South Africa to break off those relations and to cease any other form of encouragement for the policy of apartheid.

(10) Stress the great responsibility incurred by the colonial authorities of territories neighboring on South Africa for the pursuit of the policy of apartheid.

(11) Condemnation of racial discrimination in all its forms in Africa and all over the world.

(12) Expression of the deep concern aroused in all African peoples and governments by the measures of racial discrimination taken against communities of African origin living outside the continent and particularly in the United States of America. Expression of appreciation for the efforts of the Federal Government of the United States of America to put an end to these intolerable malpractices which are likely seriously to deteriorate relations between the African peoples and governments on the one hand and the people and government of the United States of America on the other.

III. Africa, Non-Alignment, and the United Nations

The Summit Conference, *believing* that the United Nations is an important instrument for the maintenance of peace and security among nations and for the promotion of the economic and social advancement of all peoples; *reiterating* its desire to strengthen and support the United Nations; *noting* with regret that Africa as a region is not equitably represented in the principal organs of the United Nations; *convinced* of the need for closer cooperation and coordination among the African states members of the United Nations:

(1) *Reaffirms* its dedication to the purposes and principles of the United Nations Charter, and its acceptance of all obligations contained in the Charter, including financial obligations;

(2) *Insists* that Africa as a geographical region should have equitable representation in the principal organs of the United Nations, particularly the Security Council and the Economic and Social Council and its Specialized Agencies;

(3) *Invites* African governments to instruct their representatives in the United Nations to take all possible steps to achieve a more equitable representation of the African region;

(4) *Further invites* African governments to instruct their representatives in the United Nations, without prejudice to their membership in and collaboration with the African-Asian Group, to constitute a more effective African Group to bring about closer cooperation and better coordination in matters of common concern.

IV. GENERAL DISARMAMENT

The Summit Conference, *having considered* all aspects of the questions of general disarmament; *unanimously convinced* of the imperious and urgent necessity of coordinating and intensifying their efforts to contribute to the achievement of a realistic disarmament program through the signing, by all states concerned, of a Treaty on general and complete disarmament under strict and effective international control; *have agreed* unanimously to concert and coordinate their efforts and action in these various fields, and to this end have decided on the following measures:

(1) To declare and accept Africa as a denuclearized zone, the banning of nuclear and thermonuclear tests; the peaceful use of nuclear energy and the banning of the manufacture of nuclear weapons.

(2) The destruction of existing nuclear weapons.

(3) The removal of military bases from Africa and disentanglement of African countries from military pacts with foreign powers.

(4) To appeal to the great powers to: (a) reduce conventional weapons; (b) put an end to the arms race; and (c) sign a general and complete disarmament agreement under strict and effective international control.

(5) To appeal to the great powers, in particular to the Soviet Union and the United States of America, to use their best endeavors to secure the objectives stated above.

(6) To undertake to bring about by means of negotiation the end of military occupation in the African continent, the elimina-

tion of military bases and nuclear tests which constitute an essential element of African independence and unity.

V. ECONOMIC PROBLEMS

The Summit Conference, *concerned* with the active share of the developing countries in world trade and at the persistent deterioration of the terms of trade in these external commercial relationships; *conscious* of the fact that owing to its extreme dependence on the export of primary products, Africa and Madagascar more than any other developing region are adversely affected by persistent deteriorations in export earnings; *convinced* of the necessity for concerted action by the African countries and Madagascar in order to ensure a much more remunerative price from the sale of their primary products; *mindful* of the need to eliminate the barriers to trade between the African states and thereby to strengthen their economies; *considering* that economic development, including the expansion of trade on the basis of fair and remunerative prices, should tend to eliminate the need for external economic aid, and that such external economic aid should be unconditional and should not prejudice the independence of African states; *considering* the imperative necessity for African countries to pool their resources and harmonize their activities in the economic field; *aware* of the necessity for the joint utilization of river basin resources, the study of the use of Saharan zones, the coordination of means of transport and communication systems, and the provision of research facilities, all of which serve to stimulate economic growth and expansion of trade, both regionally and inter-regionally; *convinced* that the acceleration of the rate of economic and social development of the various African countries lies in the industrialization of these countries and the diversification of their production; *considering* the serious problems arising from the great shortage of trained and skilled personnel, the lack of qualified staff, scarce capital resources, grossly inadequate infrastructure, limited outlets for industrial products and the far too inadequate participation of Africans in the economic construction of their countries; *desiring* to explore the effects of regional economic groupings of the

African economy; *noting* with satisfaction that the Executive Secretary of the Economic Commission for Africa has decided to convene a Conference of African Ministers of Finance, to be held in Khartoum (Sudan) in July, 1963, with a view to setting up an African Development Bank; *resolves to:*

(1) Appoint a preparatory economic committee to study, in collaboration with governments and in consultation with the Economic Commission for Africa, *inter alia,* the following questions and submit their findings to member states: (a) the possibility of establishing a free trade area between the various African countries; (b) the establishment of a common external tariff to protect the emergent industries and the setting up of a raw material price stabilization fund; (c) the restructuralization of international trade; (d) means for developing trade between African countries by the organization of and participation in African trade fairs and exhibitions and by the granting of transport and transit facilities; (e) the coordination of means of transport and the establishment of road, air, and maritime companies; (f) the establishment of an African Payments and Clearing Union; (g) a progressive freeing of national currencies from all non-technical external attachments and the establishment of a Pan-African monetary zone; (h) ways and means of effecting the harmonization of existing and future national development plans;

(2) Invite the Economic Commission for Africa to request their Executive Secretary to give the Commission of Experts all the necessary support and assistance which it may require in the fulfillment of its assignment;

(3) Welcome the forthcoming Conference of African Ministers of Finance and give the respective Ministers of Finance instructions to take the necessary measures for the rapid establishment of the African Development Bank;

(4) The Summit Conference of Independent African States note with satisfaction the progress achieved by the Economic Commission for Africa in establishing the Dakar Institute of Economic Development and Planning and affirm their profound interest in that Institute and their intention of giving it appropriate financial and other support;

(5) Welcome the forthcoming World Conference on Trade and Development which is to examine international trade problems in relation to the economic development of emerging countries;

(6) *Urge* all states concerned to conduct negotiations, in concert, with a view to obtaining from the consumer countries real price stabilization and guaranteed outlets on the world market so that the developing countries may derive considerably greater revenue from international trade.

VI. THE FUTURE OF THE CCTA

The Summit Conference, *considering* that at the last CCTA session in Dar es Salaam in January to February, 1963, the final adoption of the new CCTA convention was deferred until the Heads of African States had had an opportunity to consider and direct on the role of the CCTA within the overall context of Pan-African cooperation; *and in view* of the fact that Article 23 of this new convention lays down as follows: *"Pending the signature and the ratification of this convention as provided in Article 16, the Parties having initialled this convention agree to apply it provisionally as if it had entered into force as from the date of initialling, subject to any decision which may be taken by the Heads of African States at the Conference of Addis Ababa or at any subsequent conference on the role of the CCTA within the overall context of Pan-African cooperation"; decides* to reconsider its role in order to bring it eventually within the scope of the organization of African states which will have, as one of its arms, an organ for technical, scientific, and cultural cooperation.

3. The OAU Charter

We, the Heads of African States and Governments assembled in the city of Addis Ababa, Ethiopia;

CONVINCED that it is the inalienable right of all people to control their own destiny;

CONSCIOUS of the fact that freedom, equality, justice and dignity are essential objectives for the achievement of the legitimate aspirations of the African peoples;

CONSCIOUS of our responsibility to harness the natural and human resources of our continent for the total advancement of our peoples in spheres of human endeavor;

INSPIRED by a common determination to strengthen understanding and cooperation among our states in response to the aspirations of our peoples for brotherhood and solidarity, in a larger unity transcending ethnic and national differences;

CONVINCED that, in order to translate this determination into a dynamic force in the cause of human progress, conditions for peace and security must be established and maintained;

DETERMINED to safeguard and consolidate the hard-won independence as well as the sovereignty and territorial integrity of our states, and to fight against neo-colonialism in all its forms;

DEDICATED to the general progress of Africa;

PERSUADED that the Charter of the United Nations and the Universal Declaration of Human Rights, to the principles of which we reaffirm our adherence, provide a solid foundation for peaceful and positive cooperation among states;

DESIROUS that all African states should henceforth unite so that the welfare and well-being of their peoples can be assured;

RESOLVED to reinforce the links between our states by establishing and strengthening common institutions;

HAVE agreed to the present Charter.

ESTABLISHMENT

Article I. (1) The High Contracting Parties do by the present Charter establish an organization to be known as the "Organization of African Unity."

(2) The organization shall include the continental African states, Madagascar, and other islands surrounding Africa.

PURPOSES

Article II. (1) The organization shall have the following purposes: (a) to promote the unity and solidarity of the African states; (b) to coordinate and intensify their cooperation and efforts to achieve a better life for the peoples of Africa; (c) to defend their sovereignty, their territorial integrity, and independence; (d) to eradicate all forms of colonialism from Africa; and (e) to promote international cooperation, having due regard to the Charter of the United Nations and the Universal Declaration of Human Rights.

(2) To these ends, the member states shall coordinate and harmonize their general policies, especially in the following fields: (a) political and diplomatic cooperation; (b) economic cooperation, including transport and communications; (c) educational and cultural cooperation; (d) health, sanitation, and nutritional cooperation; (e) scientific and technical cooperation; and (f) cooperation for defence and security.

PRINCIPLES

Article III. The member states, in pursuit of the purposes stated in Article II, solemnly affirm and declare their adherence to the following principles:

(1) the sovereign equality of all member states;

(2) non-interference in the internal affairs of states;

(3) respect for the sovereignty and territorial integrity of each member state and for its inalienable right to independent existence;

(4) peaceful settlement of disputes by negotiation, mediation, conciliation or arbitration;

(5) unreserved condemnation, in all its forms, of political as-

sassination as well as of subversive activities on the part of neighboring states or any other states;

(6) absolute dedication to the total emancipation of the African territories which are still dependent;

(7) affirmation of a policy of non-alignment with regard to all blocs.

MEMBERSHIP

Article IV. Each independent sovereign African state shall be entitled to become a member of the organization.

RIGHTS AND DUTIES OF MEMBER STATES

Article V. All member states shall enjoy equal rights and have equal duties.

Article VI. The member states pledge themselves to observe scrupulously the principles enumerated in Article III of the present Charter.

INSTITUTIONS

Article VII. The organization shall accomplish its purposes through the following principal institutions:

(1) the Assembly of Heads of State and Government;

(2) the Council of Ministers;

(3) the General Secretariat;

(4) the Commission of Mediation, Conciliation, and Arbitration.

THE ASSEMBLY OF HEADS OF STATE AND GOVERNMENT

Article VIII. The Assembly of Heads of State and Government shall be the supreme organ of the organization. It shall, subject to the provisions of this Charter, discuss matters of common concern to Africa with a view to coordinating and harmonizing the general policy of the organization. It may in addition review the structure, functions, and acts of all the organs and any specialized agencies which may be created in accordance with the present Charter.

Article IX. The Assembly shall be composed of the Heads of State and Government, or their duly accredited representatives, and it shall meet at least *once a year.* At the request of any member state, and on approval by a two-thirds majority of the member states, the Assembly shall meet in extraordinary session.

Article X. (1) Each member state shall have one vote.

(2) All resolutions shall be determined by a two-thirds majority of the members of the organization.

(3) Questions of procedure shall require a simple majority. Whether or not a question is one of procedure shall be determined by a simple majority of all member states of the organization.

(4) Two-thirds of the total membership of the organization shall form a quorum at any meeting of the Assembly.

Article XI. The Assembly shall have the power to determine its own rules of procedure.

THE COUNCIL OF MINISTERS

Article XII. The Council of Ministers shall consist of Foreign Ministers or such other Ministers as are designated by the Governments of member states.

The Council of Ministers shall meet at least twice a year. When requested by any member state and approved by two-thirds of all member states, it shall meet in extraordinary session.

Article XIII. The Council of Ministers shall be responsible to the Assembly of Heads of State and Government. It shall be entrusted with the responsibility of preparing conferences of the Assembly.

It shall take cognizance of any matter referred to it by the Assembly. It shall be entrusted with the implementation of the decisions of the Assembly of Heads of State and Government. It shall coordinate inter-African cooperation in accordance with the instructions of the Assembly and in conformity with Article II (2) of the present Charter.

Article XIV. (1) Each member state shall have one vote.

(2) All resolutions shall be determined by a simple majority of the Council of Ministers.

(3) Two-thirds of the total membership of the Council shall form a quorum for any meeting of the Council.

Article XV. The Council shall have the power to determine its own rules of procedure.

GENERAL SECRETARIAT

Article XVI. There shall be an Administrative Secretary-General of the organization, who shall be appointed by the Assembly of Heads of State and Government, on the recommendation of the Council of Ministers. The Administrative Secretary-General shall direct the affairs of the Secretariat.

Article XVII. There shall be one or more Assistant Secretaries-General of the organization, who shall be appointed by the Assembly of Heads of State and Government.

Article XVIII. The functions and conditions of service of the Secretary-General, of the Assistant Secretaries-General and other employees of the Secretariat shall be governed by the provisions of this Charter and the regulations approved by the Assembly of Heads of State and Government.

(1) In the performance of their duties the Administrative Secretary-General and the staff shall not seek or receive instructions from any government or from any other authority external to the organization. They shall refrain from any action which might reflect on their position as international officials responsible only to the organization.

(2) Each member of the organization undertakes to respect the exclusive character of the responsibilities of the Administrative Secretary-General and the staff and not to seek to influence them in the discharge of their responsibilities.

COMMISSION OF MEDIATION, CONCILIATION, AND ARBITRATION

Article XIX. Member states pledge to settle all disputes among themselves by peaceful means and, to this end, decide to establish a Commission of Mediation, Conciliation, and Arbitration, the composition of which and conditions of service shall be defined by a separate protocol to be approved by the Assembly of Heads of State and Government. Said protocol shall be regarded as forming an integral part of the present Charter.

SPECIALIZED COMMISSIONS

Article XX. The Assembly shall establish such Specialized Commissions as it may deem necessary, including the following:

(1) Economic and Social Commission;
(2) Educational and Cultural Commission;
(3) Health, Sanitation, and Nutrition Commission;
(4) Defence Commission;
(5) Scientific, Technical, and Research Commission.

Article XXI. Each Specialized Commission referred to in Article XX shall be composed of the Ministers concerned or other Ministers or Plenipotentiaries designated by the Governments of the member states.

Article XXII. The functions of the Specialized Commissions shall be carried out in accordance with the provisions of the present Charter and of the regulations approved by the Council of Ministers.

THE BUDGET

Article XXIII. The budget of the organization prepared by the Administrative Secretary-General shall be approved by the Council of Ministers. The budget shall be provided by contributions from member states in accordance with the scale of assessment of the United Nations; provided, however, that no member state shall be assessed an amount exceeding twenty percent of the yearly regular budget of the organization. The member states agree to pay their respective contributions regularly.

SIGNATURE AND RATIFICATION OF CHARTER

Article XXIV. This Charter shall be open for signature to all independent sovereign African states and shall be ratified by the signatory states in accordance with their respective constitutional processes.

The original instrument, done, if possible, in African languages, in English and French, all texts being equally authentic, shall be deposited with the Government of Ethiopia, which shall transmit certified copies thereof to all independent sovereign African states.

Instruments of ratification shall be deposited with the Government of Ethiopia, which shall notify all signatories of each such deposit.

ENTRY INTO FORCE

Article XXV. This Charter shall enter into force immediately upon receipt by the Government of Ethiopia of the instruments of ratification from two-thirds of the signatory states.

REGISTRATION OF THE CHARTER

Article XXVI. This Charter shall, after due ratification, be registered with the Secretariat of the United Nations through the Government of Ethiopia in conformity with Article 102 of the Charter of the United Nations.

INTERPRETATION OF THE CHARTER

Article XXVII. (1) Any question which may arise concerning the interpretation of this Charter shall be decided by a vote of two-thirds of the Assembly of Heads of State and Government of the organization.

ADHESION AND ACCESSION

Article XXVIII. (1) Any independent sovereign African State may at any time notify the Administrative Secretary-General of its intention to adhere or accede to this Charter.

(2) The Administrative Secretary-General shall, on receipt of such notification, communicate a copy of it to all the member states. Admission shall be decided by a simple majority of member states. The decision of each member state shall be transmitted to the Administrative Secretary-General, who shall, upon receipt of the required number of votes, communicate the decision to the state concerned.

MISCELLANEOUS

Article XXIX. The working languages of the organization and all its institutions shall be, if possible, African languages, English, and French.

Article XXX. The Administrative Secretary-General may accept on behalf of the organization gifts, bequests, and other donations made to the organization, provided that this is approved by the Council of Ministers.

Article XXXI. The Council of Ministers shall decide on the privileges and immunities to be accorded to the personnel of the Secretariat in the respective territories of the member states.

Cessation of Membership

Article XXXII. Any state which desires to renounce its membership shall forward a written notification to the Administrative Secretary-General. At the end of one year from the date of such notification, if not withdrawn, the Charter shall cease to apply with respect to the renouncing state, which shall thereby cease to belong to the organization.

Amendment to the Charter

Article XXXIII. This Charter may be amended or revised if any member state makes a written request to the Administrative Secretary-General to that effect, provided, however, that the proposed amendment is not submitted to the Assembly for consideration until all the member states have been duly notified of it and a period of one year has elapsed. Such an amendment shall not be effective unless approved by at least two-thirds of all the member states.

In faith, whereof, We, the Heads of African State and Government, have signed this Charter.

Done in the City of Addis Ababa, Ethiopia, this 25th day of May, 1963.

1. Algeria: Premier Ahmed Ben Bella
2. Burundi: King Mwambutsa
3. Cameroun: President Ahmadou Ahidjo
4. Central African Republic: President David Dacko
5. Chad: President François Tombalbaye
6. Congo-Brazzaville: President Fulbert Youlou
7. Congo-Leopoldville: President Joseph Kasavubu
8. Dahomey: President Hubert Maga
9. Ethiopia: Emperor Haile Selassie I
10. Gabon: President Leon M'Ba
11. Ghana: President Kwame Nkrumah
12. Guinea: President Sékou Touré
13. Ivory Coast: President Félix Houphouet-Boigny
14. Liberia: President William V. S. Tubman

15. Libya: King Idris I.
16. Malagasy Republic: President Philibert Tsiranana
17. Mali: President Modibo Keita
18. Mauritania: President Mokhtar Ould Daddah
19. Niger: President Hamani Diori
20. Nigeria: Prime Minister Alhaji Sir Abubakar Tafawa Balewa
21. Rwanda: Foreign Minister Callixte Habamenshi for President Grégoire Kayibanda
22. Senegal: President Léopold Sédar Senghor
23. Sierra Leone: Prime Minister Sir Milton Margai
24. Somali Republic: President Aden Abdullah Osman
25. Sudan: President Ibrahim Abboud
26. Tanganyika: President Julius Nyerere
27. Tunisia: President Habib Bourguiba
28. Uganda: Prime Minister Milton Obote
29. United Arab Republic: President Gamal Abdul Nasser
30. Upper Volta: President Maurice Yameogo

Not Present:
1. Morocco: King Hassan II
2. Togo: President Nicolas Grunitzky

CHART 4. THE AFRICAN STATES AND THE U.N.: FINANCIAL ACCOUNTING
(as of June 1, 1963)

Country	1963 Scale of assessments as percentage of total U.N. budget	1963 Assessment for working capital fund	1963 Assessment for regular budget	Amount due to working capital fund and to regular budget	Amount due to special account emergency fund[a]	Amount due to Congo ad hoc special account[b]	Total due
Algeria[c]							
Burundi[c]							
Cameroun	0.04	$ 6,431.00	$ 1,965.00	Paid	Paid	Paid	Paid in Full
Central African Republic	0.04	6,431.00	1,965.00	$ 38,396.00	Paid	Paid	$ 38,396.00
Chad	0.04	6,431.00	1,965.00	Paid	$ 777.00	$ 12,814.50	13,591.50
Congo-Brazzaville	0.04	6,431.00	1,965.00	38,396.00	Paid	Paid	38,396.00
Congo-Leopoldville	0.07	11,256.00	56,018.00	Paid	Paid	Paid	Paid in Full
Dahomey	0.04	6,431.00	1,965.00	54,250.89[d]	1,158.93	6,246.06	61,665.88[d]
Ethiopia	0.05	7,392.00	39,930.00	Paid	65,084.00	34,365.50	99,449.50
Gabon	0.04	6,431.00	1,965.00	38,396.00	Paid	Paid	38,396.00
Ghana	0.09	13,715.00	71,973.00	85,688.00	Paid	Paid	85,688.00
Guinea	0.04	6,431.00	1,965.00	Paid	8,219.00	Paid	8,219.00
Ivory Coast	0.04	6,431.00	1,912.00	38,343.00	Paid	Paid	38,343.00
Liberia	0.04	6,000.00	1,965.00	37,965.00	Paid	Paid	37,965.00
Libya	0.04	6,000.00	1,965.00	Paid	34,108.00	Paid	34,108.00
Malagasy Republic	0.04	6,431.00	1,912.00	Paid	Paid	17,330.00	17,330.00
Mali	0.04	6,431.00	1,965.00	Paid	15.50	14,321.00	14,336.50
Mauritania	0.04	16,000.00	2,071.00	76,939.00[e]	1,196.00	7,277.00	85,412.00[e]

Country	1963 Scale of assessments as percentage of total U.N. budget	1963 Assessment for working capital fund	1963 Assessment for regular budget	Amount due to working capital fund and to regular budget	Amount due to special account emergency fund[a]	Amount due to Congo ad hoc special account[b]	Total due
Morocco	0.14	21,000.00	111,876.00	131,515.00	Paid	117,823.00	249,338.00
Niger	0.04	6,431.00	31,965.00	40,179.00[d]	4,983.00	15,386.50	60,548.50[d]
Nigeria[c]	0.21	33,767.00	167,814.00	Paid	Paid	Paid	Paid in Full
Rwanda[c]							
Senegal	0.05	8,040.00	39,930.00	44,677.00	971.00	7,944.00	53,592.00
Sierra Leone	0.04	16,000.00	32,071.00	Paid	Paid	Paid	Paid in Full
Somali Republic	0.04	6,431.00	31,965.00	38,396.00	Paid	7,507.07	45,903.07
South Africa	0.53	79,176.00	403,749.00	24,406.50	Paid	1,249,477.00	1,273,883.50
Sudan	0.07	10,608.00	55,965.00	68,965.00[d]	71,118.00	Paid	140,083.00[d]
Tanganyika	0.04	16,000.00	32,071.00	Paid	Paid	Paid	Paid in Full
Togo	0.04	6,431.00	31,965.00	38,396.00	4,983.00	15,386.50	58,765.50
Tunisia	0.05	7,500.00	39,956.00	27,086.00	Paid	Paid	27,086.00
Uganda[e]							
U.A.R.	0.25	37,320.00	195,532.00	315,120.68[d]	284,742.00	258,155.00	858,017.68[d]
Upper Volta	0.04	6,431.00	31,965.00	25,744.00	8,745.00	16,452.00	50,941.00
Total for Africa	2.27	373,808.00	1,790,290.00	1,162,859.07	486,100.43	1,780,485.13	3,429,444.63

[a] The Special Account Emergency Fund maintains the United Nations field mission on the border between Israel and Egypt. The figures include arrears from all years prior to 1963.

[b] The Congo *Ad Hoc* Special Account maintains the United Nations military forces and technical missions in the Congo. The assessments were made in three periods: November 1, 1961–June 30, 1962; January 1, 1961–October 31, 1961; and July 14, 1960–December 31, 1960. The figures cited here include arrears for all previous years.

[c] The assessments for the states admitted at the Seventeenth Session of the General Assembly have not been established.

[d] The figure includes arrears due the Working Capital Fund and the Regular Budget for 1962.

[e] The figure includes arrears due the Working Capital Fund and the Regular Budget for 1961 and 1962.

SOURCE: Compiled by C. Allen Foster from materials supplied by the United Nations.

PART FOUR

Contemporary African Poetry and Prose

1. *South Africa: Literature of Protest*
LEWIS NKOSI

The world of Negro writers in South Africa is a familiar one to those who have lived in race-torn areas: the ugly leer on the claustrophobic face of violence, the sweltering heat of talk about to simmer into social explosion, the senseless arbitrary death, the frenzied quest for emotional release in sex and drink. They are concerned with the fantasies evoked by a black-and-white world which, though divided, simultaneously seeks and is terrified by social fusion.

South African fiction is loud, melodramatic. Its language is brassy, it concerns itself with a particular moment in a series of socially incoherent events. This moment may be one of sudden death, as in Peter Kumalo's story "A Death in the Sun," or it may be a mere passing gesture of defiance against the political order, as in Richard Rive's "The Bench," ending, predictably enough, in arrest.

The political order against which the writer seeks definition for himself and his characters is disturbingly permanent: The past is dim and opaquely unfamiliar, the future inscrutable. The African writer seizes upon the moment in space and time as concealing the dramatic, the most arresting truth about his rootless life. Black writers describe this world with anger, sometimes with zest, again with scornful condescension or hearty cynicism. Their heroes are rude to whites, amoral, and unspeakably cunning. When in a joyous mood, they are likely either to break chairs or stick a knife in somebody's back; it all goes to make the moment more memorable.

This phase of African literature resembles the Elizabethan period of cloak-and-dagger stories, violence, and intrigue. Here is a society in transition, full of sound and fury, reflecting the dislocation of tribal social structure, the release of peasant populations into crowded cities, and the consequent shifting of values. But also, as in Shakespeare's cloak-and-dagger stories, violence masks the real energy awaiting expression in something creative and socially valuable.

This eventful world, as the short stories of Bloke Modisane demonstrate, leaves little to the imagination. Its gargantuan reality impinges so strongly upon the imaginative world that the temptation is often compelling to use the ready-made plots of violence, chicanery, and racial love tragedies as representing universal truths, when, in fact, actual insight into human tragedy may lie beneath this social and political turbulence. Even when the writer eschews melodrama but seizes upon tableaux of the social world of South Africa and presents them as fictionally and artistically meaningful in themselves, the writer falls into the trap of giving us only glimpses of the vast machinery of political suppression, rather than of the workings of human character. Sooner or later, character is subordinated to situation; the whites in these stories are flat, insensate beings, mere ciphers explaining white oppression.

If one assumes that some whites experience anguish and doubt about the colossal hoax now being perpetrated upon South Africa by Dr. Verwoerd and his followers, this possibility has no place in these stories. White characters always leer, underpay and abuse servants, pinch the maid's bottom; they callously reject or eject the black man from the drawing room. A corrupt, hard-drinking lot, they manage to keep their society together only by the elaborate machinery of force. Why these people are as they are— that is a profounder truth seldom explored. Only occasionally does the writer peep behind the mask of violence on a policeman's face, as Alex la Guma does in his long story *A Walk in the Night,* to see the lurking terror and insecurity.

These writers provide an interesting contrast to the generation dominant between 1900 and 1950. The current writers are describing impulses of a generation that grew up under the shadow of Dr. Malan's government, or reached maturity at about the same time that the Boer government was taking over the country and firmly putting the blacks in their place. Consequently they regard Rev. Kumalo, hero of Alan Paton's *Cry, The Beloved*

Country, not so much with annoyance as with uncomprehending scorn. To them, he represents the genuflections and awkward gestures of a generation that believed in the good faith of White South Africa. The loud chorus of derision that greets Rev. Kumalo from the younger generation of Africans, especially those who stay with the story until the man of God ascends a mountain to offer his last prayer, is the same chorus of derision that greeted a film called *The Defiant Ones* in Harlem, especially when Sidney Poitier jumped off the train to rescue Tony Curtis, his white fellow prisoner. "There was a tremendous roar of fury from the audience," James Baldwin said later in an interview. "They told Sidney to 'Get back on the train, you fool.' "

Even after the war, when African rights had already been whittled away, it was still possible for the older poet, J. J. R. Jolobe, to urge African relatives of those who died in the fight against fascism and totalitarianism to "weep not" but to "take comfort and rejoice." Assuming a somewhat Hyde Park corner posture, he passionately harangued them:

> They laughed at danger and despised gaunt Death;/They looked beyond and saw the fruit, vast gains/To their own race, to mankind and the world.

As every Negro boy in South Africa now knows, the promise was shamefully hollow; though Jolobe's rhetoric sprang from nobler sentiments, the bitterness has not been assuaged; among the younger writers it has merely given birth to a new kind of hero—rude, cynical, violent, amoral, resolutely refusing, when put in his place, to remain there for long.

In Woodie Manqupu's story set in the Alexandra backyards, where bootleg liquor is concealed underground to elude police detection, the author happily juxtaposed images of the sinful with images of the pious in a kind of gay cynicism not merely of his own invention but representing the struggle between good and evil in the community—the impulse toward the ecstasy of religious life and the contradictory impulse toward loose living. He wrote:

> The woman walked over to the corrugated-iron fence and after removing a lot of dirty sacking, a tin of liquor was visible. She filled the mug

with beer and tottered back to the door, humming a church hymn under her breath.

There is reason to believe that the juxtaposition of hymn singing, representing Christian institution, and liquor-running, representing the profane, was fully intended and was not merely ac-
cidental. In fact, the gay irreverence toward the solemn, the pious,
and the traditional is what distinguishes the heroes and heroines
in the writings of this present generation of black writers in South
Africa.

The older writers, such as R. R. R. Dhlomo and J. J. R. Jolobe,
were very much influenced by the missionaries who pioneered
African writing; their writing shows itself to be motivated by
the missionary zeal to instruct and to reform a backsliding generation in much the same way that the Rev. Kumalo tries to in *Cry,
The Beloved Country*. The younger writers have had a much
more secular education. They remain unimpressed by Dhlomo's
brand of morality and Rev. Kumalo's touching sincerity; in fact,
Dhlomo's embarrassing moral indignation at the corruption into
which he saw the African people sinking, especially in the urban
areas of South Africa, seems to cause the young genuine anguish.
In a novel published in the early 1940's by the missionary press,
a slight work called *An African Tragedy,* Dhlomo, the Zulu
writer, abandoned the narrative midway and began to sermon-
ize:

> Do these people who have the welfare of our nation at heart, ever visit
> these dark places and try to win back the straying young? . . . Do Chris-
> tians who profess to love God, seek to do His will, ever visit such places
> —not as they do on Sunday afternoons when the people in the yards
> are already half mad with drinks and evil passions—but in the quiet
> during the week when these people are more amenable to reason?

Contrast this with the mocking tone in which Marks Dikobe
Ramitloa in his forthcoming novel, *Marabi Dance,* describes an
African priest:

> He was illiterate and had learned to 'read' the Bible by memorizing
> what he had heard. When conducting a service, he hid his illiteracy by
> looking closely into the Bible from his place behind the pulpit; he
> never made the mistake of 'reading' anything that was not written in

the book. He was greatly helped in his work by the street corner services and funerals he attended.

Though violence plays a large part in the works of all these writers, nowhere is it explored with such frightening effect as in the works of four Cape Town writers, Peter Clark, who sometimes uses the pen name Peter Kumalo, Richard Rive, James Matthews, and Alex la Guma. In Peter Clark's "A Death in the Sun" and Richard Rive's "Willyboy," the violence portrayed has gone beyond the physical reality to become a quiet, brooding thing that is a state of mind—of the national mind, even. These stories remind one strongly of books such as *Black Boy* or *Native Son* by the American Negro writer Richard Wright.

Even the burning heat is used by these writers to evoke the atmosphere of brooding violence that lies like a blanket over South Africa. In Rive's story "Willyboy," in which a skollie who has been humiliated by other thugs outside a cinema throttles an old woman in an attempt to reclaim his dignity, the writer begins his story with these lines:

> When the world feels hot it's hot as hell in District Six. The sky is sweet red Muscatel and the moon melts . . . and some say the world becomes a bit soiled and dirty, but the world laughs back richly and tells them to go to hell.

Thus is set the general tone of the story, a mixture of threatening violence and rebellion, and the social claustrophobia that presses upon the derelict ghetto of Cape Town's District Six, captured admirably in a few brush strokes. Peter Clark ends his story with these lines:

> And the afternoon sun shone, a great glowing ball suspended in the afternoon sky, fierce in its summer heat, casting its warm radiant light like a golden mantle, but for a little group of three people its light had gone out suddenly as if a great black cloud had descended and they were left weeping in unbounded darkness.

The profound disillusionment with the South African color-bar society and the accompanying revolt or protest against that society takes various forms in these writers, according to their bent. Sometimes it is an amoral attitude or complete negation of moral law. In a society that has subverted human morality and substituted a morality based on color in its place, small wonder that these sensitive ones delight in siding with those who live outside the pale of any moral law. Their tone is that of the young who have concluded that it is futile to try to live honestly in a society whose basic assumptions are patently dishonest. Bloke Modisane peoples his stories with engaging pickpockets who live by their wits, preying on white women in the streets of Johannesburg and rifling handbags. He significantly titled one "The Respectable Pickpocket."

In another story, "The Dignity of Begging," Modisane writes of an African cripple who discovers that he can live better by begging in the streets than he can by joining the joyless queues of clock-punchers. So he exploits his physical deformity to escape the clutches of the law, only too happy to feed on the underbelly of a corrupt society. After being turned loose by a judge, Nathaniel, the hero of the story, reflects cynically:

> If the magistrate had seen the big grin on my face as we leave the court, he would have thrown my deformed carcass in gaol and deliberately lost the key. He does not see it though.

In a later moment of inspiration, the hero unburdens himself:

> One of these days when I'm on my annual leave, I hope to write a book on begging, something like a treatise on the subject. It will be written with sensitivity and charm, brimful with sketches from life, and profusely illustrated with colored photographs, with easy-to-follow rules on the noblest and oldest occupation in the world: Begging! It will be a textbook for all aspiring beggars, young and old, who will reap a wealth of knowledge from my personal experiences and genius.

Humor and satire are possibly the most neglected elements in the writing of black South Africans. When they do occasionally manage to achieve a certain degree of detachment from a situation that lends itself too readily to protest and melodrama, some delightful moments of trenchant satire are captured for the reader. In Richard Rive's recent novel, *Emergency*, a Colored man who is all but white has difficulty buying a train ticket from a white clerk, who tells him to go to the window "reserved for Europeans":

It was Abe's turn to look surprised.

"Now let's not be difficult," Abe began. "I prefer to be served here."

"I'm not allowed to serve Europeans here."

"I'm not a European. I've never been to Europe in my life."

Later he remarks to his friends:

"So I have to fight in order to establish my non-white status."

"It's the shape of things to come," his friend says—with a sudden flash of eschatological truth.

Senior of the black writers in South Africa is Ezekiel Mphahlele. Among other works, he has published *The Living and the Dead,* a collection of stories with a zany assortment of Newclare Township characters who earn their living precariously by selling bootleg liquor carried in coffins. Mphahlele is one of the few Johannesburg writers whose stories are something more than protest; the white world is there, to be sure, but one is given to understand that the existence of the black world is not always contingent upon the existence of the white one. His characters have their own lives, become involved with each other as black people. In his celebrated story "The Suitcase," the hero picks up a case left by a girl in the bus. After much trouble getting it home, he discovers, in a final ironical twist, that the case contains the body of a small baby.

Unless one is thinking of vernacular literature, these African writers do not really represent a school of writing different from that of their white counterparts such as, for example, Barney Simons and Athol Fugard. There certainly is no new experimentation with language or syntax. What they do bring to the literature, however, is a view of the society as seen from the bottom. No white writer in South Africa can deal at present with the subject matter that Casey Motsisi has made popular in his sketches, for the simple reason that the twilight world of "speakeasies" or "shebeens" that Casey Motsisi writes about is not so accessible to white writers. There is a unique vigor and vitality in the work of the Negro writers that has been forced upon them by the very rawness and uncouthness of their materials.

Critics have hailed Todd Matshikiza (*Chocolates for My Wife*) as an innovator and experimenter with language. Yet, at his most intelligible, Todd Matshikiza merely appropriated the jazz language of the Johannesburg musicians and tried to extend its vocabulary to express a variety of emotions. Some of them were much too subtle for this kind of forced dialect; its limitations immediately became obvious. At worst, Todd made an effort to hide these limitations by inventing a gibberish that became a kind of private soliloquy, intelligible to nobody except to himself. It is possible that Matshikiza, were he a gifted creative writer, might have finally arrived at some kind of synthesis of various idioms consisting of the jazz argot, African rhythms, and ordinary English. Unfortunately, we must wait for another experimenter to come along.

What is negritude? The Negro writers of South Africa were never aware of such a movement until the Congress of Negro Culture took place in Paris some years ago. Ezekiel Mphahlele introduced dialogue on negritude in the pages of the newspaper *Fighting Talk,* but there has been little discussion of it by southern writers. The controversy raging through West Africa has left them comparatively untouched. Certainly most Africans in South Africa react violently to Dr. Verwoerd's exhortations that Africans should go back to their tribal roots, to his assertion that they are unfit by nature to participate in Western culture. Any talk of tribal roots smacks of apartheid. Musicologists such as Hugh Tracy, for example, meet a wall of distrust and suspicion every time they talk of "traditional music." The perennial theme of this new literature is that of the hero who escapes from the traditional rule of chiefs in the rural areas to seek his fortunes in the crowded, brawling cities.

Arthur Fula broke away from this theme to write a novel in Afrikaans callèd *Janie Giet die Beeld (Janie Casts the Image).* The story provoked tremendous fury among non-whites because it suggested, by implication, that the solution to the African problem lay in returning to the countryside and, symbolically, to the traditional way of life. Ezekiel Mphahlele writes bitterly of characters "who go limping back to the countryside" after a brief encounter with the industrial society.

In contrast with the total lack of interest in tribal society, southern African writing deals again and again with the problems of mixed identities, the ways of survival in a hostile color-bar society.

With boring frequency, as in Casey Motsisi's sketches, they roam the speakeasies, jive haunts, and brothels in a futile quest for the satisfying experience. Only when African intellectuals are somehow finally integrated into the society, one feels, will they have enough courage to see beyond Dr. Verwoerd's nonsense about "Bantu culture" and be able to look back to their origins. Today they write with him staring over their shoulders. This severance from tradition has impoverished African writing to a certain extent; at best, the novels and short stories of this generation tend to be merely reportorial, not interpretive. A writer such as Casey Motsisi merely paints what he sees going on in his community; nobody is exploring the wider reaches of the African soul. The folk myths, as West Africans have shown, can infuse a new vitality into the literature.

Vernacular literature is more or less moribund. The reasons are many. First, writers seek a wider audience than can be provided by vernacular readers—mostly school children. Since the government decides which books are suitable for reading in school, vernacular literature is subject to close official scrutiny. Controversial works dealing with sex, politics, and religion are automatically excluded. When an Afrikaans publishing company organized its first literary competition for African novels in the 1950's, it announced that works treating these three controversial themes would be excluded from consideration. Concluding that there was nothing else to write about, serious writers declined to submit their works to the publishers. English remains the dominant medium of expression at the moment, despite the fact that the government is making serious efforts to supplant it with Afrikaans in both white and African schools.

Apart from Peter Abrahams, black writers in South Africa have not produced novels of any competent execution. They use mainly the short story and sketch as vehicles. Ezekiel Mphahlele has attempted to explain away this lack by claiming that the social and political pressures in South Africa make it almost impossible emotionally to sustain a work of great length. This does not seem to me to be an entirely satisfactory answer. Part of the reason is sheer sloth. Also, some magazines have employed such low standards of selection that beginning writers began to get the idea that one could detour from the long and dreary labor of good writing by bashing out a short story in a matter of a day or two and getting it published immediately.

This is not to minimize the serious problems facing the black South African writer: physical rootlessness, emotional instability, lack of contact with the outside world, and disbarment from such local cultural activities as theater, serious film exhibition, musical concerts.

Despite all these handicaps, there are indications that the 1960's are going to see a new burst of literary activity in South Africa. Already, a number of Negro writers have completed or are about to complete their first novels. André Deutsch is publishing Alex la Guma's novella *A Walk in the Night.* Arthur Maimane, now living in London, has a completed manuscript of a novel. Richard Rive's first novel, *Emergency,* has already been published. Marks Dikobe Ramitloa has finished the major portion of his novel called *Marabi Dance.*

Also, a little magazine for literature has been started under the editorship of Nathaniel Nakasa, a young Johannesburg writer. It is hoped that the magazine will be a spur to local writing. The magazine, which is called *The Classic,* has taken its name from a Johannesburg "shebeen" where most of the African writers centered around *Drum* Magazine repaired for their daily dose of bootleg liquor. The magazine has been helped by funds from the Fairfield Foundation, but will need much more financial support before it can begin to attract the attention of subscribers and advertisers.

So burdened are we with personal anecdotes, small autobiographies celebrating some personal worth in the face of Dr. Verwoerd's repressive regime, that we need more creative fiction now than ever before to provide us with less superficial insights into the nature of the South African tragedy.

2. English-Speaking West Africa: Synthesizing Past and Present

LEWIS NKOSI

One of the first things one notices upon arriving in West Africa, especially in Nigerian cities, is the easy coexistence of the old and the new modes of living. It is not so much a question of the traditional way of life giving way before the remorseless advance of a grinding technological civilization from the West as it is a mere accommodation of the new, an acceptance of the inevitable, without too great a retreat from the traditional outposts.

Ibadan, for instance, is truly an African city with no counterpart anywhere in Europe. "It does not look like a big European town," Janheinz Jahn writes in his book *Through African Doors*, "but like a cluster of endless villages with one- or two-story buildings, mostly with corrugated iron roofs. There are only a few big surfaced roads dividing it into irregular parts, the settlements straddling many hills."

It is not only that architectural styles have found a new synthesis in some of the buildings here: The very spirit that motivates city life is uniquely African. The "feel" of a West African city is as distinguishable from that of cities in other parts of the world as a European city is distinguishable from an American city. And it is this uniquely West African mood that distinguishes the literature of West Africa from that of South Africa. Whereas the contemporary fiction of West Africa seems to be almost saturated with the spirit of traditional myths, the literature of South Africa reflects the great gulf existing there between the urban and the rural communities and between the industrial and the traditional societies.

In visiting the rural reserves of South Africa, one has the feeling that one has crossed a psychic threshold into a much older, dimly remembered past. In West Africa, there is no such noticeable schism. The cities here seem to form confluences where the new and traditional cultures meet. A transformation often takes place with a minimum of psychic damage to the community.

In view of the comparative gentleness of the impact of the modern technological civilization upon tradition in West Africa, it seems paradoxical that the Nigerian novelist is so preoccupied with the theme of cultural conflict. Perhaps it is because his own culture is still so visible, and not because it has been irreparably damaged, that the writer of West Africa is so sensitive to the impact of Western culture upon his mode of life.

Another paradox to be noted is the great part played by religion, or religious feeling, in West African writing. Although the writers, especially the younger ones, are often secular in outlook and, technically at least, greatly indebted to modern European literature, they continuously make forays into religious beliefs and mythologies belonging to a social order that they have personally rejected on rational grounds. It is as though a modern European writer were to compose a work motivated by a belief in Fates he assumed did not exist. Indeed, the reader is not always sure whether the writer is merely portraying a community that is now alien to him and where traditional beliefs still linger, or whether he actually identifies himself with such beliefs and writes from inside as an extension of that tradition. In South Africa, this question never arises.

The vitality afforded West African writing by a conscious borrowing from fables, traditional myths, and folklore is perhaps nowhere better illustrated than in stories by Amos Tutuola, the only Nigerian writer who can be described as a traditional story-teller upon whom European influences are minimal, if not entirely absent. Mr. Tutuola's works—*The Palm Wine Drinkard, My Life in the Bush of Ghosts, Simbi and the Satyr of the Dark Jungle, The Brave African Huntress, The Feather Woman of the Jungle*—all borrow both plots and storytelling forms from traditional Yoruba myths.

Tutuola, one of the best known of Nigerian writers abroad, remains a controversial figure at home. His first work, *The Palm Wine Drinkard*, published in 1952, was widely acclaimed by

European critics. Dylan Thomas, writing in the London *Observer,* described the work as a "brief, thronged, grisly, and bewitching story" and claimed that "nothing was too prodigious or trivial to put down in this tall, devilish story." The younger West African writers remain skeptical of Mr. Tutuola's talents, however. While admitting to Tutuola's prodigious inventive powers, they suspect that his lack of inhibitions in the use of language is largely attributable to an inadequate education and suggest that his success abroad derives from European critics' interest in a "primitive" storyteller who has bent the English language to suit his own resources.

In a review of Tutuola's latest work, *The Feather Woman of the Jungle,* Wole Soyinka, one of Nigeria's best-known poet-playwrights, alleges that Tutuola borrows largely from the works of an indigenous novelist, D. O. Fagunwa, whose *Ogboju Ode* is a best seller in Nigeria. "Few writers," observes Mr. Soyinka, "have aroused as violent extremes of opinion as Amos Tutuola has done in four books. Tutuola was taken into the literary bosom of the European coterie, a rather jaded bosom which rings responses most readily to quaint and exotic courtiers. This was a red flag to his educated compatriots. And indeed, most of their charges were true." The fact remains, however, that the publication of Tutuola's *The Palm Wine Drinkard* in 1952 began a new literary era in English-speaking West Africa, which has clearly not yet reached its peak.

Most of the young Nigerian writers are graduates of the English Department of Ibadan University College, and they follow each other's works with intense interest. (The closeness of their relationship does not necessarily make them more charitable in their criticism of each other's works, however!) The Mbari Writers and Artists Club at Ibadan serves as a focus for the literary life of these writers, and a major portion of West African writing, including that from the French-speaking territories, has been published by Mbari, or its quarterly journal, *Black Orpheus.* Mbari, which leads a hand-to-mouth existence, is housed in a rundown building in Ibadan. Its only luxuries are a library of Negro books, an exhibition room, and an open-air theater.

Among Nigerian poets, European influences are particularly

noticeable. Modern poets such as T. S. Eliot and Ezra Pound are favorites; however, the work of the African writers is informed by a vigor and vitality often lacking in today's European literature. In Europe, there is a tendency to conceal lack of content (or even passion) by experimenting with technique. In the end, one is likely to remember how something was said rather than what was said.

In contrast, the young African writers use techniques merely to signify a social reality or mental order. (It is a reality that often remains obscure to the European reader.) Their imagery gains in vigor by containing references to a particular world that is all theirs, whether physical or mental. In Gabriel Okara's poem "One Night at Victoria Beach," there is a passing reference to "haggling sellers and buyers," but for those who have ever been in West African cities or villages, an entire world is evoked:

> The wind comes rushing from the sea,
> the waves curling like mambas strike
> the sands and recoiling hiss rage
> washing the Aladuras' feet pressing hard
> on the sand and with eyes fixed hard
> on what only hearts can see, they shouting
> pray, the Aladuras pray; and coming
> from booths behind, compelling highlife
> force ears; and car lights startle pairs
> arm in arm passing washer-words back
> and forth like haggling sellers and buyers.

Note the vigor of imagery in John Pepper Clark's description of the god of creation inspired by a piece of batik:

> Those stick-insect figures!
>   they rock the dance
> Of snakes, dart after Him
>   daddy long-arms,
> Tangle their loping strides to
>   mangrove stance
> And He, roped in the tightening
>   pit of alarms
> Dangles in his front, full
>   length,

> Invincible limbs cramp'd by
> love of their strength. . . .

Wole Soyinka has a satirical talent that he wields like a surgical scalpel. It cuts both ways, inward and outward. The "African Immigrant" in Europe who tries to clothe himself with the false dignity of his colonial master's garb is sometimes the target, as in these lines:

> My dignity is sewn
> Into the lining of a three-piece suit.
> Stiff, and with the whiteness which
> Out-Europes Europe.

But in his "Telephone Conversations" the same scalpel is turned against a white prostitute who displays snobbish prejudice when her services are solicited for the pleasure of a black man. When he is asked over the telephone whether or not he is black, his reply comes like a sweeping sickle:

> 'Facially, I am brunette, but madam, you should see
> The rest of me. Palm of my hand, soles of my feet
> Are a peroxide blonde. Friction caused—
> Foolishly madam—by sitting down, has turned
> My bottom raven black. . . .'

Nigeria's Christopher Okigbo, whose long poem "The Limits" will be published soon by Mbari, is noted for the way he turns the English language into a musical instrument. He is a virtuoso with verbal sounds and can be highly evocative. Okigbo claims that he keeps himself "in trim," when not actually writing poetry, by translating Greek verse into English. Here is an example of Okigbo's intense vision from a collection of his first poems in *Heavensgate*:

> Bright
> with the armpit-dazzle of a lioness,
> she answers,
>
> wearing white light about her;
>
> and the waves escort her,
> my lioness,
> crowned with moonlight.

So brief her presence—
match-flare in wind's breath—
so brief with mirrors around me.

Downward . . .
the waves distil her:
gold crop
sinking ungathered.

Watermaid of the salt emptiness,
grown are the ears of the secret.

Okigbo detests hackneyed phrases or slogan-poetry and is per-haps the bitterest critic of the negritude school of poets led by Senegal's Léopold Senghor. In Okigbo's view, Senghor and others of this school fall into predictable postures of soapbox rhetoric every time they experience emotion.

Of the novelists, Nigeria's Chinua Achebe is the best to have come out of English-speaking West Africa. In his first novel, *Things Fall Apart,* Achebe wrote with masterly detachment, affec-tion, and simplicity a story of the encounter between Western cul-ture and the Ibo way of life. Though some may not agree, I think that *Things Fall Apart* is the more powerful of the two novels Achebe has written. Even the texture of the prose is more finished in his first work than in the more technically complex *No Longer at Ease.* Okonkwo, the central figure, is not merely pathetic but is truly a tragic character. His destruction comes out of strength, out of an unbending commitment to a social order that is already fall-ing apart.

Achebe borrows freely from traditional proverbs and the phi-losophy of the tribe to enrich his work, but he also owes a special debt to Conrad. Very often, his work reminds the reader of Con-rad's novella *Heart of Darkness.* Although a superficial reading of Conrad might lead one to think that he viewed Africans as sav-ages far below the European standards, more careful scrutiny makes it clear that he sees little distinction between the African and the European types of savagery—except perhaps to suggest that the African expression of it is more open and honest than the bourgeois colonial greed. Conrad would seem, when the chips are down, to plump for the noble savagery of the Congo forest.

Achebe, in his dilemma, also declines to resolve the issue as easily as the missionaries want him to. He does not see the technological civilization of the West as providing much of an alternative to his traditional society. Okonkwo once had to kill his ward because tribal law demanded this brutal act, but his grandson, who becomes a Christian and later works in the civil service of modern day Lagos, is just as sunk in corruption.

Apart from a number of short stories, Cyprian Ekwensi has given us three novels, not all of which were wholly successful. Cyprian Ekwensi knows Lagos life and his best descriptive passages evoke, with a few brush-strokes, this teeming cacophonous city. Indeed, his first novel, *People of the City,* is memorable only because of its faithful depiction of the atmosphere of Lagos. His second novel, *Jagua Nana,* tells the story of the declining fortunes of a Lagos prostitute; film rights were purchased by an Italian company. The younger Nigerian writers, who dismiss Ekwensi with incautious disdain as a "good journalist," contend that *Jagua Nana* was written straight for the screen. It is long on violence and sex and shows little concern for motivation. His latest novel, *Burning Grass,* also starts well and later peters out.

Onuora Nzekwu has written two books, *Wand of Noble Wood* and *Blade Among the Boys.* Nzekwu's books are marred by what seems to be an unconquerable passion to inform; they are all laden with an abundance of anthropological information. When Nzekwu concerns himself solely with character and action, however, he often reveals surprising comic talent. In *Wand of Noble Wood,* for example, he shows a wonderful sense of comedy in a scene recording the gossip of two women at a dance.

Abioseh Nicol, in Sierra Leone, writes short stories that are deceptively easy-paced. He often seems without passionate concern for the feelings of his characters, and yet character itself is sometimes startlingly revealed through small incidents. His poetry leans heavily toward the negritude school of French-speaking Africans.

Whereas Nigeria lacks a strong sense of centralism, and gives the impression of lively intellectual disorder, Ghana is self-conscious of its position as a small but influential power in African affairs. In the arts, especially in writing, this translates itself into an intense urge to make self-vindicatory statements about Africa and its statesmen, especially in support of Ghana and its political leaders. Ghanaians do not, on the whole, seem to be able to stand outside of themselves or to achieve the detachment that the young Nigerian writers so readily evince.

Apart from a small body of vernacular literature, very little creative writing has been published in Ghana. So far, the best thing that has come from Ghana to add to the body of "Anglo-African" literature in West Africa is an anthology of poems and tales, mostly translations from vernacular, called *Voices of Ghana*. Among poets of note represented here are Frank Parkes, Albert Kayper Mensah, and Kwesi Brew. When the volume was published, its editor, Henry Swanzy, made this comment: "To say that the collection fills a long-felt want is no mere figure of speech. There is nothing at the moment in print, apart from political and biographical writing, led by Dr. Nkrumah's autobiography. . . . Here we have no Cyprian Ekwensi, no Camara Laye, no Amos Tutuola."

From time to time, Mr. Mensah does achieve lyrical power which is highly individual. His poem "In God's Tired Face" has especially rich imagery. Perhaps because many of these stories were written for Radio Ghana in the vernacular and later translated into English, they are much closer to the oral tradition of African literature. Andrew Amankwa Opoku's story "Across the Prah," is typical of these. It tells of a family that decides to leave its clan to resettle in a cocoa-farming district and to amass a fortune for itself and its relatives. As sometimes happens in oral tradition, when the tale has to be told over several days, "Across the Prah" is divided into sections: "Departure," "The Journey," "The Farm Chosen," etc. Also in the best of the oral tradition, the story seeks to impart to the listeners the wealth of tribal wisdom through proverbs, wise sayings, and moral dicta. The story-teller is the repository of such traditional knowledge. Mr. Opoku's story abounds in proverbs, but they are so finely interwoven in the story that they do not, as so often happens in the self-conscious use of traditional folklore, become obtrusive.

Ghana also has a fine Drama Studio in Accra, built with the assistance of two American donors by the Ghanaian Government.

The Studio is largely the brainchild of the Ghanaian poetess Efua Sutherland, and has put on indigenous drama as well as Greek plays such as *Antigone* staged in a stylized African idiom. Efua Theodora Sutherland herself is a fine writer, a poetess who combines vivid imagery and strong sense of rhythm. Though Cambridge-educated, her poems, stories, and plays seem to utilize the cadences of her own vernacular language to charge what might otherwise have been rather jejune English with a new vitality. The following passage from her story "New Life at Kyerefaso" reflects her fascination with traditional folklore:

> Shall we say
> Shall we put it this way
> Shall we say that the maid of Kyerefaso, Foruwa, daughter of the Queen Mother, was a young deer, graceful in limb? Such was she, with head held high, eyes soft and wide with wonder. And she was light of foot, light in all her moving.

The work of Frank Parkes, a Ghanaian now living in London, shows how close some of the Ghanaians are to the French West African writers in ideology if not in technique. There is the same preoccupation with the African personality, the loss of innocence through the ravages of colonialism. His poem "African Heaven" derives from a vision of Africa as a custodian of innocence and virtue:

> Admit
> Spectators
> That they may
> Bask
> In the balmy rays
> Of the
> Evening Sun
> In our lovely
> African heaven.

Most Ghanaian poetry is not only appallingly romantic; it utilizes some archaic forms of expression, and borrows heavily from the lush imagery of eighteenth- and nineteenth-century English poetry. Sometimes a Keats or Wordsworth seems to have been removed from the English soil lock, stock, and barrel.

"Only a Dream," by Dei-Anang, for instance, is not only derivative, but sheer romantic nonsense:

> Last night, while nature's wondrous calm
> Brooded o'er roof and palm,
> Two immortal Muses transported me
> To their sacred springs of poesy.

The muses might have transported Mr. Dei-Anang, but the poetry is not likely to transport a discriminating reader. After so much bulldozing by Ezra Pound and T. S. Eliot, who but Mr. Dei-Anang and his compatriots would have the courage to rest in his "simple bower"?:

> When day's much burdened tasks are o'er
> And in my simple bower I rest. . . .

"Are we never going to know what a Ghanaian feels and thinks as he teeters on the brink of violent change or crashes into contemporary ideas like socialism . . . ?" asks Ezekiel Mphahlele in a recent article titled "Ghana: On the Culture Front."

French-African literature is, of course, in a class by itself. Suffice it to note here that the Africans of Dakar and Abidjan not only speak a different language from the Africans of Nigeria and Ghana and Sierra Leone. Their entire mode of thought reflects their French education. No English-speaking African could ever come up with so abstruse a definition of a nation as Senegal's Mamadou Dia does in his book *The African Nations and World Solidarity:* "a collective vocation." This tendency toward abstraction is characteristic of the creative literature of French-speaking Africa as well. Blackness is conceptualized into a new mystical mode of being. Hegelian and Marxian philosophies are combined to create a literature that relies on dialectical assault against Western culture, upon retraction and reformulation. "Blackness is not absence," says a Martinique poet, "but refusal."

This refusal gives rise to a poetry of gesticulating rhetoric, as in Senghor and David Diop. When their writing occasionally becomes more personal, such writers can be masters of evocative, picturesque imagery. For example, Senghor's tender poem "Black Woman" and some passages in his long poem "New York," achieve tremendous lyrical power. However, Senghor's picture of American Negro soldiers during World War II as God's avenging angels wreaking havoc on decadent Europe is not only lush and embarrassingly sentimental, but downright silly. The imagery becomes so stilted that one can only wonder whether it was honestly felt as a poetic statement. What is one to make of these lines?:

> Oh, black brothers, warriors whose
> mouths are singing flowers—
> Delight of living when winter is
> over—

My reaction to the literature of French-speaking Africa is widely shared in the English-speaking writing circles, and the widening gap between the two schools is disturbing. Nigerian and Ghanaian writers (as well as South African ones) tend to dismiss offhand the writing by French Africans as mawkish and romantic; the French Africans, on the other hand, regard the English-speaking Africans as superficially educated and sadly ill equipped to engage in intellectual gymnastics with them.

The truth may lie somewhere between the two extremes. For, in a sense, the works of both French-speaking and English-speaking West Africans are forms of romanticism. The French-speaking Africans defend their idealized conception of African society with ringing rhetoric that is not always meaningful. But the younger writers of Nigeria can also be charged with a local form of romanticism: Too often, they regard their writing as a private human activity. The symbolism of their soliloquies becomes convoluted, private, and obscure. When Wole Soyinka was queried in London recently about the obscurity of the message in his play *A Dance in the Forest,* the young playwright ignored the question and explained that his only responsibility to the public was to provide them with good theater. This sharp separation between literature as an art form and its content has resulted in a kind of poetry and drama that seems to shy away from social criticism.

One day, perhaps, West African writers will turn their satire to the moral flabbiness near at home.

3. French-Speaking Africa's Poètes-Militants

PAULIN JOACHIM

In reviewing the literary creations of French-speaking Africa, one is immediately struck by the decided preference for poetry at the expense of the novel and the theater. Some people read into this an inclination on the part of Africans to flee reality or an incapacity to work with prose or formulate a concrete thought. Rather, one must understand that Africa is the land of poetry, *par excellence*.

Each African, on his arrival in this world, is imbued with the gift of poetry. It flows in his veins from morning to evening, infusing meaning into his every act—the greeting, the farewell, ritual ceremonies, and declarations of love to a woman. *L'homme noir* possesses incomparable emotional power; when his soul expresses itself, poetry gushes forth like a bubbling spring.

But this is only a partial explanation of the African writer's preference for the medium of poetry. The novel is like a difficult, affected woman who must be equipped with the proper shade of make-up, words precisely suited to the occasion, and a carefully studied manner of behavior before she can present herself to the public. Poetry, by contrast, flows forth with unaffected spontaneity. It is thus the perfect medium for the African who has his emotions on the tip of his tongue and longs to shout his sufferings to the rooftops of the world—to proclaim Africa's anxiety to rid itself of foreign domination and to assert the African's existence as a whole man with a separate identity.

The first French-speaking African writers felt above all the need to regain their lost sense of human dignity and of racial pride, to cleanse the stains of history from Africa's past, and to replace shame with solemn glory. Negritude had its origins in the heart of the Latin Quarter in Paris around the years 1933–35. Its goal was to purge *l'homme noir* of Westernism and to restore his pride in his Negro-African cultural heritage. The most familiar of the *poètes-militants* of negritude are Léopold Sédar Senghor, the President of Senegal; Aimé Césaire of Martinique; and Léon Damas from French Guiana. Assimilation was to them a form of suicide.

Aimé Césaire disowned his own identity to take up the fight with bare fists: *"Mon nom: offense; mon prénom: humilité; mon état: révolté; mon âge: l'âge de la pierre; ma religion: la fraternité."* His course was not limited to the peoples of Africa, but extended itself to all those oppressed peoples of the world who existed in a *"cul-de-sac innommable de la misère et de la faim."* His mouth, he proclaimed, would be *"la bouche de celles qui s'affaissent au cachot du désespoir. . . ."* With clenched fists and volcanic fury, he cried to his white masters: *"Accommodez-vous de moi, je ne m'accommode pas de vous."* Sounding the same theme in a more nostalgic vein, Léon Damas weeps for his stolen Africa—"Give me back my black dolls that I may play with them/ The naïve games of my instincts. . . ."

In his poem "Femme noire," Léopold Senghor extolled the beauty of the black woman and gave the concept of negritude its credentials of nobility:

Femme nue, femme noire
Vêtue de ta couleur qui est vie, de ta forme qui est beauté!
J'ai grandi à ton ombre; la douceur de tes mains bandait mes yeux. . . .

. . .

Femme nue, femme obscure
Fruit mûr à la chair ferme, sombres extases du vin noir, . . .

. . .

Huile que ne ride nul souffle, . . .
Gazelle aux attaches célestes, les perles sont étoiles sur la nuit de ta peau

Délices des jeux de l'esprit, les reflets de l'or rouge sur ta peau qui semoire

A l'ombre de ta chevelure s'éclaire mon angoisse au soleil prochain de tes yeux. . . .

In his collections of poems entitled *Ethiopiques* and *Nocturnes,* the Senegalese poet-statesman eulogizes Africa with majesty and patriotic loyalty, and gives us some bits of inspired verse as powerful as those of Paul Claudel or St. John Perse. These *chants* come directly from his native Sine Saloum and are always accompanied by traditional instruments such as the kahalam, the balafong, or the kora.

There are other Senegalese apostles of negritude who have tirelessly sought to illustrate the dignity of *l'homme noir* and to define and affirm the originality of African culture. *Coups de pilon,* a collection of poems by the late David Diop, a young poet with a warm and generous heart, is a work of profound faith in *l'homme noir.* In his finely textured *Contes d'Amadou Koumba,* Birago Diop exhumes the cultural values of the black race that have so long been stifled by colonialist oppression and imparts to them a pearly luster for all mankind to see. His stories contain some of the most beautiful examples of Negro-African self-expression in print.

Now that the colonial masters have left French Africa and independence has been regained, this poetry of combat and of bitterness has lost its *raison d'être.* The poets have a continuing duty, however, to delve into their cultural patrimony and the little-known values of their ancestors. As Aimé Césaire has pointed out, Africa must play a role in *"le rendez-vous du donner et du recevoir."* Black writers can bring fresh blood to world culture and add a new dimension to modern man.

While the novel in French-speaking Africa has not reached the same creative level as the poetry produced there, a few examples are worthy of note.

The young Guinean, Camara Laye, has produced an autobiographical novel written in an elegant, poetic style—*L'enfant noir* —which won *le prix Charles Veillon* in 1953. In it, he recreates the image of traditional Africa with its magic spells, its legends, and its passionate poetry. His second novel, *Le regard du Roi,* is less interesting, principally because its form is no longer original or African and it approaches too closely current European writing.

Mongo Beti, a young Camerounian professor, is undoubtedly the most gifted of the French-speaking African writers. This was quickly recognized after the publication of his first book, *Le pauvre Christ de Bomba,* which he wrote under the pseudonym of Eza Boto. It portrays two Africans, a priest and an administrator, who are wearied by the mediocrity of the men they were charged with leading. Despite their good intentions, they eventually acquire both the self-centeredness of Europeans and the grasping materialism of those Africans who exploit the authority delegated to them.

The heroes of the second book, *Mission terminée,* are alert young men with the aura of prestige that a secondary-school education gives in Africa. They consider themselves ahead of their times and strangers to the life of the village in which they were born. This work is rich in local color and is punctuated by a lively and often malicious humor. The same ideas are found in a third novel, *Le roi miracule,* which also elicits one's admiration for the author's talents.

Another Camerounian, Ferdinand Oyono, has written two excellent satirical novels—*Une vie de boy* and *Le vieux Nègre et la mèdaille.* These depict masterful scenes of everyday African life in which he emphasizes the role of oral tradition.

A young novelist from the Ivory Coast, Ake Loba, has written *Kocumbo, l'étudiant noir,* which won the Prix de Littérature de l'Afrique d'expression française. In it the author analyzes the difficulties that Africans and Europeans experience in living together—that is, the barriers that arise between individuals who base their reasoning and conception of life on diametrically opposed standards.

A similar theme is found in *L'Aventure ambiguë,* a stimulating novel by the young Senegalese, Cheikh Hamidou Kane. It portrays two civilizations which lack the same heritage and the same laws, but which fundamentally are made to complement each other. This book is remarkable for the manner in which it stimulates the reader's thinking and for the high intellectual level on which it is written.

These books raise the hope that the coming years will see a flowering of romantic works in Africa, now that it has been liberated from the yoke which stifled its creative genius. Certainly there is much hope for the future of the novel here, for the African is clearly capable of becoming an excellent novelist. He lives in close contact with nature, is deeply rooted in the cosmos, and is endowed with the perceptiveness and sensitivity that enable one to grasp elusive ideas and nuances. Above all, the African novelist does not need to invent life—he lives it with a fullness that is rare.

The African novel will begin an authoritative existence the day its writers abandon a sterile imitation of Western forms of expression and return to their native land to search for originality and a specifically African style. So far, the majority of African novelists are really writing for another audience, which they are trying too hard to please, and not for their own people.

4. The Somalis: A Nation of Poets in Search of an Alphabet*

JEANNE CONTINI

The struggle to establish a national identity is common to all newly emerging independent countries, but the three-year-old Somali Republic faces a special problem, as basic as it is unusual in this day and age. It is still searching for a written alphabet to express the language spoken by the 4 million to 5 million Somalis of the African Horn.

While a Somali from Djibouti on the coast of French Somaliland can speak in the same tongue as a Somali living in Mogadiscio or in the Northern Frontier District of Kenya, they must write to each other in a foreign language. Three foreign languages are used in the republic today—English in the formerly British-protected north, Italian in the south, and Arabic as the language of Islam, the state religion.

The capital city of Mogadiscio is an administrative Tower of Babel, with the result that translators rate high in the hierarchy of foreign experts. All official documents, including legislation, verbatim records of parliament, treaties, etc., must be translated eventually into all three languages. Public-school children speak Somali at home and in the classroom, but are taught to read and write in either English or Italian plus Arabic, depending on where the school is situated. This state of affairs clearly hinders the advance of literacy, and complicates the whole educational system.

More poignant is the gradual loss of the nation's literature, a rich body of poetry and legend tenuously preserved in the minds of a few old men. The most gifted of the new generation are swept

* Expanded for *Africa Report* from a brief article that appeared earlier in the *Reporter*, New York.

off to Europe, Asia, or America where, if they are writers, they absorb the literary traditions and mannerisms of the host nation in spite of themselves. One of the most popular dreams among the young intellectuals, home for a brief holiday, is to collect, translate, and someday publish an anthology of Somali poetry. To date, however, only a tiny coterie of foreign scholars have published samples of Somali poetry. Nothing comprehensive has been undertaken because of the difficulty of digging out the source material, although the British sociologist I. M. Lewis is currently working on a serious anthology nourished by months of research in the Somali bush.

There are many reasons for the flowering of literature to the exclusion of other arts in Somali life. Originally a pastoral people, about 70 per cent of Somalia's population are still nomads today. The nomad considers that the most honorable profession for a man is to own a hundred camels, many horses, some mules, and flocks of sheep and goats, which he leads on foot at a dignified pace through the bush in search of water and grazing land. For centuries his wandering has been determined by the seasons of erratic rainfall brought by the monsoon winds, alternating with periods of merciless heat and drought. He holds any kind of manual labor in contempt, as fit only for women or menials. I know of no other country in the world where calling a man a "tailor" or "shoemaker" is a legally libelous insult.

The deeply rooted Moslem faith prohibits man-made images of God's works, whether human, fauna, or flora, as acts of presumptuous impiety. This religious factor, combined with the poverty of raw materials in the Somali landscape, has effectively discouraged the development of painting and sculpture, as well as of the decorative elements in local handicrafts. Somali reverence for the artfully spoken word, however, is all pervasive. Poetry, which is always chanted rather than spoken, has been a traditional vehicle for transmitting folk wisdom from leader to followers, parent to child; for recording great historical events; for controlling tempers during public debate at the *shir* or tribal assembly; for refreshing the long night treks of shepherds or warriors.

Poetry also became a redoubtable propaganda weapon and a

means of communicating secret military commands in the mouth of Somalia's most controversial personality—the "Mad Mullah," Sayyid Mohammad Abdullah Hassan. Born late in the nineteenth century in what is now Ethiopia's Ogaden Province, he began his career as a religious reformer, rallying converts for a particularly austere Moslem sect. He was educated at Koran school like the average Somali boy, but subsequently enhanced his reputation for piety and his knowledge of classical Arabic by making several pilgrimages to Mecca.

At first, the British colonial regime regarded the rise of the Mullah to prominence as a force for stability, but he soon developed into a fierce nationalist leader with a genius for guerrilla warfare that was to plague British military forces for twenty-one years. From 1899 to 1920, when the Mullah and his legendary dervishes were finally defeated by aerial attack, Sayyid Mohammad Abullah Hassan held the British at bay. In those days, too, he compelled the inner circle of his loyal followers to commit all of his poetry to memory. It is the few venerable survivors of the Mullah's campaigns who are the living archives both of his literature and his strategy. The cruelty he showed not only his enemies but also his own countrymen (who were slaughtered by the thousands for incurring his displeasure) deprived Somalia's first brilliant nationalist general of the hero's status he might otherwise have achieved. No one, however, challenges his supremacy as the nation's greatest poet.

The Mullah composed some of his best lyric poetry about his favorite horses for whom he—like most Somalis—felt an extraordinary tenderness and esteem. The following excerpts from an ode to one of his horses were translated by John Drysdale, a former British foreign service official and expert on Somali culture:

> . . . He carries skins of fresh cool milk
> which bring about repletion.
> A leather-covered saddle too,
> A halter and a bit.
> Amulets of shining brass,
> A swinging collar, colored wool.
> A large embroidered rhino shield,
> A nicely polished riding whip.

And my long spears,
And I, who talk.
All this he carries
On himself.
And, like a mad bull-elephant,
He has a trotting gait.
Nay! he never tires.
Is he not incredible?
If I ride at early morn,
or even after noon,
He is like unrivaled shade.
Is he not a wafting breeze?
If I ride at dead of night,
in the coolness of the night,
He shields me from the watery dew.
Is he not a cloak to me?
If I turn him sharply,
He spins around and darts ahead
Like a vibrant ostrich.
If I should ever lose him,
No greater sadness on this earth,
My grief will surely kill me,
For is he not my only heart? . . .

The *gabay* (or long epic poem), reserved to male poets, is the most important classic form of Somali poetry. It is a strictly disciplined, complicated framework used chiefly to celebrate great events and figures, or deep emotions—friendship, betrayal, patriotism, love. Alliteration rather than rhyme is one of the obligatory rules of composition, and must appear in two key words of each line. Repetition of the same verb in any single *gabay* is regarded as exposing poverty of imagination on the part of the poet. An enormous vocabulary is required, which is often beyond the understanding of the average Somali listener. No aspiring young poet has arrived until he can compose a top-notch *gabay*.

This is a very approximate translation of a verse from one of the Mullah's unpublished *gabays* expressing his bitter contempt for the Isaak tribe, which refused to join him:

They [the Isaak] fast, they pray, they pay taxes and give alms to the poor,

But all this parade of righteousness will never earn them a place in
  Heaven
Because they call the foreigner 'sahib.'

The original Somali, written phonetically, looks like this:

> Soonkiyo salaaddiyo sokada, sadagaddii iidda
> Aawaab kama helayaan wahhay amal smaysteene
> Saana wahh ugu wa'an waa kufriga, saab la leeyhaye.

There are several forms of poetry—the *geraar,* the *jiifto,* the
masafa, to mention three—all differing in structure, length, and
meter. Sixty years ago, Scek Ahmed Gabiou sat before his door
in Itala in the early evening, sipping a cool draught of camel's
milk and thinking deeply on the future as he watched the first
stars flicker over the sea. He composed a *masafa,* whose prophetic
last lines are quoted below:

Before the end of the world the Somalis shall be divided in three:
One will live in a palace surrounded by his guards,
One will continue living in the bush, drawing sustenance from the sale of
  milk, which he will carry to town in his tunji:
One will die in the dusty street crying out 'Somalia!'

Another kind of poetry, which may be sung by either men or
women, is the two-line *wilgo.* Its traditional low-pitched tones
make it a favorite for sentries singing to keep awake during the
long night watch over a sleeping village, and as a secret language
for courting couples. For example, there is an exchange between
an impatient lover and the pretty wife of an elderly man who re-
turns home unexpectedly. The youth sings as he dances with
companions on the other side of the village:

> 'How long, oh Aweeya, my beautiful Aweeya
> Is your village going to stay awake?'

The wife replies as she is milking:

> 'Oh my brown cow, my gentle lovely cow
> Your owner is back seated in front of the house waiting your milk!'

The husband, listening, decides to put a stop to the nonsense
by singing:

'I may be no longer young, but am learned in the arts of war
Thus it is still dangerous to cross my keen-edged sword.'

While there are established settled areas along the fertile banks
of Somalia's two serpentine rivers, the unpredictability of rainfall
over vast stretches of the country's waterless bush has encouraged
the Somali people to rely traditionally on livestock rather than
agriculture. More important, perhaps, is the nomad view that it is
primitive and too trying of man's patience to work the soil and
stay in one place all year round. A nostalgic farmer composed this
expressive lament:

Clouds cover the heavens, rain is falling everywhere but in my garden.
I cannot pierce the sky above it,
Nor can I chase the garden like a flock of camels
Who run with the swiftness of deer
To slake their thirst in the nearest pond—
Oh, that my garden too might run, drink, and come back to me.

From the *wilgo* comes the modern *hello* (pronounced "halo"),
the vehicle for current popular songs. A contemporary poet from
the northern city of Hargeisa dedicated this forceful, rhythmic
hello to Somali President Aden Abdullah Osman:

Haseehhàn, haseehhàn, haseehhàn!
Nin lagù seehhdòw
Hhil baad siddaa
Haseehàn, haseehhàn, haseehhàn,
    haseehàn, haseehhàn, haseehhàn!

It means:

Never sleep, never sleep, never sleep!
Man thou dost carry a heavy burden
Never sleep, never sleep, never sleep, etc.

Some poetry is political. While a great many *gabays* have been
inspired by Somali's independence, the 1961 constitutional referendum, etc., and are generally laudatory to the present government, others are frankly critical. For example, a *gabay* by the
Hargeisa poet Abdi Iddaan addressed this observation to the
ministers of the central government:

Possession of handsome cars and clean clothes
As well as many flights around the world in the company of beautiful girls
Will never make the idea of Greater Somalia
A reality.

Grass-roots politics are often conducted in poetry, with the campaigning party representatives wooing new adherents at a bush rally via chants. When a deputy goes home to face his constituents, he is likely to be greeted by a local poet who has improvised a *gabay* in his honor. Tucked away between the strophes paying homage to his accomplishments and ancestors may be a sharp reprimand for his neglect of certain issues of special concern to local voters.

The Somali love for a well-turned metaphor infuses the body of folk legends, whose plots often turn on phrases or messages with hidden meanings. There is a long series of tales about a couple named Cab-Alaf and Huryo, who were well matched in terms of wit. Huryo, though lovely and having many other qualities prized in a wife, was a domestic tyrant. One of the most popular stories illustrates how Cab-Alaf tactfully manages to reassert some of his rights as a husband:

> Whenever the couple sat down to their main meal of the day, consisting of finely ground millet cooked into a porridge, it was Huryo's custom to place the appetizing ghee [clarified butter] and fragrant spices on her side of the common bowl, leaving her husband to eat his portion with milk. Cab-Alaf grew heartily bored with this bland though nourishing diet.
>
> One evening, while Huryo was preparing dinner, Cab-Alaf asked her to allow him to set out the food. When she consented, he placed the milk in front of his wife and seasoned his own side of the bowl with ghee and spices. Huryo sat down, and after thinking, said in a reproachful voice: 'Cab-Alaf, something you said to me yesterday smote my heart in two, just like this!' She leaned over, and with her fingers drew a sharp line across the millet so that all the ghee ran down the depression to her side of the bowl.
>
> Undaunted, Cab-Alaf sat for a moment in silence. Then he said: 'Oh my beautiful Huryo, the very thought of offending you churns my innards thus!' And with a circular motion of his finger, he stirred the porridge mixing milk, butter, and spices. The result was so good that millet is eaten that way to this very day.

Under Moslem law, a man may have as many as four wives simultaneously, provided that each wife receives equal affection, housing, possessions, etc., from her husband. These conditions are so difficult to fulfill, both emotionally and economically, that few Somalis today take full advantage of the privilege. Moreover, because of the omnipresent menace of drought and subsequent famine in this barren land, a female glutton—no matter how ravishing—is regarded as a marital liability. The following story makes the point:

A man who had just taken a beautiful young girl as a fourth wife still owed his in-laws 25 cows as part of the dowry paid the bride's family. Some time after the wedding, he was visited by his new kinsmen. The husband invited them into a well-shaded 'zariba' [acacia-wood picket fence enclosing a clean-swept yard that serves as outdoor sittingroom] to rest and refresh themselves. He ordered a camel slaughtered in their honor, as was fitting. When the meat was prepared, out of sight but within hearing of his guests, the husband called his wives and cutting off a portion for each, said to the first wife:
'Take this piece for me.'
To the second, he said: 'Take this piece for the children.'
To the third, he said: 'Take this piece for us.'
To the fourth, the recent bride, he said: 'Take this piece for yourself.'
When the guests had eaten, the husband exchanged the usual courtesies and offered to show them his cattle in order for them to choose the 25 cows for which they had come. But the guests, who had divined the various relationships implied by what they had overheard, thanked their host for his hospitality and bade him farewell, saying they considered his debt already amply paid.

Unlike the bards and poets, there are no professional storytellers. "Every Somali is supposed to be one," said the man who told me both of the foregoing tales, with a glint of irony in his dark eyes. It is true that this is a nation of spellbinders. Indeed, many popular proverbs caution against the Somali power of eloquence. For example:

Warran badaan guran ma noqdo.
[Many words do not necessarily become a Koran.]
Ninki af kaa badiyo dahaal adoga wa-ku-la wadaga. [He who is more eloquent than you, will share with you the inheritance of your father.]

For such an articulate people, the lack of an alphabet is a particular loss. Recognizing this, Somali scholars have been trying, ever since the end of World War I, to devise an alphabet that would be acceptable to all elements of the population.

Since Arabic is familiar to Somali students of the Koran, it was natural that all the initial efforts to find an alphabet should be based directly or indirectly on Arabic script. Around 1920, three Somalis (unknown to each other) were all trying to transcribe Somali in Arabic symbols. One was the famous Sayyid Mohammad Abdullah Hassan, who was searching for a permanent means of recording his works for posterity. Another was the Chief Qadi of Borama. The third was Mohammad Abdullah Mayal of Berbera. Some thirty other alphabets devised by Somalis during the last forty years derive from Arabic. Some of these pioneers persevered despite threats on their life by religious compatriots who feared that any attempt to write Somali would diminish interest in the *shariah* (the body of sacred Islamic law). Quite aside from these problems, the effort to use Arabic as a base eventually foundered because of basic structural differences in the two languages, including the almost total absence of vowel symbols in Arabic.

In the early 1920's, a Somali poet and leader of the Sultanate of Hobia, Osman Yusuf Kenadid, decided to invent his own characters. His script, known as *Osmania,* is the only original alphabet to achieve a degree of success. When the news that Osmania was being taught in the schools of Osman's Sultanate reached the ears of the ruling Italian colonial administrators, he was jailed in Mogadiscio. With his arrest, all efforts to devise a means of writing Somali came to an end in the territory for twenty-five years.

The rise of nationalism that followed World War II, and specifically the birth of the nationalist Somali Youth League in 1943, brought about a revival of Osmania. Osman was one of the founding members of the SYL, which is today the governing party of the republic. Under his sponsorship, Osmania was introduced into the schools of Mogadiscio and other southern centers during the late 1940's. Several fundamental weaknesses were soon revealed, however. These included the impossibility of applying Osmania to more than one of the three or four main Somali dialects, and the militant resistance of its sponsors to any criticism of the script. There was increasing suspicion that the advocates of Osmania were motivated by regional pride and personal loyalty to Osman rather than by an objective appraisal of his script.

The language issue flared again during the ten-year Italian Trust Administration (1950–60). In 1950, Professor M. M. Moreno, who later published two Somali grammars based on Latin script, urged the authorities to realize that the speedy adoption of an alphabet was an indispensable step in the preparations for independence. But when the proposal was put to the first Somali legislature, the Consiglio Territoriale, the deputies decided to table the question because of its political implications until it could be resolved without pressure or interference from the outside. Five years later, Bruno Panza, an Italian elementary school teacher, wrote a Somali language primer, again based on Latin script, and obtained the tacit permission of several high-placed Somali officials to teach his students to read and write according to his own system. Meanwhile, the local Italian-language newspaper introduced a daily page in Somali based on Panza's script. The page was abolished after two weeks, however, and the whole Panza initiative had to be halted because of opposition from the conservative Moslems who considered the Latin "Christian" script unsuitable for a Moslem state. Stacks of Panza's primers are still moldering in a government warehouse.

In September, 1960, a few months after independence, the National Assembly asked the government to appoint a committee to undertake an investigation of the best means of writing Somali. The nine-man committee was chaired by Mussa Galaal, a civil servant in the Ministry of Education who had studied the language dilemma for fifteen years. While training at the London School of Oriental and African Studies, Mussa had worked for four years with Professor Andrzejewsky on a British Colonial Office research project on the Somali alphabet problem. He also helped him to produce *Hikmaad Soomali,* a collection of Somali stories with an introduction to Somali grammar (Oxford University Press, 1956).

The committee concentrated on the three most important potential alphabets of the many submitted for consideration—Arabic, Osmania, and Latin. After a year of weighing the pros and cons of each, it turned in a report in January, 1962, favoring the Latin alternative. The positive reasons advanced for this decision were both technical and practical. As explained by Frank Mahoney, an American anthropologist who has spent two years in Somalia studying the language: "Latin script offers the best phonetic fit for Somali." There is a broad continuum of language throughout the republic, whose differences are no greater than those between British and American English. The Latin alphabet is apparently flexible enough to embrace the variations in dialect, whereas Osmania is not.

From the practical viewpoint, it is relevant that Latin characters are already used by about seventy countries and are employed internationally for telegraphy and higher mathematics. In addition, adoption of a Latin script would make it possible to acquire modern printing equipment at moderate prices. Though now partly outdated by new methods of reading and language instruction, a small international library of Somali grammars based on Latin script already exists, prepared experimentally by British, German, and Italian scholars since the turn of the century. In short, it would be quicker and easier to take advantage of this spadework than to strike out in a brand new direction.

Whether a solution based on logic, economy, and efficiency will carry the day is still far from certain, however. The Somali alphabet search has exposed raw nerves in the cultural tissue of the country, and the profound religious feeling that binds Somalis to the rest of the Moslem world may eventually triumph over the obstacles to the adoption of Arabic symbols. On the other hand, the satisfaction of utilizing Osmania may provide a sufficiently strong incentive to iron out the difficulties in this product of Somali ingenuity.

One can only hope that the lodestars of literacy and a proud literary heritage will pull the Somalis toward a decision on the alphabet issue before the new generation loses touch with its roots.

Maps

CEUTA MELILLA

IFNI MOROCCO

TUNISIA

SPANISH SAHARA

ALGERIA LIBYA UNITED ARAB REPUBLIC

MAURITANIA MALI NIGER CHAD SUDAN

FRENCH SOMALILAND

GAMBIA SENEGAL

PORT GUINEA

GUINEA UPPER VOLTA

SIERRA LEONE IVORY COAST

LIBERIA GHANA TOGO DAHOMEY NIGERIA

ETHIOPIA

SOMALI REPUBLIC

CAMEROUN FEDERATION

FERNANDO POO RIO MUNI

PRINCIPE

SAO TOME GABON

ANNOBON

CONGO CONGO

CENTRAL AFRICAN REPUBLIC

UGANDA KENYA

RWANDA

BURUNDI

PEMBA

CABINDA TANGANYIKA ZANZIBAR

ANGOLA N. RHODESIA

MOZAMBIQUE

SOUTH WEST AFRICA S. RHODESIA

BECHUANALAND

MALAGASY REPUBLIC

SWAZILAND

REPUBLIC OF SOUTH AFRICA BASUTOLAND

MAP 1

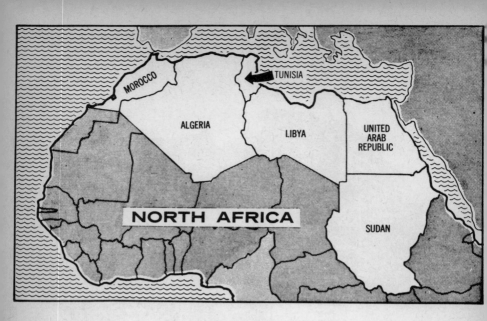

MAP 2

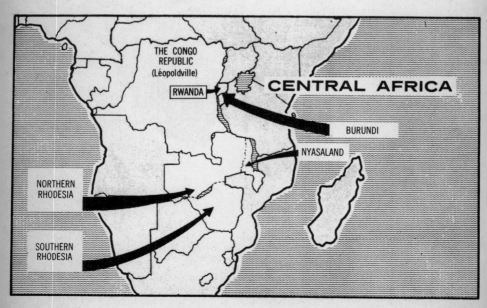

MAP 3

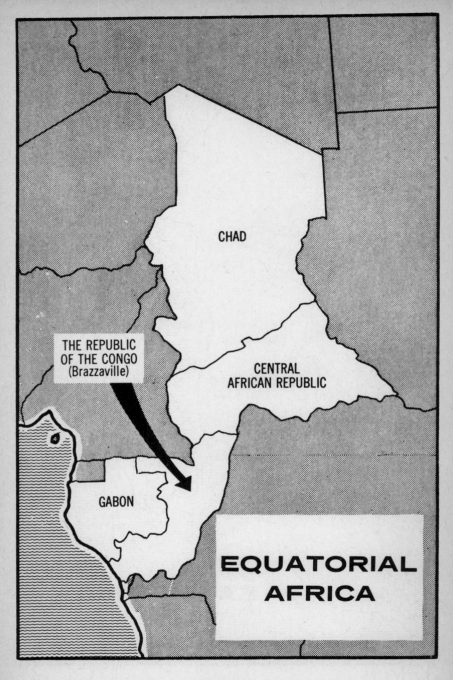

CHAD

THE REPUBLIC
OF THE CONGO
(Brazzaville)

CENTRAL
AFRICAN REPUBLIC

GABON

EQUATORIAL
AFRICA

MAP 4

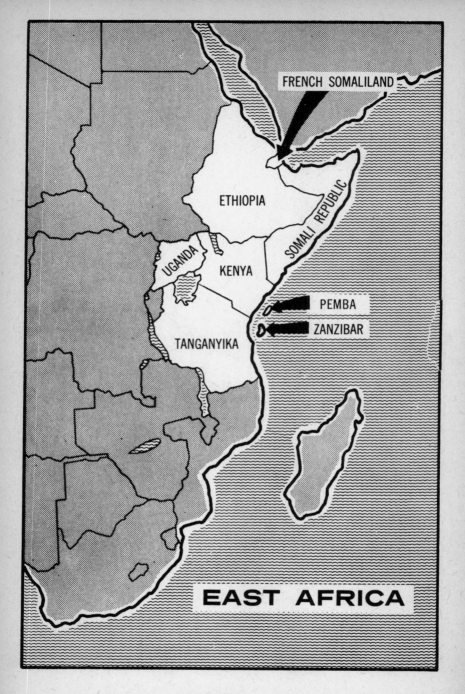

MAP 5

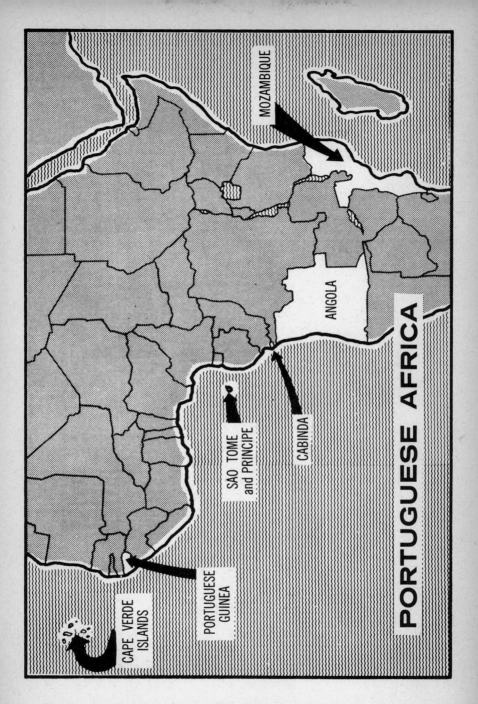

PORTUGUESE AFRICA

MAP 6

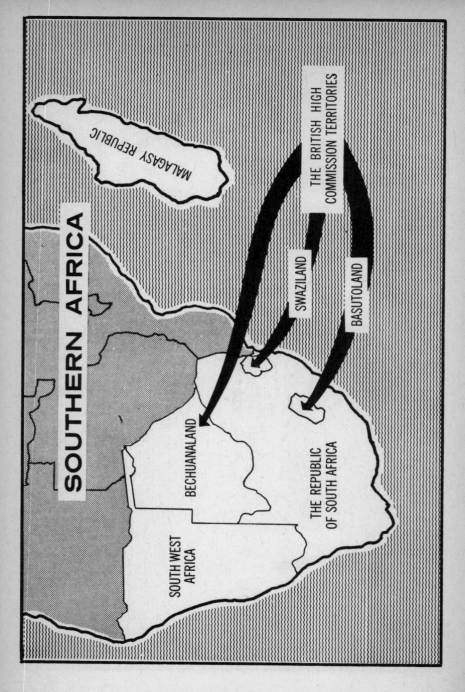

MAP 7

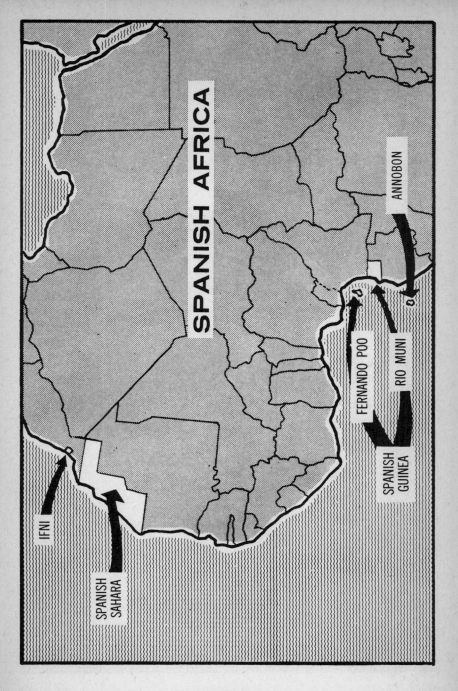

MAP 8

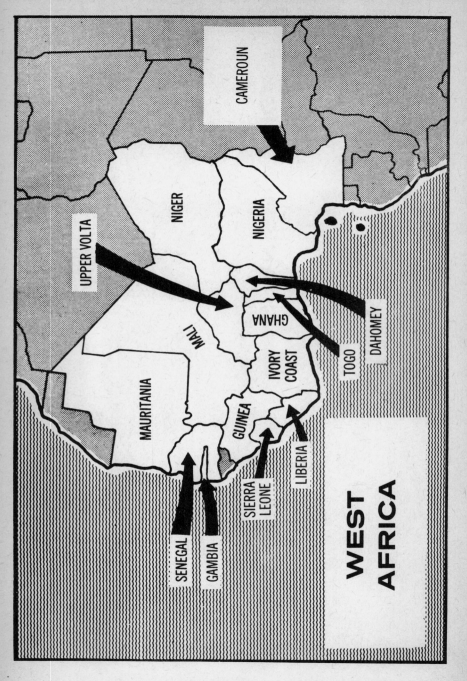

WEST AFRICA

MAP 9

DATE DUE